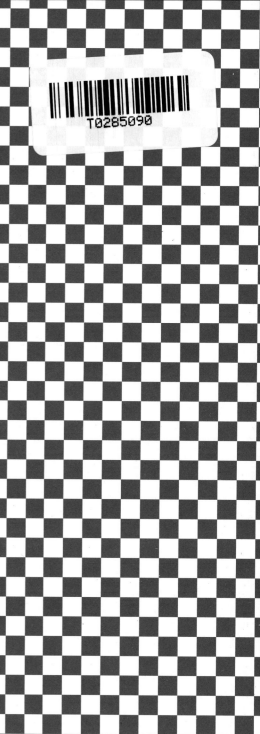

T0285090

Pizza Night

To my husband, Ben

Pizza Night

Deliciously Doable Recipes for Pizza and Salad

Alexandra Stafford

Photographs by Eva Kolenko

Clarkson Potter/ Publishers New York

Contents

Summer

Fall

Winter

Spring

Pizza Night:
An Introduction

I was seven when my parents divorced. It was the eighties, everyone was getting divorced, but I remember feeling sad anyway, sitting with my older sister on her bed while my mother, gently rubbing our backs, consoled us, teary-eyed and confused. In my memory, her voice sounded like the adults in a *Peanuts* cartoon, muffled and muted, an incomprehensible babble.

But then, piercing through the prattle, came, "When we move, we'll have pizza every Friday."

Those three words—*pizza every Friday*—washed away every tear, dried up every worry, and provided immediate clarity. Pizza. Every. Friday. Everything would be fine.

And everything was fine. We moved across town from our creaky old house on busy Main Street to one with wall-to-wall carpeting on Clear View Drive. In our new house, my sister and I spent hours choreographing gymnastics routines to Madonna and rollerblading in the basement to Cindy Lauper. This new neighborhood, with rows of houses each just a hair different than the next, felt like Utopia, home to kids of all ages, instant playmates for my siblings and me. We biked, jumped rope, and played hockey in the street.

And, as promised, we had pizza every Friday.

I remember so looking forward to hearing the doorbell ring, to tipping the driver the few dollars my mother had handed me, to opening the box to reveal an enormous, cheesy, pepperoni-topped pie, a dinner followed by "TGIF," two hours of TV, our allotment for the week. Fridays were a dream.

Like many Americans, my love for pizza began as a child. The local pizza parlor, Louie's, was where we wrapped up every soccer season, where we drank Fanta with abandon, where we celebrated every birthday, every recital, every milestone. It's also, incidentally, where my aunt, in town for the weekend, jumped over a booth to perform the Heimlich on a blue-faced customer, dislodging a clam from his throat, which, as I remember, soared across the room.

Clam pizza was popularized by Pepe's Pizzeria Napoletano in New Haven, Connecticut, twenty minutes from my home. Pepe's thin-crust pies with charred edges, along with those from Sally's, just down the street, and Modern, a few blocks away, gave New Haven a national name for pizza.

But this was not the pizza I grew up on. Like most children, I didn't appreciate blistered edges or burnished undercarriages, and I didn't mind excess: the cheesier and greasier the better. Back then, I didn't see the beauty in the less-is-more approach, in a lightly topped, lightly cheesed, lightly sauced pie.

That appreciation would come years later when I moved to New Haven for college. There I did what many did: waited in line at Sally's, Pepe's, and Modern, so I could weigh in on the best-pizza debate. In between these research outings, I had my fair share of late-night dollar slices, floppy and foldable on grease-soaked paper plates, showered with pepper flakes and parmesan. Oil dripping down my chin, I loved them all, but it was the pizza at Bar, lesser-known (on a national level, at least) but closer to campus, that stole my heart. It's also where I fell in love.

I met Ben, now my husband, at the end of my sophomore year. He was a senior and would be gone in three months, but we gave it a go and soon found a common love: eating. I know: *At that age, who doesn't share that love?* But still, we liked to eat, and we ate a lot: wings at Archie Moore's, burgers at The Doodle, falafel at Mamouns, grilled cheese and black bean soup at Atticus, chicken souvlaki at Yorkside, and more burgers at Louie's Lunch.

But as time went on, and in the years after Ben graduated, we mostly found ourselves at Bar, for their good beer, their one salad, and their pizza, namely their white clam pizza, made in the style of Pepe's: sauceless and strewn with tender clams, lots of garlic, olive oil, a modest amount of Romano cheese, and a sprinkling of oregano. With a squeeze of lemon, nothing was better. Truly, I don't think anything is better to this day.

Ben and I married a few years after I graduated. In the years that followed, we moved around a lot, from the East Coast to the West Coast and back again, settling finally in Upstate New York, where we've been for over ten years now. During this decade, we had four children, so while my memory of most of it is a blur, I could describe in detail the pizzas we ate along the way.

There was the boxed Margherita pizza from Marra's that we brought home when Ben withdrew from medical school to join the Marine Corps—a decision that inspired our worried-sick parents to drop in to our South Philadelphia apartment to intervene, hoping to change his decision, the one, they would learn, finally allowing him to fall asleep at night.

There were the many wood-fired Neapolitan pies with their ballooned edges at 2Amy's in Washington, DC, where Ben and I met every few weeks when he was stationed in Quantico, Virginia. And the decidedly not-Neapolitan

pizza we ate beneath surfboards dangling from the ceiling, surrounded by diners sporting flip-flops, trucker hats, and hoodies, at Pizza Port in Carlsbad, California, where we ended our two-week cross-country drive.

There was the speck-topped pie at Pizzeria Mozza in Los Angeles, the last meal we ate before Ben deployed, and the Margherita pizza topped with house-made mozzarella at Pizzeria Bianco in Phoenix, where we ate when he returned.

There was the Grimaldi's pizza lunch under the Brooklyn Bridge, surrounded by friends who were in town for a dear friend's wedding. And the "bee-sting" pizza at Roberta's, where we ate before flying out of town for another dear friend's funeral.

There was the boxed pie we inhaled after hiking Mount Marcy, a trek that left us utterly and completely spent, and the New Haven–style pizzas we ate in my parents' backyard the night before my brother got married, an event that made me wonder why all weddings weren't giant pizza parties.

I could go on, but you get the idea—pizza gets you through it: divorce, marriage, death, birth, triumph, defeat. It's no wonder every culture, or nearly every one anyway, has developed some sort of pizza-ish creation, dough baked with toppings, a mingling of humble ingredients, their union so much more than the sum of their parts.

As I get older, I love pizza more and more. Saying I could live on it would be bold, but I do know this: There is no food I'd wait in line longer for, there is no food I'd go more out of my way for, there is no food I'd travel farther for. Pizza is what I find myself dreaming about before bed, a subject I never tire of reading about, and the one food I plan trips around. Because time has proven, pizza is worth it. It's the ultimate comfort food. Every Friday. And beyond.

ABOUT THE PIZZA IN THIS BOOK

This is not a book about the merits of New Haven-style pizza over Detroit or Neapolitan pizza over Sicilian or any other category of pizza. It's about how to make good pizza at home, whether you have a baking stone or steel, a sheet pan or a cast-iron skillet, a backyard wood-burning oven or a portable pellet-burning inferno. This book is about how to make pizza night a routine and a ritual, predictable but never boring in execution. There are fifty-two pizza recipes in this book, each with a salad to accompany it, along with five simple desserts, classics that belong in everyone's repertoire.

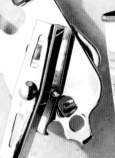

Tools, Ingredients, and Tips for Success

Pizza, at heart, is a simple food: dough, topped in various ways, baked in a hot oven. Simple though it may be, the right tools can make the pizza-making process more efficient and enjoyable, and in doing so help make it a routine. Good ingredients, furthermore, will make your efforts all the more worthwhile—if you start with bad flour, neither a three-day ferment nor a fancy pizza oven will make your pizza taste any better.

Pizza Tools

Digital scale

Please use a scale. Please use a scale. Please use a scale. The single most important step you can take to make homemade pizza a simpler and more foolproof process is to use a digital scale. Measuring by weight is the only way to know you are truly measuring accurately. When we measure with cups, we all measure differently. If 50 people measure 4 cups of flour, the weight of each of those 4 cups of flour will be different. If 50 people measure 550 grams of flour using a scale, every bowl of flour will weigh exactly 550 grams.

Measuring by weight also allows you to troubleshoot in a meaningful way. If you live in a humid environment, for instance, you may need to use less water to get your dough to the proper consistency, and holding back a precise amount will help you more quickly pinpoint the right ratio of flour to water.

Finally, using a scale to measure is also faster than measuring by cups. Once you start baking by weight, you'll never go back.

Mixing bowl

A large (4-quart) mixing bowl is what you'll need for most of the recipes in this book. A lidded bowl is ideal because the lid will protect the dough from drying out as it rises.

Good silicone spatula

I am partial to the GIR brand of spatulas. Some spatulas are too stiff, and some are too flimsy. GIR is just right— it stands for "get it right" actually—and it feels like an extension of the arm. Bonus: Unlike wooden spatulas with removable rubber heads, which can trap moisture and small bits of food, GIR spatulas are all one piece, making them easy to clean and less susceptible to mold growth. They're heat-resistant and dishwasher-safe, to boot.

Clear straight-sided container with lid

A 2- to 4-quart clear straight-sided container is particularly helpful with sourdough recipes, because it allows you to see more accurately how much your dough has increased in volume, thereby helping you determine when the bulk fermentation is complete. A lid, moreover, will ensure your dough does not dry out.

Bench scraper

For dividing masses of dough into smaller portions and for cleaning work surfaces of stuck-on dough bits, there is no better tool than a bench scraper. I like metal bench scrapers for the reasons just mentioned, but flexible dough scrapers have their advantages, too, namely for releasing dough clinging to the sides of bowls.

Parchment paper

You can assemble your pizzas directly on parchment paper and use your pizza peel to transfer the pizza parchment paper and all directly onto the hot surface. Note that most brands of parchment paper will warn against using their parchment paper above 450°F, but I have never had parchment paper catch fire even with my oven at 550°F. Do not, however, use parchment in an outdoor pizza oven or under the broiler, where it *will* catch fire.

Baking steel

The single most important tool to invest in to make better pizza in a home oven is a baking steel. A baking steel is similar to a baking stone or pizza stone, but is a better conductor of heat, as steel transfers heat to the dough faster, which in turn causes the dough to spring in the oven, leading to glorious bubbles throughout. Steel also retains heat better than stone, so it will help keep your oven at the proper temperature as you open and close it while launching and removing pizzas. I recommend the Original Baking Steel made by a company called Baking Steel. Note: If you don't have a baking steel or pizza stone, you can use an old sheet pan—one you don't care about, however, because it may warp—turned upside down.

Pizza peel

For non-pan pizzas, you'll need a peel to both transfer the pizza to the oven and retrieve it when it's done. I am partial to wooden peels, which I find naturally more nonstick than metal. I particularly like the Epicurean 14 × 21-inch peel; it's large enough for my thin-crust pizzas, which are 13 inches in diameter, but not so large that it doesn't fit in my outdoor oven. (Do, however, measure your outdoor oven before purchasing a peel.) Note: If you don't have a peel, you can use a thin cutting board or the back of a 13 × 18-inch sheet pan (topped with parchment paper for ease) to make the transfer.

Turning peel

If you have an outdoor pizza oven, in addition to the pizza peel, you'll need a specialized peel for turning the pizza frequently to ensure even cooking. A turning peel has a smaller head than a pizza peel and a longer handle, allowing for more nimble movements.

Lloyd baking pans

For Detroit-, Sicilian-, and grandma-style pizzas, steel baking pans ensure that the bottoms of your pizzas crisp and brown properly. For Detroit-style pizza, I recommend the 10 × 14-inch pan from LloydPans, and for Sicilian- and grandma-style pizza, I recommend the 12 × 16-inch pan from LloydPans. Winco, another brand, makes a slightly larger (12 × 18-inch) steel pan, which also is great for Sicilian- and grandma-style pizzas.

Cast-iron skillets

If you are not ready to invest in a baking steel or stone or a Lloyd baking pan, you can make excellent pizza using a cast-iron skillet, which retains heat well and can be used on the stovetop in addition to the oven to help crisp up the crust. See Cast-Iron Skillet Meatball Pizza with Caramelized Onions and Mozzarella (page 129).

Microplane grater

Finishing pizzas with a fine shaving of parmesan or pecorino cheese is a great way to add a hint of salt and umami. These are also terrific for finely grating garlic, zesting citrus, and shaving chocolate.

Pizza cutters

I have a pair of "pizza scissors," which the kids love using and which is the safest option for them, though any kitchen shears will work. I also love the R. Murphy Knives Pizza Rocker, which is 13 inches across and equipped with a sharp carbon steel blade.

Outdoor pizza oven

Ooni, Gozney, and other portable outdoor pizza oven manufacturers have revolutionized the "wood-burning" pizza game for home cooks. For a fraction of the cost of a wood-burning oven, these portable pizza ovens reach the same temperatures, allowing you to quickly churn out pizzas with excellent results.

Infrared thermometer

Equipped with a laser pointer, an infrared thermometer allows you to instantly and accurately measure the temperature of your cooking surface. This is particularly helpful for outdoor ovens, but you can use it on your baking steel or stone, too.

Dough containers

Once you divide your dough into balled portions, you need containers to proof and store them in. Many grocery stores sell 1-quart lidded food storage containers, which are perfect: This size will allow the dough to grow (which it will do in the fridge), and the lid will protect it from drying out. Deli quart containers are great for storing dough as well. For storing Sicilian, Detroit, and grandma dough balls (see Pan Pizza Dough, page 30), you'll need a larger storage container: roughly 2 quarts. Once you remove the dough from the fridge, you'll need a roomier vessel to proof the dough balls in at room temperature: a 9 x 13-inch pan or something similar works well, and you'll want to cover it with plastic wrap to ensure the dough balls do not dry out. If you have the space, DoughMate trays (roughly 13 × 18 inches) are lidded, stackable, airtight containers designed for storing and proofing dough.

Large wooden boards for serving

Wooden cutting boards can double as serving platters for pizza. It's ideal to have two or more large rectangular boards, roughly 14 × 20 inches, for serving and cutting your pizza.

Salad Tools

Peelers

Great for transforming vegetables such as carrots and asparagus into long, ribbony strips.

Mandoline

For shaving hard vegetables like radishes, turnips, and beets, there is no better tool than a mandoline. I am partial to the Benriner mandoline for its slim profile, which makes it easy to store.

Chef's knife

A good, sharp 8-inch chef's knife is what I use most often for prepping ingredients—onions, carrots, tomatoes, cucumbers, etc.

Ingredients

Flours

A variety of different flours are called for in the pages that follow. Depending on the style of pizza you are making and the type of oven you are using, you'll want to use different flours:

BREAD FLOUR AND ALL-PURPOSE FLOUR

Each of the recipes in this book has been tested with both all-purpose flour and bread flour. I recommend using King Arthur Flour, but you can use any other unbleached, unbromated flour that has a protein level of 11% to 13% (which yields a strong but tender crust). KAF bread and all-purpose flours (as well as several other commercial brands, such as Bob's Red Mill) also contain malted barley flour, which has enzymes that convert the starches in the flour into sugars, which in turn helps the crust to brown better. This is why for most of my home-oven pizza doughs, I prefer using bread flour or all-purpose flour—as opposed to tipo "00" flour (see page 17), which does not contain malt. Bread flour also has the added benefit of absorbing more liquid than all-purpose flour, which is helpful if you live in a humid environment and find your dough to be wet and difficult to handle.

TIPO "00" FLOUR

Tipo "00" flour is a finely milled flour, the "00" denoting the finest grade in the Italian classification system. This flour is known for producing a dough with a gluten structure that is very extensible, meaning the dough will stretch out easily. I love using it in my Thin-Crust Pizza Dough (page 26). The Antimo Caputo "00" Pizzeria flour is my preference for tipo "00" flour.

SEMOLINA FLOUR

Semolina flour is coarse in texture and, for home-oven pizzas, is sprinkled on pizza peels to help prevent the dough from sticking to the peel. It also adds a subtle crunch to the finished pizza.

SEMOLA RIMACINATA

Semola rimacinata is a high-protein flour made from durum wheat, like semolina, but milled twice, making it much finer in texture. In pizza dough, it helps create a crust with both a crisp and pliable texture, which is why I use it in my Thin-Crust Pizza Dough (page 26). I recommend Antimo Caputo's Semola Rimacinata.

RICE FLOUR

Rice flour, which is gluten-free, can also be used as a nonstick barrier on a pizza peel. Rice flour doesn't burn the way wheat flour does, making it an especially good option for pizza peels used with an outdoor oven.

FRESHLY MILLED FLOUR

If you're looking to add some nutrition to your homemade pizzas, your best bet is to use wheat that is freshly stone-milled, a process that preserves more of the bran and the germ, which contain many of the grain's nutrients, antioxidants, oils, and flavors. Using small amounts of stone-milled flour in your pizza dough recipes will provide so much more by way of flavor and aroma than commercial whole wheat flour. If you wish to use stone-milled flour in any of the dough recipes, simply swap in 30% stone-milled flour for an equal weight of the white flour.

A few mills I love include Cairnspring Mills, Anson Mills, Community Grains, and Red Tail Grains.

Water

Use cold water straight from the tap or room temperature water. It should be roughly 60°F.

Salt

In pizza dough, salt is important not only for flavor but also for strengthening gluten and slowing down fermentation. The weight of the salt in any pizza recipe should be roughly 2% to 3% the weight of the flour. As such, the salt range for the pizza dough recipes in this book, which call for 550 grams of flour, is 11 to 16.5 grams. I find 15 grams of salt to be perfect, but feel free to experiment with more or less within this range. Important: I use Diamond Crystal kosher salt for my pizza dough recipes. The volume equivalent of 15 grams of Diamond Crystal kosher salt is roughly 5 teaspoons. The volume equivalent of 15 grams of Morton kosher salt is 3 teaspoons, and the volume equivalent of 15 grams of fine sea salt is 2½ teaspoons.

FLAKY SEA SALT

For seasoning salads and sprinkling over unbaked pizzas ready for the oven, I use flaky sea salt. I am partial to Maldon sea salt, which is readily available.

Rising agents

INSTANT YEAST

Sometimes labeled as "rapid-rise," "fast-rising," or "bread machine yeast," instant yeast is more concentrated than active dry yeast and doesn't have to be "bloomed" with water before using—it can be whisked directly into the dry ingredients. SAF Instant yeast is my preference, and it can be found in some grocery stores and many online sources as well. After opening it, transfer it to a lidded container, and store it in the fridge or freezer for up to 1 year.

ACTIVE DRY YEAST

None of the recipes in the book calls for active dry yeast, but if it's all you have or can find, you can use it in place of the instant yeast. To do so, simply sprinkle the same amount called for in the recipe over the water and let it stand for 10 minutes before proceeding.

SOURDOUGH STARTER

This is a fermented mix of flour and water containing wild yeasts and bacteria (lactobacilli). A bubbly and active sourdough starter is what will make your sourdough pizza rise. For the sourdough recipes in this book, use a 100% hydration sourdough starter, meaning a starter that is composed of equal parts flour and water by weight.

Before using, it should be at least doubled in volume since its last feeding, roughly 6 to 8 hours prior. While you can build a sourdough starter from scratch, I am a huge proponent of purchasing one, namely because with a strong, vigorous starter on hand, you can start making pizza with confidence right away.

Note: A sourdough starter must be fed and maintained, and if you need guidance on doing so, I have a detailed post on my website, alexandracooks.com, called "How to Feed, Maintain, and Store a Sourdough Starter."

Pantry

CANNED SAN MARZANO PLUM TOMATOES
For both the No-Cook Tomato Sauce (page 34) and Simple Tomato Sauce (page 34), you'll need canned peeled San Marzano tomatoes. La Valle is my favorite, and I also love DiNapoli and Afeltra.

PICKLED CHILES AND PASTES
Pickled chiles—including banana peppers, hot cherry peppers, jalapeños, and Calabrian chiles—are a great way to add acidity, heat, and brightness to a pizza.

EXTRA-VIRGIN OLIVE OIL
For its flavor and richness, I use extra-virgin olive oil to drizzle over pizza, dress vegetables, and whisk into salad dressings. I love California Olive Ranch, which is widely available.

VINEGAR
White balsamic vinegar, for its sweetness and acidity, is my favorite for salads. I am partial to the Colavita brand, which is readily available and reasonably priced. Rice vinegar, apple cider vinegar, or white wine vinegar can also be used, but you may have to adjust the sweetness of the dish to account for the increase in acidity.

HOT HONEY
Popularized by Mike Kurtz of Mike's Hot Honey, chile-spiked honey complements many a pie in this book. Zab's Hot Honey is excellent, too.

Dairy

MOZZARELLA
I often call for low-moisture whole-milk mozzarella (I like the Calabro brand); the low-moisture content keeps your pizza from being soggy. Fresh cow's or buffalo milk mozzarella can work if making a pizza in an outdoor oven because the cook time is short, which allows the cheese to stay fresh and creamy. But in a home oven, they tend to break or overmelt, turning rubbery in the process.

PARMIGIANO-REGGIANO, PARMESAN, AND PECORINO
Many of the recipes call for Parmigiano-Reggiano, which is imported from Italy, and which I prefer to American parmesan for its nutty flavor and buttery texture. For simplicity, *parmesan* is included in the recipe titles. Some of the recipes call for Pecorino Romano, which is an Italian sheep's milk cheese, which I love for both its sharpness and saltiness. Finally, a handful of recipes call for finely grated Pecorino Romano or parmesan cheese, for which you'll want the pregrated type sold in deli quart and pint containers.

RICOTTA
Several of the recipes call for whole milk ricotta, which I always add post bake to preserve its creaminess. I also like to whip it in the food processor (see Whipped Ricotta, page 41), which removes its graininess and lightens its texture. I like the Calabro brand.

CRÈME FRAÎCHE
Similar to sour cream but thicker, richer, and less sour tasting, crème fraîche makes an excellent base for white pizza.

HEAVY CREAM
Several of the recipes call for beating heavy cream until slightly thick and spreadable, and some call for simply drizzling the cream over the dough.

5 KEYS TO HAVING SUCCESS WITH PIZZA AT HOME
1. Use a digital scale.
2. Don't be afraid of salt. It not only ensures your crust is seasoned, it also controls fermentation and strengthens gluten.
3. Don't be afraid of water (and a wet, sticky dough ball). High hydration doughs take practice getting used to. Use flour as needed.
4. Invest in the right tools, namely a baking steel.
5. Preheat your oven sufficiently: one hour for a baking steel in a home oven; 30 to 45 minutes for an outdoor oven.

The Doughs

There are four main dough recipes in this book: Neapolitanish pizza dough, thin-crust pizza dough, pan pizza dough, and gluten-free pizza dough.

Each dough recipe starts with 550 grams of flour, 15 grams of salt, and 2 grams of instant yeast. And there are sourdough variations for each of the dough recipes with the exception of the gluten-free dough recipe. The water amount will vary depending on the style of pizza you are making—more water for pan pizzas, for example, less water for thin-crust pizzas—and the thin-crust pizza dough also includes olive oil.

Why 550 grams of flour? This amount of flour produces what I find to be the perfect amount of dough, enough for four 10- to 13-inch round pizzas or one to four pan pizzas, depending on the style you are making. The recipes can be halved if the yield is too high for you, and the doughs can be used over the course of 3 days (and for as long as a week, in fact, but with less reliable results). The yeast-leavened doughs, moreover, can be frozen, and all of the doughs can be parbaked and frozen (see How to Freeze Pizza Dough, page 248).

All of the recipes call for cold water, a room-temperature rise, and just enough yeast to ensure the dough won't overferment while it sits on the counter all day or overnight (roughly 6 to 10 hours). None of the doughs requires kneading or a machine for mixing, and all of the doughs follow the same basic method: Mix, let rise at room temperature, portion, ball, refrigerate, proof at room temperature, then bake. There are notes on how to speed up the timeline, if necessary, but should time permit, do allow for a long, slow room-temperature rise followed by some fridge time.

Timelines

24- to 48-hour timeline

Here's an example of how these timelines work. For 48 hours: Because my family's pizza night often is Friday, I like to mix my dough on Wednesday morning, let it rise all day, ball it up in the evening, and stick the dough balls in the fridge until Friday. For 24 hours: If I don't have time Wednesday morning, I'll mix the dough Wednesday evening or Thursday morning.

Same-day timeline

Mix the dough in the morning, let it rise all day at room temperature, portion, ball, and use 1 hour later.

3- to 4-hour timeline

If you would like to speed up any of the yeast-leavened dough recipes in the book, in place of cold water, use lukewarm water and increase the yeast to 4 grams. Let the dough rise in a warm spot for 1½ to 2 hours, turn it out, portion it, ball it up, then proceed with the recipe, transferring any dough balls you don't plan on cooking to airtight containers and storing in the refrigerator for 1 to 3 days.

Neapolitanish Pizza Dough

For a pizza to be considered truly Neapolitan, its production must adhere to strict rules ranging from the ingredients used in the dough to the fermentation and baking process. In short, true Neapolitan pizza is made with only flour, water, salt, and yeast in specified ratios to produce a dough that is 55% to 62% hydration. Moreover, it must be baked in a wood-burning oven at 900°F for 60 to 90 seconds.

For these reasons, I am using "Neapolitanish" to describe this dough, which will produce a pizza that is Neapolitan in spirit: thin but not paper thin with a slightly ballooned rim. Like true Neapolitan pizza dough, this dough is made with only flour, water, salt, and yeast, but unlike true Neapolitan pizza dough, its hydration is 77%. The reason for this higher hydration is that in a home oven the dough cooks at a much lower temperature for a longer period of time, during which a significant amount of the water in the dough will evaporate. So, to prevent the dough from drying out, it needs more water in it at the start.

To adapt this dough recipe to be used in an outdoor pizza oven, you'll need to reduce the water slightly. See Outdoor Pizza Oven Dough (below). I also recommend cooking the pizza at a slightly lower temperature range (650° to 750°F) for a slightly longer period of time (2½ to 3 minutes). For more details, see Cooking Your Pizza in an Outdoor Oven (page 46).

HYDRATION
Hydration refers to the percentage of water in a dough recipe. In order to calculate the hydration of any of the dough recipes in this book, simply divide the weight of the water by the weight of the flour.

VARIATION: OUTDOOR PIZZA OVEN DOUGH
For the Neapolitanish Pizza Dough (below), use 385 grams of water. For the Sourdough Neapolitanish Pizza Dough (page 25), use 335 grams of water.

Neapolitanish Pizza Dough

Timeline: 1½ to 3 days

Makes four 245- to 250-gram balls

550 grams (about 4¼ cups) bread flour or all-purpose flour, plus more for dusting

15 grams salt (see page 17)

2 grams (about ½ teaspoon) instant yeast

425 to 450 grams (1¾ to 2 cups) cold (about 60°F) water

Extra-virgin olive oil

If you live in a humid environment or are new to pizza making, start with 425 grams of water. The dough may feel dry immediately after mixing, but as the dough rises, the flour will continue to hydrate, and when you turn out the dough to portion it, it will feel much wetter and stickier. If you are an experienced pizza maker and don't mind working with a higher hydration dough, you can use 450 grams of water to start. If you plan on baking your pizza in an outdoor pizza oven, see Outdoor Pizza Oven Dough (above).

Mix the dough: In a large bowl, whisk together the flour, salt, and yeast. Add the water and use a spatula to mix until the dough comes together, forming a sticky dough ball. If the dough is dry, use your hands to gently knead it in the bowl until it comes together. Cover the bowl with a towel and let rest for at least 15 minutes and up to 30 minutes.

Stretch and fold: Fill a small bowl with water. Dip one hand into the bowl of water, then use the dry hand

Portioning the Dough

Dust a work surface with flour.

Dust your dough with flour.

Gently deflate your dough.

Turn out onto a work surface.

Use a bench scraper to portion the dough.

Most of the dough recipes yield four portions, but if you are making Pan Pizza Dough (page 30), you will either leave your dough whole, cut it in half, or divide into four portions.

to stabilize the bowl while you grab an edge of the dough with your wet hand, pull up, and fold it toward the center. Repeat this stretching and folding motion 8 to 10 times, turning the bowl 90 degrees after each set. By the end, the dough should transform from shaggy in texture to smooth and cohesive.

Pour about 1 teaspoon of olive oil over the dough and use your hands to rub it all over. Cover the bowl tightly and

let the dough rise at room temperature until it has nearly doubled in volume, 6 to 10 hours. The time will vary depending on the time of year and the temperature of your kitchen.

Portion the dough: Turn the dough out onto a lightly floured work surface and use a bench scraper to divide the dough into 4 equal portions, roughly 245 to 250 grams each. Using flour as needed, form each portion into a ball by grabbing the edges of the dough

and pulling them toward the center to create a rough ball. Then flip the ball over, cup both your hands around the dough, and drag it toward you, creating tension as you pull. Repeat this cupping and dragging until you have a tight ball.

Store the dough: Place the dough balls in individual airtight containers (see Dough containers, page 16) and transfer to the fridge for 1 to 3 days.

Sourdough Neapolitanish Pizza Dough

Timeline: 1½ to 3 days

Makes four 245-gram balls

375 grams (about 1⅔ cups) cold (about 60°F) water

100 grams (about ½ cup) sourdough starter, active and bubbly (see Sourdough starter, page 17)

15 grams salt (see page 17)

500 grams (about 4 cups) bread flour or all-purpose flour (see Note), plus more for dusting

Extra-virgin olive oil

NOTE

This recipe calls for 500 grams of flour because it also calls for 100 grams of sourdough starter, which is made up of equal parts by weight flour and water, bringing the total amount of flour in this recipe to 550 grams.

If you plan on baking your pizza in an outdoor pizza oven, see Outdoor Pizza Oven Dough (page 22).

Mix the dough: In a large bowl, stir together the water and sourdough starter. Add the salt and stir to dissolve. Add the flour and use a spatula to mix until the dough comes together, forming a shaggy ball. You may see dry patches in the dough. This is okay. Cover the bowl with a towel and let rest for 30 minutes.

Stretch and fold: Fill a small bowl with water. Dip one hand into the bowl of water, then use the dry hand to stabilize the bowl while you grab an edge of the dough with your wet hand, pull up, and fold the dough toward the center. Repeat this stretching and folding motion 8 to 10 times, turning the bowl 90 degrees after each set. By the end, the dough should transform from shaggy in texture to smooth and cohesive.

Let the dough rest for another 30 minutes, then perform another set of stretches and folds. Repeat this process twice more, performing 4 sets of stretches and folds over the course of 2 hours. After the fourth set, you will notice a difference in the texture of the dough: It will be smoother, stronger, and more elastic. (If you are not able to tend to the dough for those 2 hours, do not worry. Perform the first set of stretches and folds, cover the bowl, and let rest at room temperature. Two hours later, or when you can get to it next, perform one more set of stretches and folds—the dough will likely be very stretchy and elastic—then proceed.)

If you have a straight-sided container, transfer the dough to it. If you don't, leave the dough in the bowl. Pour 1 teaspoon of olive over the dough and use your hands to rub it all over. Cover the bowl or container tightly and let rise at room temperature until the dough has increased in volume by 50 to 75 percent, 4 to 10 hours. The time will vary depending on the time of year, the strength of your starter, and the temperature of your kitchen.

Portion the dough: Turn the dough out onto a lightly floured work surface and use a bench scraper to divide the dough into 4 equal portions, roughly 245 grams each. Using flour as needed, form each portion into a ball by grabbing the edges of the dough and pulling them toward the center to create a rough ball. Then flip the ball over, cup your hands around the dough, and drag it toward you, creating tension as you pull. Repeat this cupping and dragging until you have a tight ball.

Store the dough: Place the dough balls in individual airtight containers (see Dough containers, page 16) and transfer to the fridge for 1 to 3 days.

I fell in love with thin-crust pizza in the summer of 2022. I had arrived in Italy with visions of poofy-rimmed Neapolitan pizza crusts in my head but left dreaming about the thin-crust *tonda* ("round") pizzas served at Da Remo, Pizzeria Ostiense, and other pizzerias throughout Rome.

Upon researching how to make this style of pizza, I found recipes that called for both tipo "00" flour and semola rimacinata (see page 17), which together make a beautiful crust, at once thin, crisp, and pliable. This 70%-hydration dough also includes a small amount of olive oil, which helps with extensibility. Rolled into a round roughly 13 inches in diameter with toppings spread all the way to the edges, it can be baked on a preheated baking steel or in an outdoor oven. It's also the dough recipe used for the grilled pizza recipes in this book.

If you love pizza with an extra-thin and crispy crust, be sure to try the Tonda Dough variation (opposite) and the Roman Pizza Margherita (page 94).

Thin-Crust Pizza Dough

Timeline: 1½ to 3 days

Makes four 245-gram balls

385 grams (about 3 cups) tipo "00" flour or all-purpose flour, plus more for dusting

165 grams (about 1 cup) semola rimacinata or all-purpose flour

15 grams salt (see page 17)

2 grams (about ½ teaspoon) instant yeast

385 grams (about 1 ⅔ cups) cold (about 60°F) water

28 grams (about 2 tablespoons) extra-virgin olive oil, plus more for drizzling

Mix the dough: In a large bowl, whisk together the tipo "00" flour, semola, salt, and yeast. Add the water followed by the olive oil and use a spatula to mix until the dough comes together, forming a sticky ball. If the dough is dry, use your hands to gently knead it in the bowl until it comes together. Cover the bowl with a towel and let rest for at least 15 minutes and up to 30 minutes.

Stretch and fold: Fill a small bowl with water. Dip one hand into the bowl of water, then use the dry hand to stabilize the bowl while you grab an edge of the dough with your wet hand, pull up, and fold the dough toward the center. Repeat this stretching and folding motion 8 to 10 times, turning the bowl 90 degrees after each set. By the end, the dough should transform from shaggy in texture to smooth and cohesive.

Drizzle about 1 teaspoon of olive oil over the dough and use your hands to rub it all over. Cover the bowl tightly and let the dough rise at room temperature until it has nearly doubled in volume, 6 to 10 hours. The time will vary depending on the time of year and the temperature of your kitchen.

Portion the dough: Turn the dough out onto a lightly floured work surface and use a bench scraper to divide the dough into 4 equal portions, roughly 245 grams (or slightly less) each. Using flour as needed, form each portion into a ball by grabbing the edges of the dough and pulling them toward the

Rolling Out the Thin-Crust Pizza Dough

On a lightly floured work surface, pinch the outermost edges of the dough, depressing the air as you press.

Flip the ball and repeat the process, depressing the air from the edges as you pinch.

Using floured hands, lightly pat the center of the dough ball to flatten it.

Using a lightly floured rolling pin, begin rolling out the dough.

Use flour as needed and flip every few strokes.

Roll until your round is 12- to 13-inches in diameter.

center to create a rough ball. Then flip the ball over, cup your hands around the dough, and drag it toward you, creating tension as you pull. Repeat this cupping and dragging until you have a tight ball.

Store the dough: Place the dough balls in individual airtight containers (see Dough containers, page 16) and transfer to the fridge for 1 to 3 days.

VARIATION: TONDA DOUGH
To make true tonda-style pizza, which is almost paper thin, divide the dough into eight 120-gram portions. Proceed with the recipe, rolling the dough into a 12- to 13-inch round.

VARIATION: SOURDOUGH THIN-CRUST PIZZA DOUGH
To make a sourdough version of this recipe, simply omit the yeast and replace it with 50 grams of sourdough starter (see page 17). Follow the process outlined in the "Mix the dough" and "Stretch and fold" steps of the Sourdough Neapolitanish Pizza Dough (page 25). When it's time to portion, divide the dough into 4 portions roughly 255 grams each.

Balling Up the Dough

Dust a dough portion with flour.

Using lightly floured hands, pull an edge up and toward the center.

Pull another edge up and toward the center.

Repeat this pulling process three or four times.

When you've created a rough ball, stop.

Turn the ball over.

Dust your hands lightly with flour.

Cup your hands together and gently pull the ball toward you, creating tension as you pull.

Repeat this cupping and pulling until you've shaped a tight dough ball. Transfer to a storage container and store in the fridge.

Stretching Out the Neapolitanish Pizza Dough

On a lightly floured work surface, pat the dough gently to flatten it.

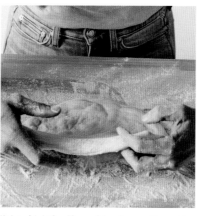

Using lightly floured hands, gently pull on an edge of the dough to stretch it out.

Repeat this gentle pulling on another edge.

Repeat again on another edge.

Using lightly floured hands, lay the dough round on the back of your hands and gently rotate it to stretch it further.

Take care not to depress the beautiful air pockets in the dough.

If the dough begins resisting, let it rest on the work surface for 5 to 10 minutes.

Continue to stretch using the back of your hands or by gently pulling on the edges.

When your dough is 10- to 11-inches in diameter, it is ready to be transferred to your pizza peel.

Pan Pizza

There are four styles of pan pizza recipes in this book: Sicilian, Detroit, grandma, and cast-iron skillet. The dough used for each of these styles is the same: a high-hydration (88%) dough that, once baked, resembles focaccia in texture. All of the styles, with the exception of the grandma, require a parbake to set the crust before the toppings are added. Sicilian pizza, which is baked on a sheet pan, is the thickest of the four styles. Grandma pizza, which is baked on a sheet pan but with half the amount of dough, is the thinnest. Detroit pizza, which is baked in a 10 × 14-inch (or similar) pan is thicker than grandma but thinner than Sicilian. And finally, cast-iron skillet pizzas, each baked separately in a cast-iron skillet, will vary in thickness depending on the diameter of the skillet used.

Pan Pizza Dough

Timeline: 1½ to 3 days

Makes 1,050 grams; enough for 1 Sicilian, 2 Detroit, 2 grandma, or 4 cast-iron skillet pizzas

550 grams (about 4¼ cups) bread flour or all-purpose flour, plus more for dusting

15 grams salt (see page 17)

2 grams (about ½ teaspoon) instant yeast

485 grams (a heaping 2 cups) cold (about 60°F) water

Extra-virgin olive oil

VARIATION: SOURDOUGH PAN PIZZA DOUGH
To make a sourdough version of this recipe, simply omit the yeast and replace it with 50 grams of sourdough starter. Follow the process outlined in the "Mix the dough" and "Stretch and fold" steps of the Sourdough Neapolitanish Pizza Dough (page 25) recipe. Proceed with the Pan Pizza Dough recipe at the "Portion the dough" step.

Mix the dough: In a large bowl, whisk together the flour, salt, and yeast. Add the water and use a spatula to mix until the water is absorbed and the ingredients form a wet, sticky dough ball. Cover the bowl with a towel and let rest for at least 15 minutes and up to 30 minutes.

Stretch and fold: Fill a small bowl with water. Dip one hand into the bowl of water, then use the dry hand to stabilize the bowl while you grab an edge of the dough with your wet hand, pull up, and fold the dough toward the center. Repeat this stretching and folding motion 8 to 10 times, turning the bowl 90 degrees after each set. By the end, the dough should be smoother and more cohesive, though still very wet.

Pour about 1 teaspoon of olive oil over the dough and use your hands to rub it all over. Cover the bowl tightly and let the dough rise at room temperature until it has nearly doubled in volume, 6 to 10 hours. The time will vary depending on the time of year and the temperature of your kitchen.

Portion the dough: Using lightly oiled hands, release the dough from the sides of the bowl.

For Sicilian pizza: Turn the dough out onto a lightly floured work surface and leave the dough whole.

For Detroit and grandma pizzas: Turn the dough out onto a lightly floured work surface and use a bench scraper to divide the dough into 2 equal portions roughly 525 grams each.

For cast-iron skillet pizzas: Turn the dough out onto a lightly floured work surface and use a bench scraper to divide the dough into 4 equal portions roughly 260 grams each.

Ball the dough: Using flour as needed, form each portion into a ball by grabbing the edges of the dough and pulling them toward the center to create a rough ball. Then flip the ball over, cup your hands around the dough, and drag it toward you, creating tension as you pull. Repeat this cupping and dragging until you have a tight ball.

Store the dough: Place the dough balls in individual airtight containers (see Dough containers, page 16) and transfer to the fridge for 1 to 3 days.

Gluten-Free Pizza

Gluten-free pizza baking is a challenge because gluten, the matrix of proteins formed when glutenous flours (those made from wheat, barley, rye, and triticale) mix with water, is what gives pizza crust a crumb with a simultaneous lightness and chew. Without gluten, dough has no strength. To compensate for a lack of gluten, gluten-free flour mixes contain stabilizers and thickeners like xanthan gum or guar gum, and gluten-free pizza and bread recipes often rely on eggs for structure.

Over the years, I have tried many gluten-free flour mixes with mixed success. So when I first made pizza dough using Antimo Caputo Fioreglut Gluten-Free Pizza Flour, I was astonished. The recipe I started with called for nothing more than the gluten-free flour, water, salt, yeast, and olive oil. And the mixed dough behaved more like wheat-flour dough than any other gluten-free dough I had previously mixed. While I couldn't lay it on the back of my hands while stretching it, it rolled out easily and it baked beautifully, emerging golden and crisp.

What's the secret? Antimo Caputo uses deglutenized wheat starch, which is a starch made from the endosperm of the wheat grain but with the gluten proteins removed. Deglutenized wheat starch is a common ingredient in gluten-free foods and has been used for decades throughout Europe and the UK. It is FDA-approved and safe for those with celiac disease. It is not, however, safe for people who have a wheat allergy. Reminder: Gluten-free does not mean wheat-free and vice versa.

Gluten-Free Pizza Dough

Timeline: 1½ to 3 days

Makes four 255-gram balls

550 grams (about 4 cups) Antimo Caputo Fioreglut Gluten-Free Pizza Flour

15 grams salt (see page 17)

4 grams (about 1 teaspoon) instant yeast (see Note)

440 grams (a scant 2 cups) cold (about 60°F) water

28 grams (about 2 tablespoons) extra-virgin olive oil, plus more for drizzling

Rice flour or more gluten-free flour, for dusting

This recipe has been specifically formulated to work with Antimo Caputo Fioreglut Gluten-Free Pizza Flour. Because all gluten-free flour mixes absorb water differently, it will not necessarily work well with other gluten-free flours.

Mix the dough: In a large bowl, whisk together the flour, salt, and yeast. Add the water, followed by the olive oil, and use a spatula to mix until the dough comes together, forming a sticky ball.

Pour about 1 teaspoon of olive oil over the dough and use your hands to rub it all over. Cover the bowl tightly and let the dough rise at room temperature until it is nearly doubled in volume, 8 to 10 hours.

Portion the dough: Turn the dough out onto a lightly rice-floured work surface and use a bench scraper to divide the dough into 4 equal portions, roughly 255 grams each. Using rice flour as needed, form each portion into a ball by grabbing the edges of the dough and pulling them toward the center to create a rough ball. Then flip the ball over, cup your hands around the dough, and drag it toward you, creating tension as you pull. Repeat this cupping and dragging until you have a tight ball.

Store the dough: Place the dough balls in individual airtight containers (see Dough containers, page 16) and transfer to the fridge for 1 to 3 days. Follow the instructions for rolling and baking in any of the recipes calling for Thin-Crust Pizza Dough.

NOTE
This dough recipe calls for slightly more yeast than the others because it needs an extra boost to compensate for the lack of gluten.

Sauces, Spreads, and Dressings

While I confess to always having a few jars of Rao's tomato sauces on hand, I do believe homemade is best. And making homemade sauce is not hard! The two tomato sauces I make most frequently—No-Cook Tomato Sauce (page 34) and Simple Tomato Sauce (page 34)—are made from canned tomatoes and just a handful of ingredients, and one of them, as you can infer, requires no cooking—simply whiz the ingredients in a blender or food processor, and you're done! The sauce tastes fresh and bright and can be ready in just about 5 minutes.

Additionally, in this chapter you'll find a few sauces made from fresh tomatoes as well as a couple of spreads—Basil Pesto (page 36), Sun-Dried Tomato Pesto (page 37), and Whipped Ricotta (page 41). There are also two vegan sauces: Butternut Squash Sauce (page 36) and Cashew Cream (page 37). Cashew cream, which I drizzle over pizzas post baking, is my go-to sauce for vegan pizzas. In addition to being incredibly tasty, it lends a creaminess and richness that I find to be a much better cheese substitute than commercial vegan cheeses, which do not melt well and often have an unpleasant mouthfeel.

If I am not a sauce purist, I am a homemade dressing evangelist, a trait I inherited from my mother, who would never purchase a bottled dressing even if pressed for time. Though there is a range of dressings in the book, a good dressing can simply come down to combining good olive oil, vinegar or fresh citrus juice, and salt. I tend to make my dressings on the more acidic side, so mellow them with more olive oil, if you prefer.

No-Cook Tomato Sauce

Makes 4 cups

1 (28-ounce) can undrained peeled whole San Marzano tomatoes

1 garlic clove, finely minced or grated on a Microplane

1 to 1½ teaspoons kosher salt

3 tablespoons extra-virgin olive oil

In a food processor, combine the tomatoes, garlic, 1 teaspoon of the salt, and the olive oil. Puree until smooth. Taste. Add another ¼ to ½ teaspoon salt, if you wish, puree again, then transfer to a storage jar and store in the fridge for up to 1 week or in the freezer for up to 3 months.

Simple Tomato Sauce

Makes 5 cups

¼ cup extra-virgin olive oil

2 cups finely chopped white or yellow onion

3 garlic cloves, minced

Kosher salt

Pinch of crushed red pepper flakes

½ cup white wine

1 (28-ounce) can undrained peeled whole San Marzano tomatoes

½ cup packed fresh basil leaves (about ½ ounce)

In a medium pot, combine the oil, onions, garlic, and a pinch of salt. Set over high heat and as soon as the onions and garlic begin simmering, stir, reduce the heat to low, cover, and cook for 10 minutes.

Uncover, stir in the pepper flakes, increase the heat to high, and add the wine. Simmer for 2 to 3 minutes to dissipate the alcohol. Using scissors, snip the tomatoes into smaller pieces as you add them to the pan. Season with a generous pinch of salt and cook at a gentle simmer for 15 minutes.

Transfer the sauce to a blender or food processor, add the basil, and puree until smooth (see Note). Taste and adjust with more salt if needed. Store in the fridge for up to 1 week or in the freezer for up to 3 months.

VARIATION: HOMEMADE VODKA SAUCE
Use vodka in place of the white wine. When pureeing the sauce, add ½ cup heavy cream.

Fresh Tomato Sauce

Makes 4 to 5 cups

2 pounds beefsteak or plum tomatoes, roughly chopped

4 red bell peppers, roughly chopped

1 cup water

1 teaspoon kosher salt, plus more to taste

4 tablespoons (½ stick) unsalted butter

⅓ to ½ cup lightly packed fresh basil leaves

In a large pot, combine the tomatoes, peppers, water, and salt. Bring to a simmer, then reduce the heat to medium and simmer gently until nearly all of the liquid has cooked off and the tomatoes and peppers are sticking to the bottom of the pot, 20 to 25 minutes more, or longer depending on the juiciness of your tomatoes.

Stir in the butter and basil, then transfer to a food processor or blender (see Note) and process until smooth. Taste and adjust with salt (I often add another teaspoon of kosher salt).

Store in the fridge for up to 1 week or in the freezer for up to 3 months.

NOTE
If using a blender, be sure to let the mixture cool off a bit first before pureeing. And start pureeing on low, with the steam vent in the blender lid removed and the lid covered lightly with a tea towel. This allows the hot air to escape and prevents an eruption of hot sauce.

Roasted Tomato "Butter"

Makes 2 cups

2 cups cherry tomatoes

1 cup diced onion

1 tablespoon extra-virgin olive oil

Kosher salt and freshly ground black pepper

¼ cup water, plus more if needed

2 tablespoons unsalted butter

Preheat the oven to 475°F.

In a 9-inch square baking dish (or something similar), toss the tomatoes and onion with the olive oil and 1 teaspoon kosher salt. Season with pepper.

Transfer the dish to the oven and roast until the tomatoes are beginning to collapse and blister lightly in spots, 25 to 30 minutes.

Transfer the tomatoes and onions to a food processor or blender (see Note, page 34). Add the water and puree until smooth. Add the butter and puree again until smooth. Taste and adjust with salt if needed. The sauce should be pourable, so add water by the tablespoon to thin it. Store in the fridge for up to 1 week or in the freezer for up to 3 months.

Butternut Squash Sauce

Makes 4 cups

¼ cup extra-virgin olive oil

1 tablespoon finely chopped fresh sage

4 cups peeled butternut squash pieces (about 1¼ pounds)

2 cups diced onion (about 1 small onion)

2 cups water, plus more if needed

Kosher salt

In a large pot, heat the olive oil over high heat. Add the sage and cook until fragrant, about 15 seconds. Add the squash, onion, water, and 1 teaspoon salt. If your squash pieces are not submerged in water, add more water just until they are barely covered. Simmer, uncovered, stirring occasionally, until the squash is very tender and the water has reduced considerably, about 20 minutes depending on the size of the squash pieces.

Transfer to a food processor or blender (see Note, page 34) and puree until smooth. (Alternatively, use an immersion blender.) Taste and adjust with salt if needed. Once cool, transfer to a storage container and store in the fridge for up to 1 week or in the freezer for up to 3 months.

Basil Pesto

Makes 1½ cups

4 cups loosely packed fresh basil leaves

2 to 4 garlic cloves, peeled

1 to 2 tablespoons fresh lemon juice, plus more to taste

Kosher salt

½ cup grated Parmigiano-Reggiano cheese

¼ cup pine nuts, almonds, or walnuts (optional), toasted (see Note)

½ cup extra-virgin olive oil, plus more to taste

In a food processor, combine the basil, garlic, lemon juice, 1 teaspoon salt, the Parmigiano, and nuts (if using) and pulse to combine. Add the oil and puree. Taste and adjust with more salt, lemon, and/or oil. Store in the fridge for up to 1 week or transfer to ice cube trays and freeze, then transfer to a zip-seal storage bag and store in freezer for up to 3 months.

NOTE

To toast the nuts, place them in a small skillet over low heat and toast slowly, stirring occasionally until golden brown and fragrant, 5 to 10 minutes depending on the nut.

Sun-Dried Tomato Pesto

Makes 1¼ cups

¼ cup almonds, any variety

½ cup oil-packed sun-dried tomatoes, drained

¾ cup grated Parmigiano-Reggiano cheese (about 2 ounces)

3 cups spinach (about 3 ounces)

1 garlic clove, peeled

3 tablespoons fresh lemon juice, plus more to taste

Flaky sea salt or kosher salt

½ cup extra-virgin olive oil, plus more to taste

In a food processor, combine the almonds, sun-dried tomatoes, Parmigiano, spinach, garlic, lemon juice, and a few pinches of flaky sea salt. Pulse 10 to 15 times, until the mixture is finely chopped but not completely pureed—I prefer this with a slightly coarse texture. Scrape down the processor and pulse again if necessary.

Transfer the contents to a bowl and stir in the olive oil. Taste and add more olive oil, lemon juice, or salt if needed. Store in a jar in the fridge for up to 2 weeks or transfer to ice cube trays and freeze, then transfer to a zip-seal storage bag and store in freezer for up to 3 months.

Cashew Cream

Makes 1½ cups

1 cup raw cashews

½ teaspoon kosher salt, plus more to taste

1 tablespoon fresh lemon juice, plus more to taste

Place the cashews in medium bowl and add water to cover by at least 1 inch. Let soak for 2 to 8 hours at room temperature.

Drain the cashews and transfer to a high-powered blender or food processor. Add the salt, lemon juice, and ⅔ cup water and process until completely smooth, stopping to scrape down the sides as needed. The process should take 1 to 2 minutes in a high-powered blender and 3 to 4 minutes in a food processor. If necessary, add more water by the tablespoon to create a creamy and very smooth consistency. Taste and adjust with salt and more lemon juice to taste. Store in the refrigerator for up to 1 week.

Lemon Vinaigrette

Makes 1⅔ cups

⅓ cup fresh lemon juice

⅓ cup white balsamic vinegar

2 teaspoons honey or maple syrup

1 teaspoon kosher salt

1 cup extra-virgin olive oil

In a medium bowl, whisk together the lemon juice, vinegar, honey, and salt. Stream in the olive oil while whisking constantly until emulsified. Transfer the dressing to a storage jar and store in the fridge for up to 2 weeks. Bring to room temperature and stir or shake the jar to emulsify before serving.

Apple Cider Vinaigrette

Makes ¾ cup

3 tablespoons fresh lemon juice

3 tablespoons apple cider vinegar

2 tablespoons honey

½ teaspoon kosher salt, plus more to taste

⅓ cup extra-virgin olive oil, plus more to taste

In a small bowl, whisk together the lemon juice, vinegar, honey, and salt. Stream in the olive oil while whisking constantly. Taste and add more olive oil by the tablespoon if the dressing is too tart and adjust to taste with salt. Store in the fridge for up to 2 weeks.

Red Wine Vinaigrette

Makes ¾ cup

2 tablespoons finely diced red onion

2 tablespoons red wine vinegar, plus more to taste

2 tablespoons fresh lemon juice

1 teaspoon kosher salt, plus more to taste

1 tablespoon honey

Freshly ground black pepper

½ cup extra-virgin olive oil

In a small bowl, combine the onion, vinegar, lemon juice, and salt. Let macerate for at least 5 minutes. Add the honey and pepper to taste and whisk to combine. Stream in the olive oil, whisking to emulsify. Taste and adjust with more salt and/or vinegar. Store in the fridge for up to 2 weeks.

Caesar Dressing

Makes 1⅓ cups

3 garlic cloves

6 olive oil–packed anchovy fillets

Flaky sea salt or kosher salt

1 large egg yolk or 1 tablespoon mayonnaise

2 tablespoons white balsamic vinegar

2 tablespoons fresh lemon juice, plus more to taste

1 cup extra-virgin olive oil

In a food processor or blender, combine the garlic, anchovies, and a pinch of salt and puree until smooth, about 15 seconds. Add the egg yolk (or mayonnaise), vinegar, and lemon juice and puree again until smooth, another 15 seconds.

With the machine running, stream in the oil very slowly until emulsified. Taste and adjust with more salt and/or lemon juice. If necessary, with the machine running, thin the dressing with 3 to 4 tablespoons of water.

Transfer the dressing to a jar and store in the fridge for up to 2 weeks.

NOTE

To make by hand, use a knife to mince the garlic and anchovies until very finely chopped. Transfer to a medium bowl, then whisk in the egg yolk (or mayonnaise), vinegar, and lemon juice until smooth. Very slowly stream in the olive oil, whisking constantly until emulsified. Taste and adjust with more salt and/or lemon. Thin the dressing with 3 to 4 tablespoons of water if needed.

Citrus-Shallot Vinaigrette

Makes 1 cup

¼ cup finely minced shallots

¼ cup white balsamic vinegar

¼ cup freshly squeezed orange juice

½ teaspoon kosher salt, plus more to taste

⅓ cup extra-virgin olive oil, plus more to taste

In a small bowl, combine the shallots, vinegar, orange juice, and salt. Let stand for 15 minutes. Whisk in the olive oil. Taste and adjust with more salt and/or olive oil. Store in the fridge for up to 2 weeks.

Italian Dressing

Makes 1⅓ cups

1 tablespoon Dijon mustard

1 teaspoon dried oregano

1 garlic clove, finely minced or grated on a Microplane

2 teaspoons sugar

2 tablespoons red wine vinegar

3 tablespoons fresh lemon juice

¾ teaspoon kosher salt

1 cup extra-virgin olive oil

In a medium bowl, whisk together the mustard, oregano, garlic, sugar, vinegar, lemon juice, and salt. Stream in the olive oil, whisking constantly until the dressing is emulsified. Transfer to a storage jar and store in the fridge for up to 2 weeks.

Mimosa Vinaigrette

Makes 1½ cups

⅓ cup freshly squeezed orange juice

⅓ cup champagne vinegar, white balsamic vinegar, or rice vinegar

2 teaspoons honey or maple syrup

1 teaspoon kosher salt

¾ cup extra-virgin olive oil

In a medium bowl, whisk together the orange juice, vinegar, honey, and salt. Whisking constantly, stream in the olive oil until emulsified. Store in the fridge for up to 2 weeks.

Blue Cheese Dressing

Makes 2 cups

¾ cup buttermilk

½ cup sour cream

⅓ cup mayonnaise

¾ teaspoon kosher salt, plus more to taste

½ teaspoon sugar

Freshly ground black pepper

2 tablespoons fresh lemon juice

1 garlic clove, minced

⅓ cup chopped fresh chives

5 ounces blue cheese, crumbled

In a bowl, whisk everything together. Taste and adjust with salt and/or pepper. Store in the fridge for up to 1 week.

Creamy Cashew Dressing

Makes 2½ cups

1 cup raw cashews

⅔ cup ice water, plus more if needed

½ cup extra-virgin olive oil

⅓ cup rice vinegar

1½ teaspoons maple syrup

1 garlic clove, peeled

2 tablespoons nutritional yeast

1 teaspoon crushed red pepper flakes

1 to 1½ teaspoons kosher salt

In a high-powered blender, combine the cashews, ice water, oil, vinegar, maple syrup, garlic, nutritional yeast, pepper flakes, and 1 teaspoon salt and blend until smooth and creamy. Taste and add the additional ½ teaspoon kosher salt, if you wish, and more ice water to thin if necessary—the dressing should be pourable.

Transfer to a storage jar and keep in the fridge for up to 1 week. The dressing will thicken further as it sits. Thin with water as needed.

Greek Yogurt Ranch Dressing

Makes 1½ cups

1 cup whole-milk Greek yogurt

3 tablespoons fresh lemon juice

1 garlic clove, minced

½ teaspoon honey

1 to 1½ teaspoons kosher salt, plus more to taste

Freshly ground black pepper

2 tablespoons minced fresh dill

⅓ cup chopped fresh chives

⅓ cup minced scallions (3 to 4 scallions)

4 tablespoons water

In a medium bowl, whisk together the yogurt, lemon juice, garlic, honey, 1 teaspoon salt, and pepper to taste. Whisk in the dill, chives, and scallions. Whisk in 2 tablespoons of the water. Taste and adjust with more salt and/ or pepper. Whisk in the remaining 2 tablespoons water to thin the dressing if needed. Store in the fridge for up to 1 week.

Herby Ranch Dressing

Makes 2½ cups

1 large egg yolk or 1 tablespoon
   mayonnaise

1 garlic clove, peeled

¼ cup fresh lemon juice

¾ cup extra-virgin olive oil

1 cup sour cream

⅓ cup buttermilk

1½ teaspoons kosher salt, plus more
   to taste

1 teaspoon honey

⅓ cup minced fresh parsley

⅓ cup minced fresh dill

⅓ cup chopped scallions
   (3 to 4 scallions)

In a food processor, combine the
egg yolk (or mayonnaise), garlic,
and lemon juice and puree for
about 15 seconds. With the machine
running, stream in the oil very slowly
and process until emulsified, 30 to
60 seconds. Add the sour cream,
buttermilk, salt, and honey and blend
until smooth.

Transfer the mixture to a medium
bowl and fold in the chopped herbs
and scallions. Taste and adjust with
salt if needed. Store in the fridge for
up to 1 week.

Green Goddess Dressing

Makes 1½ cups

1 garlic clove, peeled

1 cup packed chopped fresh herbs,
   such as parsley, tarragon, basil, and
   chives (about 1½ ounces)

4 scallions, roughly chopped

¼ cup mayonnaise

¼ cup fresh lemon juice

1 teaspoon kosher salt, plus more
   to taste

2 teaspoons honey

¾ cup extra-virgin olive oil

½ cup sour cream

In a food processor, puree the garlic,
herbs, and scallions until fine, scraping
down the sides two or three times. Add
the mayonnaise, lemon juice, salt, and
honey and process until emulsified.
Scrape down the sides again. With the
machine running, stream in the olive
oil and process until emulsified. Add
the sour cream and process again until
smooth. Taste and add more salt by
the ¼ teaspoon, or to taste. Puree one
last time. Store in the fridge for up to
1 week.

Whipped Ricotta

Makes 2 cups

If you do not want to make such a
large quantity, you can simply whip
the amount called for in the recipe in
a small bowl using a fork. The ricotta
will not transform into as silky smooth
a puree as it does when whipped in
the food processor, but whipping it
by hand will still lighten its texture
and make it less grainy.

15 to 16 ounces (about 2 cups)
   whole-milk ricotta cheese

¼ to ½ teaspoon flaky sea salt

In a food processor, puree the ricotta
with ¼ teaspoon of the salt until the
mixture is smooth, creamy, and shiny.
Taste. If desired, add the remaining
¼ teaspoon salt and puree again.
Store in the fridge for up to 2 weeks.

52
Pizzas
and
52
Salads

In the pages that follow are recipes for Neapolitan-style pizzas, thin-crust round pizzas, grilled oval pizzas, and a variety of pan pizzas. There are four seasonal chapters—Spring, Summer, Fall, and Winter—and the recipes are organized in pairs, each pizza matched with an appropriate salad mate, one whose flavors complement the pizza's sauce and toppings. You can mix and match, as of course many of the salads pair well with many of the pizzas, especially those found in the same seasonal chapter.

For simplicity, each pizza recipe calls for a specific style of dough—Neapolitanish or thin-crust, for example—but you may use toppings suggested for one style of pizza dough to another. When using toppings suggested for a Neapolitanish Pizza Dough on a Thin-Crust Pizza Dough, you'll need to increase the toppings by roughly one third. And when using toppings listed for a Thin-Crust Pizza Dough on a Neapolitanish Pizza Dough, you'll need to decrease by roughly one quarter. Use the toppings listed for an oven-baked Thin-Crust Pizza Dough recipe interchangeably with those listed for a grilled Thin-Crust Pizza Dough recipe. Use the quantities listed for sauce, cheese, and toppings on the Sicilian, Detroit, grandma, and cast-iron skillet pizzas as guides when using toppings on them from a different style of pizza.

Nearly all of the toppings in this book can be prepared ahead of time and stored in the fridge for up to 1 week. Similarly, all of the dressings and vinaigrettes for the salads accompanying each pizza can be made and refrigerated for at least 1 week. So don't be afraid to mix, chop, and whisk ahead of time!

Finally, all of the Neapolitanish pizza recipes are written for the home oven. Should you wish to cook your pizzas in an outdoor pizza oven, follow the instructions outlined in Cooking Your Pizza in an Outdoor Oven (page 46). Similarly, all of the grilled pizza dough recipes are written for a gas grill, but should you wish to cook your pizzas on a charcoal grill, follow the instructions outlined in Making Pizza on a Charcoal Grill (page 55). All of the pan pizza recipes are written for the home oven, whose even heat I find optimal for this style of pizza.

summer

Tomatoes. Farm stands. Peaches. Gardens. Corn. Camping. Canoeing. Hiking. Hammocking. Summer: It's the time of year to be outside, to turn off the oven, to embrace those low-effort meals that require assembly more than actual cooking.

If I'm being honest, here in Upstate New York, where it does not warm up till early June and begins cooling down in mid-August, it's never too hot for me to turn off the oven. I can't go more than a couple of days without baking something, be it a loaf of bread or a batch of soft pretzels, and I would never let a blazing hot day get in the way of my pizza Friday tradition.

That said, in the summer, when dinners aren't restricted to the fleeting moments between after-school activities and homework, I do take the opportunity to move the occasion outside, to fire up the grill or our outdoor pizza oven and enjoy our weekend-commencing meal on our back patio.

For the many people who can't bear to turn on the oven when the temperatures begin rising outside, never is a grill or an outdoor pizza oven more of a gift: Without having your oven at full tilt for an hour or more, warming up your kitchen, you can still make great pizza. Win-win.

In this summer chapter you'll find two pizza-cooking methods: a grilled pizza method that calls for cooking dough directly on the grill grates and an outdoor pizza oven method to be used with either a wood-burning oven or a portable pizza oven such as those made by Ooni, Gozney, and others. Of course, if you don't mind cranking up your home oven in the warmer months, the toppings used on these summer pizzas can also be used on your home-oven pizza doughs.

Accompanying these summer pizzas you'll find salads that celebrate the bounty of the season: corn as sweet as candy, peaches dripping nectar, plump tomatoes bursting at the seams. Summer is the time of year to give your favorite salad dressing a vacation and adopt a more casual approach: Scatter chopped vegetables and fruit on a platter, season with salt and pepper, dress with olive oil and vinegar or fresh citrus juice, shower with herbs, and finish, if you wish, with a bit of cheese. The dressings on these types of salads can easily be adjusted to taste, depending on your acidity preference, with a drizzle more of olive oil or vinegar, and the salads can be easily scaled up or down depending on how many people you are serving. They should take minimal time to prepare.

Cooking Your Pizza in an Outdoor Oven

Heating Your Outdoor Oven

Though many pizza ovens can reach temperatures of 900°F and beyond in 15 to 20 minutes, a longer preheat—roughly 30 to 45 minutes—will ensure the stone is sufficiently heated, which will in turn ensure your pizzas cook properly. An infrared thermometer will help you more accurately gauge the temperature of your oven and ensure you are launching your pizzas onto a thoroughly preheated surface.

Preparing Your Dough and Peel: Two Tips

Tip #1: Pop Bubbles. When stretching out your dough round, pop any large bubbles that form on the exterior crust—they will char in the high heat of the oven.

Tip #2: Use Rice Flour. Because rice flour does not burn as easily as wheat flour, I prefer using it on my peel when I am cooking pizzas in my outdoor oven. A mix of rice flour and all-purpose flour also works well.

Cooking Your Pizza

Roughly 30 to 45 minutes before you want to bake the pizza, preheat your pizza oven to between 650° and 750°F. Dust a peel lightly with rice flour or all-purpose flour. Stretch and assemble the dough on the pizza peel as directed in the recipe. Shimmy the pizza into the preheated oven.

If your oven has a dial, immediately lower the flame to its lowest setting, then bake for 2 to 2½ minutes, rotating the pizza after 45 to 60 seconds and then as needed, depending on how your pizza is browning. If you are using wood, bake for 2 to 2½ minutes, rotating and re-positioning the pizza after 45 to 60 seconds and then as needed to ensure even browning.

When the cheese has melted and the edges are beginning to char, use the peel to remove the pizza and finish the pizza as directed in the recipe.

NOTE

Depending on the temperature of your oven, the pizza may take longer to bake, 5 to 6 minutes or so. Rely on the visual cues noted before removing it from the oven.

Bufalina's Shrimp Pizza with Roasted Lemon Salsa

Makes one 12-inch pizza

1 ball Neapolitanish Pizza Dough (page 22)

All-purpose flour, for dusting

Semolina flour, rice flour, or all-purpose flour, for the peel

Toppings

5 shrimp (16/20 count), cut into ½-inch pieces

Flaky sea salt or kosher salt

Extra-virgin olive oil

3 tablespoons Roasted Lemon Salsa (recipe follows)

3 ounces low-moisture whole-milk mozzarella (see Note), pulled into ½-inch pieces (about ¾ cup)

Parmigiano-Reggiano cheese, for finishing

NOTE

If you are able to find scamorza, use half mozzarella and half scamorza.

Every summer my children spend a few weeks with my parents in Connecticut, where they get the royal treatment: pancakes for breakfast, dryer-warmed towels after showers, and dinners at their favorite pizzeria, Bufalina, a wood-fired pizza restaurant owned by Melissa and Matt Pellegrino, authors of two beautiful cookbooks on regional Italian cooking. Invariably, the children return home raving about a new favorite topping combination, and one summer, it was this shrimp pizza with roasted lemon salsa. Hoping to re-create it for them, I emailed Melissa, who kindly shared the recipe. In sum, she makes a roasted lemon salsa with parsley, garlic, and olive oil, which she spreads atop a mix of mozzarella and scamorza, an Italian cow's milk cheese shaped similarly to provolone that melts nicely. She tops the cheese with diced raw shrimp and bakes it with a bread crumb/parmesan mixture sprinkled over the top. For simplicity, I've omitted the bread crumbs here, the addition of which I'm sure would be lovely, though the pizza is absolutely divine without.

Prepare the dough: Transfer the dough from its storage container to a roomier, lightly floured, covered container (see Dough containers, page 16) and allow it to proof at room temperature for 1½ to 2 hours.

Prepare the oven and pizza peel: About 1 hour before you want to bake the pizza, place a baking steel in the top third of the oven and preheat it to 550°F convection roast (or as high as it will go). Dust a pizza peel lightly with semolina flour or top with parchment paper.

Stretch the dough: Lightly dust a work surface with flour. Using lightly floured hands, pat the dough gently to flatten it, then stretch it into a 10- to 11-inch round by laying it on the back of your hands and gently rotating it, taking care not to depress the beautiful air pockets in the dough. If the dough begins resisting, set it down on the work surface to rest for 5 to 10 minutes, then continue stretching. Transfer the stretched dough to the prepared peel and give it a shake to ensure it's not sticking.

Top the pizza: In a small bowl, combine the shrimp, a pinch of flaky salt, and a drizzle of olive oil and toss to combine. Spread the roasted lemon salsa evenly over the dough, leaving a ½-inch border. Spread the mozzarella evenly over the top, followed by the shrimp. Drizzle lightly with olive oil and season with a pinch of flaky sea salt. Stretch the dough one last time by pulling outward on the edges. Redistribute the toppings as needed, then give the peel one last shake to ensure the dough is not sticking.

Bake the pizza: Shimmy the pizza (still on the parchment if using) onto the steel and bake until the cheese is melted and the edges are beginning

Recipe continues

to char, 5 to 6 minutes. (This may take 8 to 10 minutes, depending on your oven.)

Using the peel, transfer the pizza to a cutting board (discard the parchment paper). Shave Parmigiano-Reggiano over the top to taste. Cut and serve.

Roasted Lemon Salsa

Makes about ½ cup (enough for at least two 12-inch pizzas)

2 lemons, thinly sliced

Kosher salt

2 teaspoons plus ¼ cup extra-virgin olive oil, plus more to taste

1 garlic clove, grated or finely minced

¼ cup finely chopped fresh parsley

¼ teaspoon crushed red pepper flakes, plus more to taste

Preheat the oven to 425°F. Line a sheet pan with parchment paper.

Spread the lemon slices in a single layer on the lined pan. Sprinkle with ¼ teaspoon salt and drizzle with 2 teaspooons olive oil. Transfer to the oven and roast until the edges of the lemons begin to caramelize, 15 to 18 minutes.

Transfer the slices to a cutting board. When cool enough to handle, discard the seeds and finely chop the roasted lemon. Transfer to a small bowl and season with a pinch of salt. Add the garlic, parsley, pepper flakes, and ¼ cup olive oil. Stir to combine. Adjust with more salt, olive oil, and/or red pepper flakes.

Store in the fridge for up to 1 week or in the freezer for up to 3 months.

My Mother's Horiatiki Salad

Serves 4

3 cups cherry tomatoes, halved

2 medium cucumbers, peeled and cut into 1-inch pieces (about 2 cups)

1 cup finely sliced red onion

1 red bell pepper, thinly sliced (about 1 cup)

Kosher salt or flaky sea salt

3 tablespoons extra-virgin olive oil, plus more to taste

3 tablespoons white balsamic vinegar, plus more to taste

½ cup kalamata olives

2 tablespoons capers, drained

2 tablespoons loosely packed fresh dill fronds

A big pinch of dried oregano, preferably Greek or Sicilian, to taste

4 ounces feta cheese, preferably in brine, sliced into thin slabs

If you were to order a horiatiki salad in Greece, it wouldn't look like this. Rather, it would be an arrangement of large chunks of tomatoes, peppers, and cucumbers, along with olives and sliced red onion. A slab of feta, seasoned with oregano, would sit atop the vegetables, and it would all be drizzled lightly with olive oil and red wine vinegar. Even though I love this traditional version, I love my mother's variation even more. Hers is made with a similar mix of vegetables that are chopped a touch smaller and dressed a bit heavier. She adds capers for a nice textural pop and dill, too. This is one of the salads I prepare most often throughout the summer. The sweet mix of tomatoes and peppers make it a perfect match for the lemony pizza and so many others in this chapter, namely the Summer Squash and Squash Blossom Pizza (page 65) and the Grilled Ortolona Pizza with Zucchini, Eggplant, and Olives (page 68).

In a large bowl, combine the tomatoes, cucumbers, onion, and bell pepper. Season with a big pinch of salt and toss to combine. Add the olive oil, vinegar, olives, capers, dill, and oregano. Toss again. Taste and adjust with more salt if needed. Add more olive oil or more vinegar, depending on whether you want it sharper or milder. When the salad tastes balanced, add the feta and gently toss one last time.

Grilled BBQ Chicken Pizza

Makes one 14 × 9-inch oval pizza

1 ball Thin-Crust Pizza Dough
(page 26)

All-purpose flour, for dusting

All-purpose flour or rice flour, for
the peel

Extra-virgin olive oil

Toppings

Extra-virgin olive oil

¼ cup sour cream or crème fraîche,
at room temperature

½ cup thinly sliced red onion

¾ cup (about 4 ounces) diced
BBQ Chicken (recipe follows)
mixed with 1 tablespoon of your
favorite bottled BBQ sauce

¾ cup diced peach, apricot, or
nectarine

4 ounces Monterey Jack cheese
or low-moisture whole-milk
mozzarella cheese, pulled into
½-inch pieces (about 1 cup)

Flaky sea salt

Lime wedges (optional), for
serving

Popularized by California Pizza Kitchen in the mid-eighties, BBQ chicken pizza for many is a culinary triumph. For others, just the thought of it is enough to incite apoplexy. I must admit that BBQ chicken is not my first choice as far as pizza toppings go, but is it a great way to use up leftover BBQ chicken? Absolutely! Here it's paired with sweet, juicy stone fruit, as well as sour cream or crème fraîche, whose creaminess and tartness so nicely balance the BBQ sauce's vinegary tang. One bite of this summer pie, I have no doubt, will convince any naysayers that the controversial ingredient indeed deserves a seat at the pizza-topping table.

Prepare the dough: Transfer the dough from its storage container to a roomier, lightly floured, covered container (see Dough containers, page 16) and allow it to proof at room temperature for 1½ to 2 hours.

Prepare the grill and pizza peel: Turn all the grill burners to high until it reaches 500°F. This may take 15 to 20 minutes, depending on your grill. (For making pizza on a charcoal grill, see page 55.) Dust a peel with all-purpose flour or rice flour.

Roll the dough: Lightly dust a work surface with flour. Using a rolling pin, roll the dough into a 14 × 9-inch oval, using flour as needed to prevent sticking. Place the dough on the peel and give it a shimmy to ensure it isn't sticking. Brush the top of the dough with olive oil.

Grill the pizza: Shimmy the dough, oiled-side up, onto the grates. Cover the grill and cook for 2 minutes. Uncover and use tongs to flip the

dough so that the grilled side is facing up, then immediately transfer it to the pizza peel. Turn off the middle burner and turn the remaining two burners to medium. (If your grill only has two burners, turn one off and the other to medium.) You need the grill to be around 400°F.

Top the pizza: Brush the top surface of the dough with olive oil. Spread the sour cream over the dough all the way to the edges. Scatter the onion, chicken, and fruit over the top, followed by the cheese. Drizzle with olive oil and season with a pinch of flaky salt.

Shimmy the pizza back onto the grill grates over the turned-off burner and cover the grill. Grill until the cheese is melted and the underside is evenly golden, 5 to 7 minutes.

Use tongs to transfer the pizza to a cutting board. Cut and serve, finishing with a squeeze of lime if you wish.

Recipe continues

BBQ Chicken

Serves 4 to 6

1 teaspoon cumin seeds

1 teaspoon coriander seeds

1 teaspoon smoked paprika

1½ to 2 pounds boneless, skinless
chicken thighs (about 6)

Kosher salt and freshly ground
black pepper

2 tablespoons extra-virgin olive oil

⅓ cup of your favorite bottled
BBQ sauce

Seasoned with ground toasted cumin and coriander seeds along with smoked paprika, this BBQ chicken recipe is a year-round staple in my house. Leftovers are wonderful sliced or diced to throw in a salad, and, on a non-pizza night, to tuck into a quesadilla or a wrap.

In a small skillet, toast the cumin and coriander seeds over medium heat until they begin to darken and smell fragrant, about 2 minutes. Transfer to a mortar and use a pestle to grind them to a powder. Add the smoked paprika and stir to combine.

In a large bowl, season the chicken thighs all over with salt (about 1 teaspoon per pound) and pepper to taste. Add the spice blend and olive oil and mix with your hands to evenly coat the chicken. Cover the bowl and refrigerate for at least 1 and up to 12 hours. Bring the chicken to room temperature for 1 hour before grilling.

Preheat a gas or charcoal grill to high. Lay the chicken on the grates. Close the cover and cook for 3 minutes. Flip, cover, and cook for 2 more minutes. Brush the chicken with half of the BBQ sauce. Flip the pieces so the sauced side is down. Brush the other side with the remaining sauce, cover, and cook for 1 minute. Flip, and cook for 1 minute more. Transfer the chicken to a platter and let rest for at least 10 minutes before serving.

Classic Creamy Coleslaw

Serves 4 to 6

1 head cabbage (roughly
1½ pounds), thinly sliced
(see Note)

1½ teaspoons kosher salt, plus
more to taste

2 large carrots (about 10 ounces)

½ cup finely diced white or
red onion

1 cup mayonnaise

3 tablespoons white balsamic
vinegar

2 tablespoons sugar, plus more
to taste

I have always loved the small side of creamy coleslaw that accompanies burgers, lobster rolls, and fried fish at restaurants everywhere and so have my children. Upon trying to re-create that type of coleslaw at home, I played around with using combinations of mayonnaise and sour cream or buttermilk, but they always slightly missed the mark. It wasn't until I finally made an all-mayonnaise version that my children gave me their approval, concentrating deeply as they tasted, finally agreeing: *You should put this in your book, Mom.*

Place the cabbage in a large bowl, sprinkle with the salt, and toss to disperse, massaging and squeezing the cabbage as you toss.

Meanwhile, grate the carrots on the coarse side of a box grater (or with the shredding disc of a food processor).

Add the carrots and onion to the cabbage and toss to coat. Add the mayonnaise, vinegar, and sugar and toss until evenly coated. Adjust with salt or more sugar to taste. Transfer the slaw to a storage container and refrigerate, ideally for several hours before serving. This salad tastes better as it sits, so don't be afraid to make it a day or two in advance.

NOTE
To save time, you can use two 14-ounce bags of bagged shredded coleslaw mix in place of the cabbage and carrots.

Making Pizza on a Charcoal Grill

If you are using a charcoal grill, prepare the coals however you wish to create a direct and indirect zone. Prepare the dough and peel as directed in the recipe.

Grill the dough in the indirect zone, oiled-side up, covered, for 2 minutes. Uncover and use tongs to rotate the dough 180 degrees. Re-cover the grill and cook for 2 minutes more. Use tongs to flip the dough, then immediately transfer it to the peel. Re-cover the grill.

Brush the top surface of the dough with olive oil. Top as directed, then return the dough to the indirect zone. Grill covered until the underside is evenly golden and the cheese is melted, 5 to 7 minutes more.

Use tongs to transfer the pizza to a cutting board. Cut and serve.

Grilled Pizza
with Oven-Dried Tomatoes, Mascarpone, and Basil Pesto

Makes one 14 × 9-inch oval pizza

1 ball Thin-Crust Pizza Dough (page 26)

All-purpose flour, for dusting

All-purpose flour or rice flour, for the peel

Extra-virgin olive oil

Toppings

Extra-virgin olive oil

3 tablespoons mascarpone, room temperature

2 tablespoons heavy cream

Oven-Dried Tomatoes (recipe follows)

4 ounces low-moisture whole-milk mozzarella cheese, pulled into ½-inch pieces (about 1 cup)

Flaky sea salt

3 to 4 tablespoons Basil Pesto (page 36), plus more to taste

Every year, often in early September, when it's hard to keep up with the tomato haul from our garden and weekly farm share, I make a batch of oven-dried tomatoes. It's a process that requires minimal prep but a long, slow bake in the oven, about 12 hours at 200°F. I love witnessing the transformation, from plump, juicy orbs to desiccated, anemone-like disks. And once I have those oven-dried tomatoes on hand, this is one of the first recipes I make. It's such a fun late-summer appetizer or dinner with, of course, a salad on the side. Although I love this grilled pizza with many of the salads in this chapter, while I have the grill going, I like to throw some heads of romaine lettuce on top and make the Summer Caesar Salad with Grilled Romaine, Crispy Capers, and Parmesan (page 58).

Prepare the dough: Transfer the dough from its storage container to a roomier, lightly floured, covered container (see Dough containers, page 16) and allow it to proof at room temperature for 1½ to 2 hours.

Prepare the grill and pizza peel: Turn all the grill burners to high until it reaches 500°F. This may take 15 to 20 minutes, depending on your grill. (For making pizza on a charcoal grill, see page 55.) Dust a peel with all-purpose flour or rice flour.

Roll the dough: Lightly dust a work surface with flour. Using a rolling pin, roll the dough into a 14 × 9-inch oval, using flour as needed to prevent sticking. Place the dough on the peel and give it a shimmy to ensure it isn't sticking. Brush the top of the dough with olive oil.

Grill the pizza: Shimmy the dough, oiled-side up, onto the grates. Cover the grill and cook for 2 minutes. Uncover and use tongs to flip the dough so that the grilled side is facing up, then immediately transfer it to the pizza peel.

Turn off the middle burner and turn the remaining two burners to medium. (If your grill only has two burners, turn one off and the other to medium.) You need the grill to be around 400°F.

Top the pizza: Brush the top surface of the dough with olive oil. In a small bowl, stir together the mascarpone and heavy cream. Spread the mascarpone/cream mixture over the dough all the way to the edges. Top with the oven-dried tomatoes. (Depending on the size of your tomatoes, you'll need 18 to 20.) Scatter the mozzarella evenly over the top. Drizzle with olive oil and season with a pinch of flaky salt.

Shimmy the pizza back onto the grill grates over the turned-off burner and cover the grill. Grill until the cheese is melted and the underside is evenly golden, 5 to 7 minutes more.

Use tongs to transfer the pizza to a cutting board. Drizzle with the pesto to taste. Cut and serve.

Recipe continues

Oven-Dried Tomatoes

Makes 24 tomato halves

12 plum tomatoes

Kosher salt

Preheat the oven to 200°F.

Halve each tomato lengthwise through the stem. Arrange the tomatoes, cut-side up on a sheet pan. Tomatoes should not be touching one another. Sprinkle each tomato lightly with salt.

Bake until the tomatoes are shriveled but not dry and brittle, 8 to 12 hours. Let cool completely before storing in the fridge in an airtight container for up to 2 weeks.

Summer Caesar Salad with Grilled Romaine, Crispy Capers, and Parmesan

Serves 4

4 heads romaine lettuce, halved lengthwise

4 tablespoons extra-virgin olive oil

Kosher salt

¼ cup Caesar Dressing (page 39), plus more to taste

A small block of Parmigiano-Reggiano cheese (about 1 ounce), or to taste

¼ cup capers, drained and patted dry

Freshly ground black pepper

NOTE
Preheat the broiler with a rack 6 inches from the heating element. Place the oiled and seasoned romaine heads cut-side down on a foil-lined sheet pan. Broil for 2 to 3 minutes. Flip, broil for 1 to 2 minutes more. Transfer to a platter and garnish as directed.

Though I had seen many recipes over the years for grilled lettuces, it was Susan Spungen's description in *Open Kitchen* that finally inspired me to give the method a try. She writes, "A big platter of various halved and grilled heads of slightly bitter greens is a sight to behold and a cinch to prepare." The same is true of romaine lettuce heads, which transform on a hot grill, their edges caramelizing, their frames buckling, releasing juices that bead at the surface. Off the grill, you'll drizzle the heads with Caesar Dressing and shave Parmigiano-Reggiano on top. Crispy capers, which are addictive, take this one to the next level.

Preheat a gas or charcoal grill to high. (To grill the romaine under the broiler, see Note.)

In a large bowl, drizzle the lettuce with 2 tablespoons of the olive oil and season evenly with salt, then toss to coat.

When the grill has heated, place the halved romaine heads cut-side down on the grates, cover the grill, and cook until the cut sides are lightly browned and charring at the edges, about 90 seconds. Use tongs to flip the heads and cook for another 90 seconds. Transfer the heads to a large platter, halved-sides up.

Spoon the dressing over the romaine, then use a Microplane grater or peeler to shave the Parmigiano-Reggiano over the top.

In a small skillet, heat the remaining 2 tablespoons oil and the capers over medium heat until they begin to sizzle. Increase the heat and let the capers continue to crisp and pop, 2 to 3 minutes. Once completely crisp, remove the capers, leaving the excess oil behind.

Scatter the crispy capers over the lettuce, then season with pepper to taste.

Grilled Margherita Pizza
with Fresh Tomato Sauce, Mozzarella, and Basil Pesto

Makes one 14 × 9-inch oval pizza

1 ball Thin-Crust Pizza Dough
(page 26)

All-purpose flour, for dusting

All-purpose flour or rice flour,
for the peel

Extra-virgin olive oil

Toppings

Extra-virgin olive oil

¼ cup Fresh Tomato Sauce
(page 34)

4 ounces low-moisture whole-milk
mozzarella cheese, pulled into
½-inch pieces (about 1 cup)

Flaky sea salt

Drizzle of Basil Pesto (page 36)
and/or a handful of fresh basil

Ninety percent of the year, I am happy to use sauce made from canned tomatoes, but for that short remainder, when the tomatoes are blanketing my countertops, only a fresh sauce will do. Similarly, when I can't keep up with the farm-share basil, I turn it into pesto and use it on everything: sandwiches, pastas, salads, and, of course, pizza. I love finishing this pizza with both pesto and fresh basil, but if you don't have a basil "problem" to solve, using one or the other is just fine.

Prepare the dough: Transfer the dough from its storage container to a roomier, lightly floured, covered container (see Dough containers, page 16) and allow it to proof at room temperature for 1½ to 2 hours.

Prepare the grill and pizza peel: Turn all the grill burners to high until it reaches 500°F. This may take 15 to 20 minutes, depending on your grill. (For making pizza on a charcoal grill, see page 55.) Dust a peel with all-purpose flour or rice flour.

Roll the dough: Lightly dust a work surface with flour. Using a rolling pin, roll the dough into a 14 × 9-inch oval, using flour as need to prevent sticking. Place the dough on the peel and give it a shimmy to ensure it isn't sticking. Brush the top of the dough with olive oil.

Grill the pizza: Shimmy the dough, oiled-side up, onto the grates. Cover the grill and cook for 2 minutes.

Uncover and use tongs to flip the dough so that the grilled side is facing up, then immediately transfer it to the pizza peel. Turn off the middle burner and turn the remaining two burners to medium. (If your grill only has two burners, turn one off and the other to medium.) You need the grill to be around 400°F.

Top the pizza: Brush the top surface of the dough with olive oil. Spread the tomato sauce all the way to the edges. Scatter the cheese evenly over the top. Drizzle with olive oil and season with a pinch of flaky salt.

Shimmy the pizza back onto the grill grates over the turned-off burner and cover the grill. Grill until the cheese is melted and the underside is evenly golden, 5 to 7 minutes.

Use tongs to transfer the pizza to a cutting board. Drizzle with pesto to taste and/or scatter the basil leaves over the top. Cut and serve.

Summer Squash Salad with Lemon, Mint, and Basil

Serves 4

1¼ to 1½ pounds summer squash

Kosher salt or flaky sea salt

1 tablespoon fresh lemon juice,
 plus more to taste

2 tablespoons extra-virgin olive oil

Freshly ground black pepper

A small block of Pecorino Romano
 or Parmigiano-Reggiano cheese
 (about 1 ounce)

½ cup fresh herbs, such as mint
 and basil leaves, torn if large

Everyone who eats this salad finds it revelatory: *Raw squash? Really?* Yes, really! Every year, when the summer squash begin arriving in the farm share, this is one of the first recipes I make. It's simple, it's summery, and it's especially good with the first tender squash of the season. A mandoline here makes for quick slicing work, but know that the salad can still materialize quickly using a knife.

Using a mandoline or a knife, slice the squash into ⅛-inch-thick rounds. In a large bowl, toss the squash with a big pinch of salt. Add the lemon juice, olive oil, and pepper to taste and toss again. Taste and adjust with more salt and/or pepper.

Use a vegetable peeler to shave the cheese over the squash. Add the herbs and toss again. Transfer to a serving platter.

Roasted Hatch Chile Pizza with Corn and Oaxaca Cheese

Makes one 12-inch pizza

1 ball Neapolitanish Pizza Dough (page 22)

All-purpose flour, for dusting

Semolina flour, rice flour, or all-purpose flour, for the peel

Toppings

2 tablespoons mayonnaise

⅓ cup corn kernels (stripped from ½ ear corn)

½ cup Roasted Hatch Chiles (recipe follows), chopped, or ½ cup diced canned Hatch chiles, drained

Chile powder

3 ounces Oaxaca, Monterey Jack, or low-moisture whole-milk mozzarella cheese, pulled into ½-inch pieces (about ¾ cup)

Extra-virgin olive oil

Flaky sea salt

Fresh cilantro, for serving

2 or 3 lime wedges, for serving

The combination below is inspired by esquites, a Mexican street corn salad (see Esquites-Inspired Street Corn Salad, page 74) that is dressed, among other things, with mayonnaise, lime juice, cilantro, and chile powder. I've added Hatch chiles, which I buy from the Fresh Chile Co. and roast at home, but you could use poblanos or even red or green bell peppers (see Roasted Red Peppers, page 195) in their place. Oaxaca cheese can be hard to find but it's worth seeking out for its flavor and texture—it melts so well and has a nice creaminess. Monterey Jack or mozzarella will work in its place. Note: If you're eyeing the mayonnaise in the ingredient list skeptically, I see you. Trust me, it's good.

Prepare the dough: Transfer the dough from its storage container to a roomier, lightly floured, covered container (see Dough containers, page 16) and allow it to proof at room temperature for 1½ to 2 hours.

Prepare the oven and pizza peel: About 1 hour before you want to bake the pizza, place a baking steel in the top third of the oven and preheat it to 550°F convection roast (or as high as it will go). Dust a pizza peel lightly with semolina flour or top with parchment paper.

Stretch the dough: Lightly dust a work surface with flour. Using lightly floured hands, pat the dough gently to flatten it, then stretch it into a 10- to 11-inch round by laying it on the back of your hands and gently rotating it, taking care not to depress the beautiful air pockets in the dough. If the dough begins resisting, set it down on the work surface to rest for 5 to 10 minutes, then continue stretching. Transfer the stretched dough to the prepared peel and give it a shake to ensure it's not sticking.

Top the pizza: Spread the mayonnaise over the dough, leaving a ½-inch border. Scatter the corn and roasted chiles over the top. Season with a big pinch of chile powder. Top with the cheese. Drizzle olive oil over the top and season with a pinch of flaky salt. Stretch the dough one last time by pulling outward on the edges. Redistribute the toppings as needed, then give the peel one last shake to ensure the dough is not sticking.

Bake the pizza: Shimmy the pizza (still on the parchment if using) onto the steel and bake until the cheese is melted and the edges are beginning to char, 5 to 6 minutes. (This may take 8 to 10 minutes, depending on your oven.)

Using the peel, transfer the pizza to a cutting board (discard the parchment paper). Sprinkle cilantro over the top. Cut and serve with lime wedges on the side.

Recipe continues

Roasted Hatch Chiles

**Makes about 1 packed cup
(enough for two 12-inch pizzas)**

Extra-virgin olive oil (optional)

6 Hatch green chiles or poblano
  peppers, halved lengthwise and
  seeded

Preheat the oven to 450°F. Line a
sheet pan with parchment paper (or
rub it with a small amount of oil).

Place the chiles cut-side down on the
pan. Roast until the skin is blistery and
charred, 30 to 40 minutes. Don't be
impatient here: If the skin isn't

blistered enough, the peppers will be
difficult to peel.

Place the chiles in a large bowl and
cover with a plate or kitchen towel.
Let rest for at least 20 minutes or up
to 5 hours. Peel off the skin. Store the
chiles in their juices in the fridge for up
to 1 week or freeze for 3 months.

Melon, Cucumber, and Mint Salad

Serves 4

2 cups cantaloupe or honeydew
  melon cubes (about ¾ inch)

2 cups watermelon cubes
  (about ¾ inch)

2 cups cucumber cubes
  (about ¾ inch)

Kosher salt or flaky sea salt

3 tablespoons extra-virgin olive oil,
  plus more to taste

3 tablespoons white balsamic
  vinegar, plus more to taste

5 ounces feta cheese, cut into
  ¾-inch cubes (about
  1 heaping cup)

⅓ cup fresh mint leaves, torn if
  large

The night before my brother's wedding, my parents threw a big pizza party. In
addition to the New Haven–style pizzas cooked in an antique truck outfitted
with a wood-burning oven, there were a few simple salads, including one
designed for the children: a mix of cubed watermelon, cantaloupe, and
cucumbers dressed lightly in a mint vinaigrette. It was so refreshing, and
although the bulk of the composition was fruit, the herby, sharp dressing
scooted it out of fruit salad territory. There was no cheese in the salad, but I
love the addition of feta, which is always a nice match for watermelon and other
summer melons. Sometimes with this salad, I'll add a pinch of Silk Chili (chile
flakes from the Turkish version of Aleppo pepper), and if I have an avocado on
hand, I'll add that, too.

On a large platter, combine the melon,
watermelon, and cucumber. Season
all over with a big pinch of salt. Drizzle
with the olive oil and vinegar and toss
gently. Taste and adjust with more
salt, olive oil, and/or vinegar. Add
the feta and mint leaves and stir gently
to combine.

Summary Squash and Squash Blossom Pizza

Makes one 12-inch pizza

1 ball Neapolitanish Pizza Dough
(page 22)

All-purpose flour, for dusting

Semolina flour, rice flour, or all-
purpose flour, for the peel

Toppings

1 small zucchini or summer squash
(about 5 ounces), thinly sliced
lengthwise (see Note)

Kosher salt

3 tablespoons crème fraîche, at
room temperature

Crushed red pepper flakes

½ cup grated Parmigiano-
Reggiano cheese

12 squash blossoms (about
2 ounces), stems removed
(see Note)

Extra-virgin olive oil

Flaky sea salt

NOTE
If you have a mandoline, use it
to slice the squash as thinly as
possible, ¹⁄₁₆- to ⅛-inch thick.
Otherwise, slice as thinly as
possible using a knife. Squash
blossoms can be found at most
farmers' markets from the late
spring to the early fall. If you
can't find them, you can simply
omit them.

If you garden or subscribe to a farm share, you cannot have too many summer squash recipes in your repertoire. Pizza is a great use for any variety of summer squash you might have on hand, and the key is to salt it briefly and let it drain in a colander. The salt will draw out the water in the squash, which will prevent the crust of the pizza from becoming soggy. When assembling this pizza, you'll think you are using way too many squash blossoms, but know that upon hitting the hot oven, the flowers collapse, melting into the layers of squash, cheese, and dough beneath them.

Prepare the dough: Transfer the dough from its storage container to a roomier, lightly floured, covered container (see Dough containers, page 16) and allow it to proof at room temperature for 1½ to 2 hours.

Prepare the oven and pizza peel: About 1 hour before you want to bake the pizza, place a baking steel in the top third of the oven and preheat it to 550°F convection roast (or as high as it will go). Dust a pizza peel lightly with semolina flour or top with parchment paper.

Prepare the toppings: Place the zucchini in a colander, sprinkle lightly with kosher salt, toss to distribute, and place in the sink to drain for 5 minutes.

Stretch the dough: Lightly dust a work surface with flour. Using lightly floured hands, pat the dough gently to flatten it, then stretch it into a 10- to 11-inch round by laying it on the back of your hands and gently rotating it, taking care not to depress the beautiful air pockets in the dough. If the dough begins resisting, set it down on the work surface to rest for 5 to

10 minutes, then continue stretching. Transfer the stretched dough to the prepared peel and give it a shake to ensure it's not sticking.

Top the pizza: Spread the crème fraîche over the dough, leaving a ½-inch border. Sprinkle with pepper flakes to taste. Top with the Parmigiano. Pat the zucchini dry and arrange it over the cheese. Distribute the squash blossoms evenly over the top. Drizzle it with olive oil and season with a pinch of sea salt. Stretch the dough one last time by pulling outward on the edges. Redistribute the toppings as needed, then give the peel one last shake to ensure the dough is not sticking.

Bake the pizza: Shimmy the pizza (still on parchment if using) onto the steel and bake until the cheese is melted and the edges are beginning to char, 5 to 6 minutes. (This may take 8 to 10 minutes, depending on your oven.)

Using the peel, transfer the pizza to a cutting board (discard the parchment paper). Cut and serve.

Elemental Summer Tomato Salad

Serves 4

1½ pounds beefsteak or heirloom tomatoes, sliced into ¼-inch-thick rounds

Kosher salt or flaky sea salt

1 cup yellow cherry or grape tomatoes, halved

1 cup red cherry or grape tomatoes, halved

3 tablespoons extra-virgin olive oil

3 tablespoons white balsamic vinegar

4 ounces burrata or fresh mozzarella, or whatever cheese you like

⅓ cup fresh basil leaves, torn if large

Freshly ground black pepper (optional)

This is the salad to make every night in late August, when the tomatoes are plentiful and finally taste how you've long anticipated: sweet, bright, meaty, juicy. The key for both a visually and texturally pleasing tomato salad is to use different types of tomatoes and to slice them in different ways: heirloom and beefsteak tomatoes into rounds, cherry or grape tomatoes in half. I love the creaminess that burrata adds to this salad, but fresh mozzarella, feta, goat cheese—any cheese you like (or none at all, if you prefer)—will work here. Fresh, tender basil leaves and a simple olive oil and vinegar dressing is all the adornment these summer treasures need.

On a large platter, arrange the sliced tomatoes, overlapping some of the slices if necessary. Season evenly with salt. Scatter the halved tomatoes over the top and season again with salt. Drizzle the olive oil and vinegar over the top. Use your hands to break up the burrata ball and dollop it evenly over the tomatoes. Shower the basil leaves over the top. Season with pepper if you wish.

There is no need to toss this salad. As it sits, the salt will draw out the juices from the tomatoes, which will blend with the olive oil and vinegar, making a tomato-infused vinaigrette. As you serve, spoon the juices over the tomatoes.

Grilled Ortolona Pizza with Zucchini, Eggplant, and Olives

Makes one 14 × 9-inch oval pizza

1 ball Thin-Crust Pizza Dough (page 26)

All-purpose flour, for dusting

Toppings

4 tablespoons extra-virgin olive oil, plus more as needed

1 zucchini (about 8 ounces), shredded

2 garlic cloves, finely minced

Kosher salt

Crushed red pepper flakes

2 cups ½-inch cubes eggplant

Assembly

All-purpose flour or rice flour, for the peel

Extra-virgin olive oil

12 kalamata olives, pitted and halved

4 ounces low-moisture whole-milk mozzarella cheese, pulled into ½-inch pieces (about 1 cup)

Flaky sea salt

Ortolana means "vegetable" in Italian, and my husband, Ben, and I learned the word one summer evening while strolling the streets of Caiazzo, Italy, with the uncle of one of our dear friends. As we walked with Uncle Tony toward Pepe in Grani, the renowned pizzeria located just two blocks from his home, we asked Tony what his favorite kind of pizza was, and he confessed to not liking pizza at all, which we found hilarious. With some prodding, he conceded to favoring ortolana pizza, which we ordered at 50 Kalo back in Naples the following night. Spread with a vibrant-green zucchini puree and topped with a medley of vegetables, olives, and buffalo mozzarella, the combination was the highlight of the meal, fresh and bright with pops of briny bites throughout.

Prepare the dough: Transfer the dough from its storage container to a roomier, lightly floured, covered container (see Dough containers, page 16) and allow it to proof at room temperature for 1½ to 2 hours.

Prepare the toppings: In a medium skillet, heat 2 tablespoons of the oil over high heat until it shimmers. Add the zucchini and garlic, reduce the heat to low, season with a pinch of salt and some pepper flakes, and sauté until the zucchini is very soft, 5 to 10 minutes. Transfer to a small bowl and mash with the back of a fork to create a paste. Taste and adjust with salt as needed.

In a medium skillet, heat the remaining 2 tablespoons oil over high heat until it shimmers. Add the eggplant and let it cook undisturbed for 1 to 2 minutes, or until it begins browning. Season with a pinch of salt, reduce the heat to low, and cook, stirring occasionally, until soft but caramelized at the edges, 7 to 10 minutes. Remove from the heat and transfer to a plate to cool.

Prepare the grill and pizza peel: Turn all the grill burners to high until it reaches 500°F. This may take 15 to 20 minutes, depending on your grill. (For making pizza on a charcoal grill, see page 55.) Dust a peel with all-purpose flour or rice flour.

Roll the dough: Lightly dust a work surface with flour. Using a rolling pin, roll the dough into a 14 × 9-inch oval, using flour as need to prevent sticking. Place the dough on the peel and give it a shimmy to ensure it isn't sticking. Brush the top of the dough with olive oil.

Grill the pizza: Shimmy the dough, oiled-side up, onto the grates. Cover the grill and cook for 2 minutes. Uncover and use tongs to flip the dough so that the grilled side is facing up, then immediately transfer to the pizza peel. Turn off the middle burner and turn the remaining two burners to medium. (If your grill only has two burners, turn one off and the other to medium.) You need the grill to be around 400°F.

Recipe continues

Assemble the pizza: Brush the top surface of the dough with olive oil. Spread the zucchini mixture over the dough all the way to the edges. Scatter the eggplant and olives evenly over the top. Sprinkle the mozzarella evenly over the top. Drizzle with olive oil. Sprinkle with flaky salt.

Shimmy the pizza back onto the grill grates over the turned-off burner and cover the grill. Grill until the cheese is melted and the underside is evenly golden, 5 to 7 minutes.

Use tongs to transfer the pizza to a cutting board. Cut and serve.

Summer Wedge Salad with Charred Corn, Tomatoes, and Herby Ranch Dressing

Serves 4

2 ears corn, shucked

1 tablespoon extra-virgin olive oil

Flaky sea salt or kosher salt

1 head iceberg lettuce (about 1¾ pounds), cut into 8 wedges

1½ cups cherry or grape tomatoes (about 8 ounces), halved

½ cup Herby Ranch Dressing (page 41), plus more for serving

¼ cup snipped fresh chives

Freshly ground black pepper

Next Door Kitchen and Bar, a restaurant just up the road from me in Ballston Spa, New York, is one of my favorites in the area. The menu changes seasonally, and every summer I look forward to their wedge salad, a thick slice of iceberg lettuce drizzled with a buttermilk-herb dressing and showered with house-made bacon, hard-boiled eggs, blue cheese, and tomatoes. Upon trying to re-create this salad at home, I emailed the restaurant and kindly received a reply from owner Matthew Hall, who passed along the recipe, which produces a light but creamy emulsion, not unlike a cross between an aioli and a Green Goddess dressing. It is delicious. For this wedge salad, I've kept the fixings more minimal, but I wouldn't fault you if you snuck in some crispy bacon and a blue cheese crumble or two.

Set a kitchen towel in the bottom of a large shallow bowl. Stand an ear of corn upright on the towel and use a knife to strip the kernels off the cob. Pat the kernels dry with the towel.

In a large skillet, heat the oil over high heat until it shimmers. Add the corn, season with a pinch of salt, and let cook undisturbed until the kernels begin to pop or brown at the edges, 1 to 2 minutes. Stir and continue to cook just until the corn is tender and lightly charred, 1 to 2 minutes more. Turn off the heat, set the pan aside,

and allow the corn to cool. Taste and adjust with salt if needed.

Set the iceberg wedges on a large platter and season them on both sides with some salt. Arrange them wedge-edge up. Scatter the tomatoes all around. Scatter the charred corn all around. Drizzle the dressing evenly over the top, being sure to dress each wedge generously—use more dressing as needed. Scatter the chives over the top. Season with pepper. Pass more dressing at the table.

Blistered Shishito Pizza with Onions and Monterey Jack

Makes one 12-inch pizza

1 ball Neapolitanish Pizza Dough (page 22)

All-purpose flour, for dusting

Peppers

4 ounces shishito peppers (about 1 cup)

1 teaspoon extra-virgin olive oil

Flaky sea salt or kosher salt

Assembly

Semolina flour, rice flour, or all-purpose flour, for the peel

2 tablespoons sour cream

¼ teaspoon crushed red pepper flakes

½ cup thinly sliced white onion

3 ounces Monterey Jack cheese, shredded (about ¾ cup)

Extra-virgin olive oil

Flaky sea salt

Fresh cilantro leaves, for serving

Lime wedges, for serving

Years ago at Casa Mono in Manhattan, I sat at the bar with a friend, savoring an array of Spanish tapas, most memorably the blistered salt-showered Padrón peppers. Days later, I recreated the dish at home using shishito peppers, which are similar in spirit and easier to find. They're also, as I'm told, easy to grow—my friend Sandy gives me bags of them every August. When she does, I broil and salt them, then spread them atop pizza dough with thinly sliced onions and Monterey Jack cheese. A squeeze of lime juice out of the oven brightens it all up.

Prepare the dough: Transfer the dough from its storage container to a roomier, lightly floured, covered container (see Dough containers, page 16) and allow it to proof at room temperature for 1½ to 2 hours.

Prepare the peppers: Place an oven rack 6 inches from the broiler and preheat it for 10 minutes.

Line a small sheet pan with foil. Arrange the shishitos on the pan, drizzle with the oil, sprinkle with a pinch of salt, and toss to combine. Broil until the shishitos are nicely blistered, about 5 minutes. Remove from the oven, let cool briefly, then remove any large stems. Leave small shishitos whole; cut any large ones in half crosswise.

Prepare the oven and pizza peel: About 1 hour before you want to bake the pizza, place a baking steel in the top third of the oven and preheat it to 550°F convection roast (or as high as it will go). Dust a pizza peel lightly with semolina flour or top with parchment paper.

Stretch the dough: Lightly dust a work surface with flour. Using lightly floured hands, pat the dough gently to flatten it, then stretch it into a 10- to 11-inch round by laying it on the back of your hands and gently rotating it, taking care not to depress the beautiful air pockets in the dough. If the dough begins resisting, set it down on the work surface to rest for 5 to 10 minutes, then continue stretching. Transfer the stretched dough to the prepared peel and give it a shake to ensure it's not sticking.

Assemble the pizza: Spread the sour cream over the dough, leaving a ½-inch border. Sprinkle with the pepper flakes. Top with the onion and shishitos. Top with the Monterey Jack. Drizzle olive oil over the top and season with a pinch of sea salt. Stretch the dough one last time by pulling outward on the edges. Redistribute the toppings as needed, then give the peel one last shake to ensure the dough is not sticking.

Bake the pizza: Shimmy the pizza (still on the parchment if using) onto the steel and bake until the cheese is melted and the edges are beginning to char, 5 to 6 minutes. (This may take 8 to 10 minutes, depending on your oven.)

Using the peel, transfer the pizza to a cutting board (discard the parchment paper). Sprinkle cilantro over the top. Cut and serve with lime wedges on the side.

Esquites-Inspired Street Corn Salad

Serves 4

4 ears corn, shucked

3 tablespoons extra-virgin olive oil

1 teaspoon kosher salt, plus more
  to taste

1 head romaine lettuce, finely
  chopped (about 4 cups)

¾ cup finely sliced scallions

¼ cup fresh cilantro leaves, roughly
  chopped

1 small jalapeño, seeded and
  minced

2 tablespoons mayonnaise

2 tablespoons fresh lime juice

½ teaspoon chile powder, plus
  more to taste

2 ounces cotija or feta cheese,
  finely crumbled (about ½ cup)

After sharing a corn soup recipe that called for cilantro, lime, and spices on my blog, someone emailed me asking if I had ever made esquites, a Mexican street corn salad spiced with similar seasonings and a mayonnaise-based dressing. I loved the sound of it and made it immediately, charring the corn stovetop first, then mixing it with the fresh herbs, diced jalapeños, chile powder, the dressing elements, and cotija cheese. I found it addictive—almost like a corn salsa—and so did my family. In this version I've bulked up the salad with sliced romaine lettuce, whose mild flavor plays well with the other ingredients and whose crisp texture can handle the bright, creamy dressing.

Set a kitchen towel in the bottom of a large shallow bowl. Stand an ear of corn upright on the towel and use a knife to strip the kernels off the cob. Pat the kernels dry with the towel.

In a large skillet, heat 2 tablespoons of the olive oil over high heat until it shimmers. Add the corn and kosher salt, stir to combine, and cook undisturbed until the kernels begin to pop or brown at the edges, 1 to 2 minutes. Stir, and continue to cook until the corn is tender and lightly charred, 1 to 2 minutes more. Turn off the heat, set the pan aside, and allow the corn to cool.

Transfer the corn to a large bowl. Add the remaining 1 tablespoon olive oil, the romaine, scallions, cilantro, jalapeño, mayonnaise, 1 tablespoon of the lime juice, and the chile powder. Toss to combine. Taste and add more salt as desired along with the remaining 1 tablespoon lime juice for more bite. Add the cotija, stir one last time, then transfer to a serving platter.

Grilled Pizza
with Ratatouille, Goat Cheese, and Fresh Basil

Makes one 14 × 9-inch oval pizza

1 ball Thin-Crust Pizza Dough (page 26)

All-purpose flour, for dusting

All-purpose flour or rice flour, for the peel

Extra-virgin olive oil

1¼ to 1½ cups Ratatouille (recipe follows)

3 ounces honey goat cheese or regular goat cheese, crumbled (about ¾ cup)

Flaky sea salt

A handful of fresh basil, torn if large

NOTE
Plan ahead. The ratatouille requires 1½ hours of cooking.

Whenever anyone visiting town asks me for a lunch recommendation, I suggest The Whistling Kettle, a tea shop located just down the road in Schenectady. And though I don't like to be bossy, I do strongly encourage them to order a pot of the Snowflake tea, a black tea flavored with almonds, coconut, and cinnamon, as well as the ratatouille and goat cheese crepe. It occurred to me one day that TWK's vegetable-and-goat-cheese filling would make an excellent grilled pizza topping, and so a few days later, I put the idea to the test: Shortly after pulling a large pan of roasted ratatouille from the oven, I spread the jammy mixture over grilled flatbread and topped it with crumbles of honey goat cheese. The result, well, how could it be bad? I suppose if you don't like goat cheese, in which case, use anything you like in its place, such as feta or mozzarella. Another fun option is to grill the ratatouille-topped pizza without any cheese, then, off the grill, break a ball of burrata over the top, drizzle with olive oil, and season with flaky sea salt.

Prepare the dough: Transfer the dough from its storage container to a roomier, lightly floured, covered container (see Dough containers, page 16) and allow it to proof at room temperature for 1½ to 2 hours.

Prepare the grill and pizza peel: Turn all the grill burners to high until it reaches 500°F. This may take 15 to 20 minutes, depending on your grill. (For making pizza on a charcoal grill, see page 55.) Dust a peel with all-purpose flour or rice flour.

Roll the dough: Lightly dust a work surface with flour. Using a rolling pin, roll the dough into a 14 × 9-inch oval, using flour as needed to prevent sticking. Place the dough on the peel and give it a shimmy to ensure it isn't sticking. Brush the top of the dough with olive oil.

Grill the pizza: Shimmy the dough, oiled-side up, onto the grates. Cover the grill and cook for 2 minutes. Uncover and use tongs to flip the dough so that the grilled side is facing up, then immediately transfer to the pizza peel. Turn off the middle burner and turn the remaining two burners to medium. (If your grill only has two burners, turn one off and the other to medium.) You need the grill to be around 400°F.

Top the pizza: Brush the top surface of the dough with olive oil. Spoon the ratatouille over the surface of the dough, spreading it all the way to the edges. Crumble the goat cheese over the top. Drizzle lightly with olive oil. Sprinkle with sea salt.

Shimmy the pizza back onto the grill grates over the turned-off burner and cover the grill. Grill until the cheese is melted and the underside is evenly golden, 5 to 7 minutes.

Use tongs to transfer the pizza to a cutting board. Sprinkle with the fresh basil. Cut and serve.

Recipe continues

Ratatouille

Makes 1 quart

1 eggplant (14 to 16 ounces), roughly chopped into ¾-inch cubes (about 5 cups)

Kosher salt

3 or 4 plum tomatoes (14 to 16 ounces), roughly chopped (about 3 cups)

1 large onion, diced (about 2 cups)

2 small zucchini (about 12 ounces), roughly chopped into ¾-inch cubes (2 to 3 cups)

2 red bell peppers, roughly chopped (about 2 cups)

4 or 5 garlic cloves, peeled

¼ cup extra-virgin olive oil

2 tablespoons white balsamic vinegar

Preheat the oven to 400°F.

Spread the eggplant cubes in the bottom of a 9 × 13-inch baking dish. Season evenly with kosher salt. Spread the tomatoes over the top and season again evenly with salt. Repeat this layering and seasoning with the onion, zucchini, peppers, and garlic. Drizzle the olive oil and vinegar over the top. Toss gently with your hands. Your pan will be filled to the brim so don't worry about tossing the vegetables evenly with the oil and vinegar at this time.

Roast in the oven for 1 hour.

Remove the pan, stir with a large spoon, and return to the oven until the juices have evaporated and the mixture is jammy in texture, another 30 minutes.

Let cool briefly, then taste and season with more salt if needed. Let cool completely before storing in the fridge for up to 1 week or the freezer for up to 3 months.

Peach and Tomato Salad with Basil and Balsamic

Serves 4

1½ pounds beefsteak or heirloom tomatoes, cut into irregular shapes and wedges

1½ pounds peaches (2 or 3), cut into ¼-inch-thick wedges

Flaky sea salt or kosher salt

3 tablespoons extra-virgin olive oil

3 tablespoons white balsamic vinegar

4 ounces burrata or feta cheese

A handful of fresh basil, torn if large

Freshly ground black pepper (optional)

Every July we spend a week at Lake George in Upstate New York with my husband's family, a mix of siblings, girlfriends, grandparents, and seven cousins who would happily spend every waking second on the lake. Although, I, too, love Lake George, I prefer admiring it from the beach or during my morning drive north to shop at the Bolton Garden Center for their prized produce: the first local corn and tomatoes of the season, and the juiciest peaches and nectarines. Every night for dinner, some sort of assembly like this peach and tomato salad materializes, usually with a mix of multiple fruits and vegetables, but this streamlined version is my favorite.

On a large platter, arrange the tomatoes and peaches. Season evenly with salt. Drizzle the olive oil and vinegar over the top. Use your hands to break up the burrata ball and drop dollops of it evenly over the tomatoes. Shower the basil leaves over the top. Season with pepper if you wish.

There is no need to toss this salad. As it sits, the salt will draw out the juices from the tomatoes, which will blend with the olive oil and vinegar, making a tomato-infused vinaigrette. As you serve, spoon the juices over the tomatoes and peaches.

Fried Eggplant Pizza with Fresh Tomato Sauce, Basil, and Parmesan

Makes one 12-inch pizza

1 ball Neapolitanish Pizza Dough (page 22)

All-purpose flour, for dusting

Eggplant

¼ cup all-purpose flour

1 large egg

1 cup fine dried bread crumbs, such as panko

½ cup grated Parmigiano-Reggiano cheese

1 small eggplant (6 to 7 ounces), cut crosswise into ¼-inch-thick slices

4 tablespoons extra-virgin olive oil

Kosher salt

Assembly

Semolina flour, rice flour, or all-purpose flour, for the peel

3 tablespoons Fresh Tomato Sauce (page 34) or No-Cook Tomato Sauce (page 34)

3 ounces low-moisture whole-milk mozzarella cheese, pulled into ½-inch pieces (about ¾ cup)

Extra-virgin olive oil

Flaky sea salt

Small block of Parmigiano-Reggiano cheese

Fresh basil leaves, torn if large

NOTE

If breading and frying eggplant feels like too much work, you can use grilled eggplant in its place.

My friend Laurie does not fancy herself a cook, but she is an excellent one, with instincts I so admire. Over the years, when I've found myself sitting next to her watching our children play hockey in many icy cold rinks, fretting about what to cook for this or that, she always has an answer. One New Year's Eve, she advised, *Just make a dip, everyone loves a dip.* She was right. One neighborhood block party, she said, *Just make a slaw, it will go with something.* She was right. One summer evening she asked me if I had ever topped pizza with breaded and fried eggplant. *It's so good,* she said. *The eggplant gets so crisp.* I loved this idea, which would put to great use the small, slender eggplant I had just received in my farm share. Later that night I launched the Laurie-inspired pizza into our pizza oven, and a few minutes later it emerged, the crispy fried eggplant rounds melting into the bubbling cheese and tomato sauce: eggplant parm in pizza form—Laurie had never been so right.

Prepare the dough: Transfer the dough from its storage container to a roomier, lightly floured, covered container (see Dough containers, page 16) and allow it to proof at room temperature for 1½ to 2 hours.

Prepare the eggplant: Set up a dredging station in three shallow dishes: Place the flour in one. Place the egg in a second and blend with a fork. Combine the bread crumbs and Parmigiano in the third.

Working with 1 or 2 slices of eggplant at a time, dredge both sides in the flour, shaking off any excess. Dip into the eggs, allowing excess to drip off. Coat evenly with the bread crumb mixture, pressing it to adhere. Place the breaded eggplant on a plate.

In a large skillet, heat 2 tablespoons of the oil over medium heat until it shimmers. Working in two batches, add a single layer of eggplant slices and season evenly with kosher salt. Cook until golden on the underside, about 2 minutes. Flip, season with kosher salt, and cook until the undersides of the slices are evenly golden, 1 to 2 minutes. Transfer to a plate to cool. Wipe out the skillet and cook the remaining eggplant rounds in the remaining 2 tablespoons oil in the same manner.

Prepare the oven and pizza peel: About 1 hour before you want to bake the pizza, place a baking steel in the top third of the oven and preheat it to 550°F convection roast (or as high as it will go). Dust a pizza peel lightly with semolina flour or top with parchment paper.

Stretch the dough: Lightly dust a work surface with flour. Using lightly floured hands, pat the dough gently to flatten it, then stretch it into a 10- to 11-inch round by laying it on the back of your hands and gently rotating

Recipe continues

it, taking care not to depress the beautiful air pockets in the dough. If the dough begins resisting, set it down on the work surface to rest for 5 to 10 minutes, then continue stretching. Transfer the stretched dough to the prepared peel and give it a shake to ensure it's not sticking.

Assemble the pizza: Spread the tomato sauce over the dough, leaving a ½-inch border. Top with the fried eggplant and mozzarella. Drizzle olive oil over the top and season with a pinch of sea salt. Stretch the dough one last time by pulling outward on the edges. Redistribute the toppings as needed, then give the peel one last shake to ensure the dough is not sticking.

Bake the pizza: Shimmy the pizza (still on the parchment if using) onto the steel and bake until the cheese is melted and the edges are beginning to char, 5 to 6 minutes. (This may take 8 to 10 minutes, depending on your oven.)

Using the peel, transfer the pizza to a cutting board (discard the parchment paper). Using a Microplane grater or a peeler, shave the Parmigiano over the top to taste, then scatter with some basil leaves. Cut and serve.

Cherry Tomato and Cherry Salad with Feta and Jalapeños

Serves 4

12 ounces cherries (2½ to 3 cups), pitted and halved

12 ounces cherry or grape tomatoes (2½ to 3 cups), halved

1 small jalapeño, seeded and minced

Kosher salt or flaky sea salt

¼ cup fresh lime juice, plus more to taste

3 tablespoons extra-virgin olive oil, plus more to taste

Fresh cilantro leaves

4 ounces feta cheese, preferably in brine, cut into ⅛-inch-thick slabs

Freshly ground black pepper

Like many, I am a devoted reader of Emily Nunn's *The Department of Salad*, a newsletter I discovered during the pandemic but now can't imagine living without. Emily is a riot, truly the bright spot in my week, the food writer I can always count on to make me laugh, the one who somehow manages to be grounding, entertaining, and informative all at once. In one of her posts, she wrote about an iconic Israeli salad made popular by Habasta, a restaurant in Tel Aviv, one she noted she could practically taste the minute she heard the ingredients: fresh cherries, jalapeño, cilantro, garlic, and olive oil. I could, too, and made it immediately, adding fresh lime juice as suggested by Emily, plus cherry tomatoes (because I had a heap on hand) and feta (because I can't resist). It's a surprising and delicious combination, perfect for just a brief period of the summer, when tomato and cherry seasons overlap.

In a large bowl, combine the cherries, tomatoes, and jalapeño. Sprinkle all over with salt. Add the lime juice and olive oil and toss gently to combine. Taste and add more salt, lime juice, or olive oil, if needed. Add the cilantro leaves to taste and toss gently. Transfer the salad to a serving platter. Scatter the sliced feta over top and season with pepper to taste.

Sausage Pizza
with Grilled Onions and Peppers

1 ball Thin-Crust Pizza Dough
(page 26)

All-purpose flour, for dusting

Toppings

1 medium red onion, cut into
½-inch-thick rounds

1 red bell pepper, sliced into
eighths

1 tablespoon extra-virgin olive oil

Kosher salt

1 link hot Italian sausage
(about 3 ounces)

Assembly

All-purpose flour or rice flour,
for the peel

Extra-virgin olive oil

¼ cup Fresh Tomato Sauce
(page 34)

4 ounces low-moisture whole-milk
mozzarella cheese, pulled into
½-inch pieces (about 1 cup)

Flaky sea salt

Though I am a big sports fan, my only memories of the professional games I attended as a child revolve around the concessions: big, salt-studded soft pretzels, melty breaded mozzarella sticks, and, my favorite: hot Italian sausages in hoagie rolls smothered with sautéed peppers and onions. Inspired by those game-day hoagies, this pizza calls for grilled sausage, peppers, and onions along with mozzarella. This less greasy take on a classic is a summer favorite, perfect for entertaining or for a simple family meal. The toppings are grilled just before making the pizza, but if you want to get a jump on the recipe, you can grill the toppings ahead of time.

I love it with the Niçoise-Inspired Salad with Blistered Green Beans, but many other salads in this chapter would pair nicely with it: Elemental Summer Tomato Salad (page 67), Cucumber Salad with Red Onion and Burrata (page 91), and My Mother's Horiatiki Salad (page 51).

Prepare the dough: Transfer the dough from its storage container to a roomier, lightly floured, covered container (see Dough containers, page 16) and allow it to proof at room temperature for 1½ to 2 hours.

Prepare the toppings: Preheat a charcoal or gas grill to high.

In a large bowl, toss together the onion and bell pepper with the olive oil and a pinch of kosher salt.

Place the onions and peppers on the grill and cook until the undersides are charred with grill marks, roughly 3 minutes for the onions and 5 minutes for the peppers. Using tongs, flip and cook for roughly the same amount of time, or until the undersides are charred with grill marks. As the onions and peppers are done, transfer them to a cutting board.

Place the sausage on the grill, cover, and cook until nicely charred all around, 4 to 6 minutes a side.

Meanwhile, finely dice the onions and peppers. Season with a pinch of kosher salt right on your board and toss to combine. Taste and add more kosher salt to taste.

Use tongs to remove the sausage from the grill. Let cool for 5 minutes, then slice into ¼-inch-thick rounds.

Prepare the grill and pizza peel: Turn all the grill burners to high until it reaches 500°F. This may take 15 to 20 minutes, depending on your grill. (For making pizza on a charcoal grill, see page 55.) Dust a peel with all-purpose flour or rice flour.

Roll the dough: Lightly dust a work surface with flour. Using a rolling pin, roll the dough into a 14 × 9-inch oval,

Recipe continues

using flour as need to prevent sticking. Place the dough on the peel and give it a shimmy to ensure it isn't sticking. Brush the top of the dough with olive oil.

Grill the pizza: Shimmy the dough, oiled-side up, onto the grates. Cover the grill and cook for 2 minutes. Uncover and use tongs to flip the dough so that the grilled side is facing up, then immediately transfer to the pizza peel. Turn off the middle burner and turn the remaining two burners to medium. (If your grill only has two burners, turn one off and the other to medium.) You need the grill to be around 400°F.

Assemble the pizza: Brush the top surface of the dough with olive oil. Spread the tomato sauce over the dough all the way to the edges. Top with 1 cup of the onion/pepper mixture. (You will likely have leftovers, which you can freeze or store in the fridge for up to 1 week.) Scatter the sausage over the top, followed by the mozzarella. Drizzle with olive oil. Sprinkle with sea salt.

Shimmy the pizza back onto the grill grates over the turned-off burner and cover the grill. Grill until the cheese is melted and the underside is evenly golden, 5 to 7 minutes.

Use tongs to transfer the pizza to a cutting board. Cut and serve.

Niçoise-Inspired Salad with Blistered Green Beans

Serves 4

5 tablespoons extra-virgin olive oil

6 garlic cloves, thinly sliced

1 tablespoon drained capers

1 pound green beans, trimmed

Kosher salt

8 ounces cherry or grape tomatoes (about 1½ cups), halved

8 ounces cucumbers, "zebra-peeled" (see Note) and cut into ¾-inch cubes (about 1½ cups)

½ cup thinly sliced red onion

Flaky sea salt

3 tablespoons white balsamic vinegar

¼ cup Niçoise (or other) olives

¼ cup finely chopped chives

Freshly ground black pepper

NOTE
To "zebra peel" a cucumber, peel the cucumbers, leaving strips of the cucumber skin still intact and creating a zebra-striped look on them.

One summer evening several years ago, in an attempt to make Sichuan-inspired green beans using less oil, I decided to broil my green beans instead of deep-frying them. The technique worked beautifully, resulting in blistered, tender, and well-seasoned beans. To make the dressing, I infused oil with garlic, capers, and red pepper flakes in a small skillet, then poured the sizzling oil over the beans. Over the years, those beans have become a jumping-off point for many a recipe, including this Niçoise-inspired salad, which unites the beans with tomatoes, cucumbers, onions, olives, and herbs. To keep it on the lighter side, I've omitted the traditionally included tuna and potatoes, but should you make this salad on a non-pizza night, those additions would make it a meal.

Place an oven rack 6 inches from the broiler and preheat it for 15 minutes. Line a sheet pan with foil.

In a small skillet, heat 2 tablespoons of the olive oil, the garlic, and capers over low heat. Let the oil slowly infuse until it begins to shimmer, 3 to 5 minutes. Remove the skillet with the garlic/caper mixture from the heat and set aside.

Meanwhile, place the green beans on the sheet pan and toss with 2 tablespoons of the olive oil and a big pinch of kosher salt. Taste a green bean raw—it should taste nicely seasoned. Transfer the pan to the broiler for 2 minutes, then check. If the beans aren't beginning to char, continue to broil for another 1 to 2 minutes. If they are charring, remove them from the oven and gently toss. Return the pan to the broiler for another 2 minutes, or until the beans are blistered to your liking. Remove the pan from the oven and set aside.

Place the cherry tomatoes, cucumbers, and red onion on a serving platter. Season evenly with sea salt. Add the vinegar and the remaining 1 tablespoon olive oil and toss gently. Scatter the olives over the top, followed by the blistered green beans.

Return the skillet with the garlic/caper mixture to medium to high heat and keep a close watch. As soon as you see the garlic beginning to brown at the edges, remove the pan from the heat and pour the warm garlic-infused oil evenly over the platter of vegetables. Scatter the chives over the platter and season with pepper to taste.

Fig Pizza
with Pickled Jalapeños, Crème Fraîche, and Arugula

Makes one 14 × 9-inch oval pizza

1 ball Thin-Crust Pizza Dough
(page 26)

All-purpose flour, for dusting

All-purpose flour or rice flour, for
the peel

Extra-virgin olive oil

3 tablespoons crème fraîche, at
room temperature

6 to 7 fresh figs, quartered or
sliced or a mix of both (about
8 ounces)

3 ounces low-moisture whole-milk
mozzarella cheese, pulled into
½-inch pieces (about ¾ cup)

¼ cup Pickled Jalapeños (recipe
follows), drained

Flaky sea salt

Handful of arugula (about 1 cup),
for finishing

Though pickled jalapeños have long been a popular pizza topping, I never thought much about them until I tasted The Colony, a pizza served at Brooklyn's Emmy Squared that combines the chiles with pepperoni and a drizzle of honey out of the oven. That pizza, with its addictive spicy-sweet flavor combinations, introduced me to the wonders of pickled jalapeños, not only as a complement to meaty items but also to fruits and vegetables. I love pairing them with stone fruits of all kinds, and, when I can find them, fresh figs. I finish this grilled pizza with a few handfuls of lightly dressed arugula, a mini salad that almost precludes the need for a side salad, though the Swiss Chard Salad with Hazelnuts and Cherries (page 88) is a particularly good match.

Prepare the dough: Transfer the dough from its storage container to a roomier, lightly floured, covered container (see Dough containers, page 16) and allow it to proof at room temperature for 1½ to 2 hours.

Prepare the grill and pizza peel: Turn all the grill burners to high until it reaches 500°F. This may take 15 to 20 minutes, depending on your grill. (For making pizza on a charcoal grill, see page 55.) Dust a peel with all-purpose flour or rice flour.

Roll the dough: Lightly dust a work surface with flour. Using a rolling pin, roll the dough into a 14 × 9-inch oval, using flour as needed to prevent sticking. Place the dough on the peel and give it a shimmy to ensure it isn't sticking. Brush the top of the dough with olive oil.

Grill the pizza: Shimmy the dough, oiled-side up, onto the grates. Cover the grill and cook for 2 minutes. Uncover and use tongs to flip the

dough so that the grilled side is facing up, then immediately transfer to the pizza peel. Turn off the middle burner and turn the remaining two burners to medium. (If your grill only has two burners, turn one off and the other to medium.) You need the grill to be around 400°F.

Top the pizza: Brush the top surface of the dough with olive oil. Spread the crème fraîche over the dough all the way to the edges. Scatter the figs, mozzarella, and pickled jalapeños evenly over the top. Drizzle with olive oil and season with a pinch of sea salt.

Shimmy the pizza back onto the grill grates over the turned-off burner and cover the grill. Grill until the cheese is melted and the underside is evenly golden, 5 to 7 minutes.

Use tongs to transfer the pizza to a cutting board. Scatter the arugula over the top. Drizzle lightly with olive oil and another pinch of sea salt. Cut and serve.

Recipe continues

Pickled Jalapeños

Makes 1 cup

½ cup water

½ cup vinegar, such as distilled white, rice, white balsamic, or apple cider

1 teaspoon sugar

1 teaspoon kosher salt

3 or 4 jalapeños, sliced thinly, no need to remove the seeds

Combine the water, vinegar, sugar, and salt in a small saucepan. Bring to a simmer and stir to ensure the sugar and salt are dissolved.

Place the jalapeños into a glass jar, such as a 2-cup Mason jar. Pour the hot pickle brine over top. Use a spoon to push the peppers down to ensure they are submerged. Let cool completely; then cover and stash in the fridge for many months.

Swiss Chard Salad with Hazelnuts and Cherries

Serves 4

⅔ cup raw (skin-on) hazelnuts

2 large bunches Swiss chard (1¼ to 1½ pounds)

Flaky sea salt or kosher salt

Grated zest of 1 lemon

¼ teaspoon crushed red pepper flakes

½ to 1 cup grated Parmigiano-Reggiano cheese, to taste

1 cup halved pitted cherries

Freshly ground black pepper

⅓ cup Lemon Vinaigrette (page 37), plus more as needed

For many years I relegated Swiss chard to the greens-that-require-cooking category and associated it with winter, something to sauté in garlicky olive oil and serve alongside roast chicken or wilt into a white bean and sausage stew. So when it began showing up in my summer farm share, I needed to reframe my thoughts about this dark leafy green. Could it, I wondered, be given the raw kale salad treatment? I turned to Food52.com and found a recipe for Swiss chard salad with parmesan, bread crumbs, and a lemony dressing, created by Merrill Stubbs, one of the website's founders and a brilliant cook and food writer. In this variation of Merrill's salad, I use my favorite lemon vinaigrette, omit the bread crumbs, and add toasted hazelnuts and cherries, which I can't get enough of during their short season.

Preheat the oven to 350°F.

Spread the hazelnuts on a sheet pan and roast until fragrant and lightly browned, about 12 minutes.

Set the pan on a wire rack and let cool for 5 minutes. Rub the hazelnuts in a clean dish towel to remove the skins. Transfer the hazelnuts to a cutting board and roughly chop.

Remove the leaves from the stems of the Swiss chard and thinly slice the leaves into ¼-inch-thick ribbons. You can do this by stacking leaves on top of each

other, rolling the stack into a tight coil, then slicing straight down crosswise.

In a large bowl, place the chard and season with a pinch of salt. Add the lemon zest, pepper flakes, ½ cup of the Parmigiano, the hazelnuts, cherries, and black pepper to taste. Toss to combine. Add the lemon vinaigrette and toss again to distribute.

Adjust with more salt and pepper to taste. Add more dressing if necessary. If desired, add the remaining ½ cup Parmigiano.

Peach Pizza
with Jalapeño, Prosciutto, and Crème Fraîche

Makes one 12-inch pizza

1 ball Neapolitanish Pizza Dough (page 22)

All-purpose flour, for dusting

Semolina flour, rice flour, or all-purpose flour, for the peel

2 tablespoons crème fraîche, at room temperature

¼ cup thinly sliced jalapeños

1 cup thinly sliced peach (about 3 ounces)

3 ounces low-moisture whole-milk mozzarella cheese, pulled into ½-inch pieces (about ¾ cup)

5 slices prosciutto

Extra-virgin olive oil

My aunt Marcy, my mother's sister, befriends—*best* friends, I should say—everyone she meets, from the grocers at her local IGA to the folks who pick up her compost to the UPS delivery person. One May at a graduation party, Marcy took a bite of the delicious pizza being served and beelined it to the outdoor pizza oven, where she met Chris Jones, the owner of Open Hearth Pizza. During their conversation, she secured a visit to his house and a promise to teach her how to make his pizza using 100 percent freshly milled flour, a sourdough starter, and his outdoor wood-burning oven. I got the invite, too, and this is how I found myself sitting on a sunny hill in Vermont with my aunt, uncle, and oldest daughter, Ella, eating pizza and calzones, with a dog at our feet. I could write pages about what I learned that day, from the grains Chris sources and the mill he uses to his mixing and baking process, but I'll skip straight to the highlight instead: this white pizza topped with peaches, jalapeños, and prosciutto, a combination that hits all of those sweet, spicy, salty notes, making it completely irresistible.

Prepare the dough: Transfer the dough from its storage container to a roomier, lightly floured, covered container (see Dough containers, page 16) and allow it to proof at room temperature for 1½ to 2 hours.

Prepare the oven and pizza peel: About 1 hour before you want to bake the pizza, place a baking steel in the top third of the oven and preheat it to 550°F convection roast (or as high as it will go). Dust a pizza peel lightly with semolina flour or top with parchment paper.

Stretch the dough: Lightly dust a work surface with flour. Using lightly floured hands, pat the dough gently to flatten it, then stretch it into a 10- to 11-inch round by laying it on the back of your hands and gently rotating it, taking care not to depress the beautiful air pockets in the dough. If the dough begins resisting, set it down on the work surface to rest for 5 to 10 minutes, then continue stretching. Transfer the stretched dough to the prepared peel and give it a shake to ensure it's not sticking.

Top the pizza: Spread the crème fraîche over the dough, leaving a ½-inch border. Top with the jalapeño and peach slices, spacing them evenly. Scatter the mozzarella evenly over the top. Lay the prosciutto slices over the top, spacing evenly. Drizzle lightly with olive oil. Stretch the dough one last time by pulling outward on the edges. Redistribute the toppings as needed, then give the peel one last shake to ensure the dough is not sticking.

Bake the pizza: Shimmy the pizza (still on the parchment if using) onto

Recipe continues

the steel and bake until the cheese is melted and the edges are beginning to char, 5 to 6 minutes. (This may take 8 to 10 minutes, depending on your oven.)

Use tongs to transfer the pizza to a cutting board (discard the parchment paper). Cut and serve.

Cucumber Salad with Red Onion and Burrata

Serves 4

1 pound cucumbers

1 teaspoon kosher salt

½ red onion, thinly sliced (about 1 cup)

¼ cup extra-virgin olive oil

¼ cup white balsamic vinegar

4 ounces burrata

Flaky sea salt and freshly ground black pepper

⅓ cup fresh basil or mint leaves (or a combination of the two), torn if large

Everyone needs a simple cucumber salad recipe in their repertoire, and this is the one I've come to make most often. The key to making a good cucumber salad is salting the cucumbers and letting them drain briefly, a step that draws moisture out of the slices, softens them, and primes them for soaking up whatever dressing comes their way. Another tip, especially with thick-skinned cucumbers, is to peel or to partially peel them in a striped fashion. I love this technique, which leaves part of the visually appealing green skin intact but removes enough of the peel to ensure the slices won't taste tough. A little red onion, some fresh herbs, and a simple dressing is all this salad needs, but a blob of burrata, broken and spread across the salad, adds a creaminess and richness, a perfect foil for those crisp, cool cukes.

Using a peeler, "zebra peel" the cucumbers by leaving strips of the cucumber skin still intact. Use a knife or mandoline to thinly slice the cucumbers into ⅛-inch-thick rounds. Place the cucumbers in a colander, add the salt, and toss to coat. Let sit for at least 15 minutes. Toss again, then transfer the cucumbers to a serving platter.

Scatter the red onion over the top, then drizzle with the olive oil and vinegar. Use your hands to break up the burrata ball and drop dollops of it evenly over the salad. Season all over with a big pinch of sea salt and pepper to taste. Scatter the herbs over the top. There is no need to toss this salad.

Apples. Pumpkins. Orchards. Cider. Mums. Chili. Squash. Soup. Fall: It's the time of year, for many, to return to routine, to turn the oven back on and start planning for the busy months ahead, for tailgates and holiday feasts, Halloween and gift giving, all the while feeling summer once again passed too quickly.

For me, September is always bittersweet. When the kids return to school, I relish the house being quiet by 8 a.m., but I dread the earlier afternoons, running from soccer field to hockey rink, nagging the children about math facts and reading, longing only to be huddled with them on the couch watching movies, a tub of popcorn nestled between us, the dog at our feet.

But I do love fall, and I do thrive on routine. Come September, the weekly rotation of meals returns: pasta, tacos, chicken, more pasta, and, of course, pizza, the best meal of the week on the one evening we often all are home, a convergence harder to come by the older the kids get, a union I remember my mother cherishing when my siblings and I were young. I finally get it.

For the children, fall pizza Friday looks much the same as it always does, their only concern being who gets to use the pizza scissor first, their discussion mostly a debate about which movie will follow dinner. For my husband, Ben, and me, it's a time to catch up after a week of what sometimes feels like barely seeing or speaking to each other, a few hours to hang before the weekend sprint begins. On Saturday mornings, as Ben and I wave goodbye while heading out in opposite directions, I often think, *See you next Friday!*

Business aside, there is much to celebrate, namely pizzas reflecting the changing season, pies covered with butternut squash purees, caramelized onions, roasted broccoli, and crispy Brussels sprouts. And as soon as the leaves start turning, I have a hard time not throwing sliced apples and pears into every salad I make. This time of year, too, I get back in the habit of making my favorite simple salad dressings, namely Apple Cider Vinaigrette (page 37) and Lemon Vinaigrette (page 37), sometimes in large batches, to have on hand for the busy weeks ahead.

All of this said, I do try to remember that the arrival of apple season does not mean tomato season is over, and I am a big proponent of celebrating summer produce to the end. Subpar tomatoes still make great sauce. Past-prime corn, charred in a skillet, adds depth to salads. Peppers, eggplant, and zucchini, once roasted, soften into super-concentrated, spreadable pastes, perfect for smearing over pizza dough.

Roman Pizza Margherita

Makes one 12-inch pizza

1 ball Tonda Dough (page 27)

All-purpose flour, for dusting

Semolina flour, rice flour, or all-purpose flour, for the peel

¼ cup No-Cook Tomato Sauce (page 34)

3 ounces low-moisture whole-milk mozzarella cheese (see Note), pulled apart into ½-inch pieces (about ¾ cup)

Flaky sea salt

Extra-virgin olive oil

Fresh basil leaves, torn if large

In the summer of 2022, my husband, Ben, and I went to Italy to, well, eat pizza. I would love to say we had more cultured goals in mind, but anyone who knows me knows my stamina in a museum is toddler-level at best. We spent three nights in Rome and two in Naples, then cruised home dreaming of all the delicious pizzas we ate in five days, from the focaccia-style slices at Bonci to the Neapolitan pies at Pepe in Grani to the thin-crusted Roman-style pizza at Da Remo and Ostiense, which, much to our surprise stole our hearts. This was the style of pizza, also known as "tonda" style, we found ourselves thinking about the most upon returning home, the one I immediately tried to re-create. A Google search led me to a video featuring Ostiense and clued me into a few important details, namely the weight of each dough ball and their use of a rolling pin to shape. I find these smaller-sized, thin-crust, minimally topped pies to be completely irresistible. They are especially good when made in an outdoor oven, though I get excellent results with my baking steel in my screaming-hot oven as well.

Prepare the dough: Transfer the dough from its storage container to a roomier, lightly floured, covered container (see Dough containers, page 16) and allow it to proof at room temperature for 1½ to 2 hours.

Prepare the oven and pizza peel: About 1 hour before you want to bake the pizza, place a baking steel in the top third of the oven and preheat it to 550°F convection roast (or as high as it will go). Dust a pizza peel lightly with

NOTE
If you have a pizza oven, you can make this with buffalo or fresh cow's milk mozzarella. Pull it into ½-inch pieces and let drain on a paper towel or kitchen towel for 10 to 15 minutes. For baking instructions, see Cooking Your Pizza in an Outdoor Oven (page 46).

semolina flour or top with parchment paper.

Roll the dough: Lightly dust a work surface and the dough ball with flour. With lightly floured hands, pinch the outermost edge of the dough to flatten and depress the air from the edges. Flip the ball and repeat the pinching at the edges. Using a lightly dusted rolling pin, roll the dough into a 12- to 13-inch round, flipping the dough every few strokes and using flour as needed. Transfer the stretched dough to the prepared peel and give it a shake to ensure it's not sticking.

Top the pizza: Spread the tomato sauce over the top all the way to the edges. Scatter the cheese over the top, again spreading it all the way to the edges. Season with a pinch of sea salt.

Bake the pizza: Shimmy the pizza (still on the parchment if using) onto the steel and bake until the cheese is melted and the edges are beginning to char, 3 to 4 minutes. (This may take 6 to 8 minutes, depending on your oven.)

Using the peel, transfer the pizza to a cutting board. Drizzle with olive oil and sprinkle with basil. Cut and serve.

Roman Pizzeria Salad

Serves 4

2 heads romaine lettuce (1¼ to 1½ pounds), finely sliced

2 cups halved cherry tomatoes

1 large carrot (about 5 ounces), julienned

Flaky sea salt

Extra-virgin olive oil

Freshly ground black pepper (optional)

After you make this salad once, you will wonder why a "recipe" for it was even included because, in fact, there is no recipe at all: You will be dressing the salad to taste using olive oil and salt alone. I first experienced this dress-it-yourself, no-acid salad in Rome, at La Gatta Mangiana, and then at many of the other pizzerias my husband, Ben, and I found ourselves at in the days that followed. As someone who loves bright, acidic salad dressings, I was shocked by how much I loved this preparation, a tribute, I realized, to the incredibly tasty produce and high-quality olive oil at hand. When I returned from Italy, it was mid-August, peak produce season in Upstate New York, and I immediately made the salad, hoping the secret ingredient did not lie in the novelty of being in Italy for the first time. Thankfully it did not. The key to having success with this salad is obvious but worth emphasizing: If you use good produce, good olive oil, and good salt, you will not fail.

In a large bowl, toss together the lettuce, tomatoes, and carrots. Season with a big pinch of salt and a drizzle of olive oil and toss. Taste and adjust with more olive oil and/or salt. If using pepper, crack some over the top.

Puttanesca Pan Pizza
with Tomatoes, Onions, Anchovies, and Olives

Makes 1 sheet pan pizza

2 tablespoons unsalted butter, at room temperature

1 tablespoon extra-virgin olive oil, plus more as needed

One 525-gram ball Pan Pizza Dough (page 30)

Toppings

4 tablespoons extra-virgin olive oil

3 cups thinly sliced onions

Kosher salt

2 garlic cloves, peeled

4 anchovy fillets

1 tablespoon drained capers

½ cup pitted kalamata or Niçoise olives

12 ounces low-moisture whole-milk mozzarella cheese, grated (about 3 cups)

1 cup quartered cherry or grape tomatoes

For many years, pissaladière, a Provençal tart smothered with anchovies and olives, was my go-to dish to bring to our annual fall block party. With its olive oil–crisped focaccia base, it sits well for hours and plays nicely with all sorts of potluck fare from grilled chicken and sausage to broccoli and pasta salads. That time of year, I love adding tomatoes. Though not traditional, they work so well with the other toppings, the combination of which evokes the sweet and salty, oily and briny, bold and aromatic flavors of pasta puttanesca. While classic pissaladière recipes call for arranging the anchovies in a diamond pattern across the dough, I make an anchovy paste instead and spread it across the dough, a move that not only more evenly disperses the intense umami flavor, but also disguises it: Those who think they dislike anchovies won't know they're there. One year on a whim, I made the pissaladière with half the amount of dough, stretched it into my grandma-style sheet pan, and added cheese to the mix. Thinner, crisper, and sturdier, this 2.0 version was primed for its best showing on the buffet yet, but it never was given the chance—it disappeared faster than ever, and just like that, thin-crust puttanesca pan pizza became the new potluck staple.

Prepare the dough: Grease a 12 × 16-inch grandma-style pan or 13 × 18-inch sheet pan with the softened butter. Pour the 1 tablespoon of olive oil into the center of the pan. Place the dough ball in the oil and turn to coat. Let rest uncovered until the dough has doubled in volume, 3 to 4 hours.

Stretch the dough: Lightly oil your hands and use your fingertips to dimple and stretch the dough to fit the pan. When the dough resists, let it rest for 30 minutes, then stretch it again using the same technique. Repeat this stretching and resting until the dough fits the pan.

Prepare the toppings: In a large sauté pan, heat 2 tablespoons of the olive oil over high heat until it shimmers. Add the onions and a pinch of salt, cover, immediately reduce the heat to low, and cook, stirring every few minutes, until the onions are lightly golden, 15 to 20 minutes.

In a food processor, mince the garlic and anchovies together, scraping down the sides of the processor as needed. Add the remaining 2 tablespoons oil and blend to combine. Add the capers and pulse to coarsely chop. Add the olives and pulse again to coarsely chop. (Alternatively, mince and chop everything by hand.)

Prepare the oven: If you have a baking steel, place it on a rack in the middle or lower third of the oven and preheat the oven to 450°F.

Recipe continues

Top the pizza: Using lightly oiled hands, stretch the dough one final time to fit the pan. Sprinkle the mozzarella evenly over the pizza, spreading it all the way to the edges. Spread the sautéed onions over the dough, followed by the anchovy puree. Scatter the tomatoes evenly over the top.

Bake the pizza: Transfer the pan to the oven and bake until the edges look very caramelized, 22 to 25 minutes. Remove the pan from the oven. Run a paring knife or spatula around the pan's edges, then, using an offset spatula, carefully remove the pizza from the pan, transferring it to a cutting board. Cut into 12 to 16 squares.

Raw Corn Salad with Cherry Tomatoes and Edamame

Serves 4

1 cup frozen shelled edamame

4 ears corn, shucked

1 pint cherry or grape tomatoes, halved

½ teaspoon flaky sea salt or kosher salt, plus more to taste

Freshly ground black pepper

¼ cup extra-virgin olive oil, plus more to taste

3 tablespoons fresh lime juice, plus more to taste

1 cup fresh basil leaves, torn if large

¼ cup fresh mint, torn if large, or finely chopped fresh chives

1 avocado, diced

4 ounces feta cheese, preferably in brine, cut into ⅛-inch-thick slabs

When local sweet corn is at its peak, it barely needs more than a pinch of salt and doesn't even need to be cooked. This raw salad, a variation of one Mark Bittman wrote about years ago in the *New York Times,* is a summer staple, one that can be riffed on endlessly depending on what you have on hand: diced bell peppers, cucumbers, peaches, nectarines, scallions, and any number of tender herbs. Its sharp dressing pushes it almost into salsa territory, and it's something I wouldn't mind eating with chips, if it didn't have a pizza by its side. You can hold back some of the fresh lime juice if you prefer a less acidic dressing.

In a small pot of boiling water, blanch the edamame for 15 seconds. Drain and rinse under cold water. Pat dry. Set a folded kitchen towel in the bottom of a shallow bowl. Stand an ear of corn upright on the towel and use a knife to strip the kernels off the cob. Repeat with the remaining 3 ears of corn.

In a large bowl, combine the corn, tomatoes, edamame, salt, and pepper to taste. Add the olive oil and lime juice and toss. Taste and adjust with more salt, pepper, lime juice, and/or olive oil (1 tablespoon at a time).

Add the basil, mint, avocado, and feta and toss gently. Serve immediately.

Halloween Pizza Night

I have never been much of a Halloween person, but in recent years my neighborhood, which is great for trick-or-treating, has become a meetup spot for friends who travel far and wide for the occasion. As soon as the candy gathering is complete, we convene at my house for dinner, and this union of costume-clad friends and children has become one of my favorite nights of the entire year, a casual kickoff to the holiday season.

I make the same menu every year: a few pan pizzas—Detroit-Style Pepperoni Pizza for the kids and Sicilian-Style Veggie-Loaded Pizza for the adults—and a large veggie platter for all, which I keep very basic: sliced-up bell peppers, baby carrots (yes, from a bag), and mini cucumbers, quartered and sprinkled with flaky sea salt. I set the veggies alongside a bowl of homemade romesco sauce and store-bought hummus, and it all disappears shockingly quickly, hands big and small swooping in, a natural need, no doubt, to balance all the chocolate-coated nuggets coursing through our systems.

Detroit-Style Pepperoni Pizza

Makes one 10 × 14-inch pizza

2 tablespoons unsalted butter, at room temperature

1 teaspoon extra-virgin olive oil, plus more as needed

One 525-gram ball Pan Pizza Dough (page 30)

1 cup preshredded cheddar cheese (4 ounces)

½ cup preshredded low-moisture whole-milk mozzarella cheese (2 ounces)

1½ cups cubed cheese (6 ounces) low-moisture whole-milk mozzarella or a mix of Monterey Jack, cheddar, and mozzarella

Heaping ½ cup Simple Tomato Sauce (page 34) or your favorite jarred sauce

2 to 3 ounces pepperoni (depending on thickness of slices)

Although this pepperoni pizza is very much inspired by the Detroit-style canon, it does not follow that style's traditional topping application: the pepperoni does not go on first, and the sauce does not go on last. While I appreciate a true DSP, I prefer when pepperoni and other toppings have the chance to crisp, and so in this DSP, I've added the toppings as follows: cheese, sauce, pepperoni. As is characteristic of any DSP, there is a "crust" of shredded cheese around the perimeter, which melts down between the pan and the pizza base, creating a frico: a lacework of caramelized cheese. For more on this style of pizza, see Detroit-Style Pizza (page 161).

Prepare the dough: Grease a 10 × 14-inch Detroit-style pizza pan or a 9 × 13-inch baking pan with the softened butter. Pour the olive oil into the center of the pan. Place the dough ball in the oil and turn to coat. Let rest uncovered until the dough has doubled in volume, 3 to 4 hours.

Stretch the dough: Lightly oil your hands and use your fingertips to dimple and stretch the dough to fit the pan. When the dough resists, let it rest for 30 minutes, then stretch it again using the same technique. Repeat this stretching and resting until the dough fits the pan.

Prepare the oven: If you have a baking steel, place it on a rack in the middle or lower third of the oven and preheat the oven to 500°F.

Parbake the dough: Dimple the dough one last time with lightly oiled hands, taking care not to dimple the perimeter. Transfer the pan to the middle of the oven and bake until

Recipe continues

the dough has puffed, released ever so slightly from the edges, and is just beginning to brown in spots, about 8 minutes. Remove the pan from the oven and using an offset spatula, carefully transfer the parbaked crust to a wire rack.

Let the parbaked dough cool upside down on the rack for 20 minutes. Do not wash the pan. (At this point, once the dough is cooled, you can transfer it to an airtight storage bag for up to 2 days at room temperature or up to 3 months in the freezer.)

Leave the oven on and reduce the temperature to 475°F.

Top the pizza: In a medium bowl, combine the shredded cheddar and mozzarella. Return the parbaked crust to the pan, bottom-side down. To make the "frico crust," spread the shredded cheese mixture around the perimeter of the parbaked crust pressing it against the sides of the pan. Sprinkle the cubed cheese over the surface of the crust inside the shredded cheese perimeter. Spread the tomato sauce evenly over the top. Spread the pepperoni evenly over the sauce.

Bake the pizza: Transfer the pan to the oven (and place on the baking steel, if using) and bake until the edges are caramelized to your liking, about 10 minutes.

Remove the pan from the oven and let the pizza rest for 1 to 2 minutes in the pan. Run a thin metal spatula around the pan's edges to release the cheese frico crust from the sides of the pan. Carefully remove the entire pizza from the pan, transferring it to a cutting board. Cut into 8 to 12 squares and serve.

Veggie Platter with Romesco and Hummus

Serves 10

2 red bell peppers, cut into
 ½-inch-thick strips

1 (1-pound) bag baby carrots

12 Persian (mini) cucumbers,
 quartered lengthwise

Flaky sea salt

Romesco Sauce (recipe follows)

1 (10-ounce) tub hummus

Romesco is a Catalonian sauce made from tomatoes, sun-dried peppers, nuts, and other seasonings. This very pared-down version has become a favorite for entertaining for several reasons, namely because it takes no time whip together, but also because it's vegan, making it friendly for many a diner. Most important: It's so tasty! I love making roasted red peppers from scratch and do not find the peeling process to be a hassle, but if you do, simply swap in 1 cup of drained jarred roasted red peppers. Final note, because nut allergies are common, I always have a tub of hummus on hand to set alongside the veggies as well.

On a large serving platter, arrange the peppers, carrots, and cucumbers. Sprinkle the cucumbers with the flaky sea salt.

Place the romesco and hummus in separate serving bowls. Set the bowls alongside the vegetables and serve.

Romesco Sauce

Makes 1½ cups

1 packed cup roasted red peppers,
 homemade (page 195) or store-
 bought (about 9 ounces)

½ teaspoon kosher salt, plus more
 to taste

1 tablespoon red wine vinegar, plus
 more to taste

¼ cup almonds, any variety

⅓ cup extra-virgin olive oil

1 garlic clove, peeled

In a blender or food processor, combine the peppers, salt, vinegar, almonds, olive oil, and garlic and blend until smooth. Taste and add more salt or vinegar to taste. Store in the fridge for up to 1 week or in the freezer for up to 3 months.

Sicilian-Style Veggie-Loaded Pizza

Makes 1 sheet pan pizza

2 tablespoons unsalted butter, at room temperature

1 tablespoon extra-virgin olive oil, plus more as needed

One 1,050-gram ball Pan Pizza Dough (page 30)

Toppings

3 tablespoons extra-virgin olive oil

8 ounces mushrooms, sliced

Kosher salt

1 bell pepper (any color), diced

1 cup thinly sliced red onion

1 heaping cup Simple Tomato Sauce (page 34) or your favorite jarred sauce

12 ounces grated cheese (about 3 cups), such as low-moisture whole-milk mozzarella or a mix of Monterey Jack, cheddar, and mozzarella

½ cup thinly sliced pepperoncini

½ cup sliced black or green olives

To ensure the Halloween pizza night menu is as friendly to the most people as possible, I always serve a vegetarian Sicilian pizza. No one seems to miss the meat, and if they do, they can snag a slice of the children's pepperoni pizza. If you think your crowd will appreciate a meatier pie, see Sicilian-Style Pizza for a Crowd with "The Works" (page 174).

Prepare the dough: Grease a 12 × 16-inch grandma-style pan or a 13 × 18-inch sheet pan with the softened butter. Pour the olive oil into the center of the pan. Place the dough ball in the oil and turn to coat. Let rest uncovered until the dough has doubled in volume, 3 to 4 hours.

Stretch the dough: Lightly oil your hands and use your fingertips to dimple and stretch the dough to fit the pan. When the dough resists, let it rest for 30 minutes, then stretch it again using the same technique. Repeat this stretching and resting until the dough fits the pan.

Prepare the oven: If you have a baking steel, place it on a rack in the middle or lower third of the oven and preheat the oven to 500°F.

Parbake the dough: Using oiled hands, dimple the dough one last time, taking care to not dimple the perimeter, which will help the dough bake more evenly. Transfer the pan to the oven (and place on the baking steel if using) and bake until evenly golden, 10 to 12 minutes. Remove the pan from oven. Leave the oven on and reduce the temperature to 475°F.

Prepare the toppings: In a large skillet, heat 2 tablespoons of the olive oil over high heat until it shimmers. Add the mushrooms and let sit undisturbed for about 1 minute. Season with salt, then stir and cook until the mushrooms are beginning to brown, 3 to 5 minutes. Transfer to a bowl.

Add the remaining 1 tablespoon oil to the skillet and add the bell pepper and onion. Cook until slightly softened, 1 to 3 minutes. Season with salt and transfer to the bowl with the mushrooms. Toss to combine. Taste and adjust with salt if needed.

Top the pizza: Spread the tomato sauce evenly over the dough all the way to the edges. Top with the grated cheese. Spread the vegetable mixture over the cheese along with the sliced pepperoncini and olives.

Bake the pizza: Return the pan to the oven and bake until the cheese is melted and just beginning to brown in spots, 10 to 12 minutes. Remove the pan from the oven and let the pizza rest for 5 minutes in the pan.

Run a knife or spatula around the pan's edges and carefully remove the pizza from the pan to a cutting board. Use a serrated knife to cut the pizza into roughly 20 squares.

Roasted Butternut Squash Pizza with Gruyère and Rosemary

Makes one 12-inch pizza

1 ball Neapolitanish Pizza Dough
  (page 22)

All-purpose flour, for dusting

2 tablespoons extra-virgin olive oil

1 garlic clove, peeled

1 small sprig fresh rosemary
  (2 to 3 inches; see Note)

¼ teaspoon crushed red pepper
  flakes

Semolina flour, rice flour, or
  all-purpose flour, for the peel

2 tablespoons crème fraîche, at
  room temperature

1 cup Roasted Butternut Squash
  (recipe follows)

3 ounces Gruyère cheese, grated
  (¾ cup)

Flaky sea salt

If you are a fan of things like butternut squash ravioli or sweet potato gnocchi or potato pierogies—in other words carbs in carbs—you will love this pizza, a recipe inspired by one in *Chez Panisse Vegetables* that I've been making for years. It's simple—in essence roasted squash slices plus cheese—but it's incredibly flavorful thanks to a rosemary-garlic oil you brush over the roasted squash slices. Here, I start by spreading the dough with crème fraîche, whose tang nicely balances the sweetness of the squash and richness of the Gruyère.

Prepare the dough: Transfer the dough from its storage container to a roomier, lightly floured, covered container (see Dough containers, page 16) and allow it to proof at room temperature for 1½ to 2 hours.

Prepare the oil: Place the olive oil in a small skillet. Finely mince the garlic or use a Microplane to grate the garlic directly into the olive oil. Add the rosemary and pepper flakes. Set the skillet over medium heat. As soon as the garlic, pepper flakes, and rosemary begin to sizzle, remove the pan from the heat.

Prepare the oven and pizza peel: About 1 hour before you want to bake the pizza, place a baking steel in the top third of the oven and preheat it to 550°F convection roast (or as high as it will go). Dust a pizza peel lightly with semolina flour or top with parchment paper.

Stretch the dough: Lightly dust a work surface with flour. Using lightly floured hands, pat the dough gently to flatten it, then stretch it into a 10- to 11-inch round by laying it on the back of your hands and gently rotating it, taking care not to depress the beautiful air pockets in the dough. If

the dough begins resisting, set it down on the work surface to rest for 5 to 10 minutes, then continue stretching. Transfer the stretched dough to the prepared peel and give it a shake to ensure it's not sticking.

Top the pizza: Spread the crème fraîche evenly over the dough, leaving a ½-inch border. Arrange the roasted squash slices over the top in a single layer. Brush half of the rosemary/garlic oil over the squash slices. Scatter the Gruyère evenly over the top. Season with flaky sea salt. Stretch the dough one last time by pulling outward on the edges. Redistribute the toppings as needed, then give the peel one last shake to ensure the dough is not sticking.

Bake the pizza: Shimmy the pizza (still on the parchment if using) onto the steel and bake until the cheese is melted and the edges are beginning to char, 5 to 6 minutes. (This may take 8 to 10 minutes, depending on your oven.)

Using the peel, transfer the pizza to a cutting board (discard the parchment paper). Transfer the remaining rosemary/garlic oil to a small bowl to serve on the side. Cut and serve.

Recipe continues

NOTE
If you don't like rosemary, you can use fresh sage or thyme in its place.

Roasted Butternut Squash

Makes 2 cups (enough for two 12-inch pizzas)

1 small butternut squash (about 1½ pounds)

1 tablespoon extra-virgin olive oil

Kosher salt

Preheat the oven to 400°F. Line a sheet pan with parchment paper.

Peel the squash, then halve it crosswise. Cut the bulbous end in half and discard the seeds. Cut the squash crosswise into ¼-inch-thick slices.

Arrange the squash slices on the lined pan. Drizzle with the olive oil, season evenly with kosher salt, toss to coat, then redistribute in one layer. Roast the squash until fork-tender, 20 to 25 minutes. (Store in the fridge for up to 1 week or in the freezer for up to 3 months.)

Classic Kale Salad with Pepper Flakes, Parmesan, and Lemon Vinaigrette

Serves 4

1 pound lacinato (Tuscan) kale

Flaky sea salt

Grated zest of 1 lemon

¼ teaspoon crushed red pepper flakes

½ cup finely grated Parmigiano-Reggiano cheese, plus more for shaving

Freshly ground black pepper

⅓ cup Lemon Vinaigrette (page 37), plus more to taste

My introduction to kale salads came by way of True Food Kitchen, a restaurant my aunt and I frequented for lunch when I was living in California. At TFK, they marinated the kale in lemon and olive oil, then tossed it with bread crumbs and parmesan. This was in 2010, and back then, eating kale raw was still novel, but it quickly became an obsession and a favorite salad to make at home. In the years that followed, when I discovered the probable origins of the TFK kale salad (the one created by Joshua McFadden at Fanny's in Brooklyn and popularized by Melissa Clark in a 2007 *New York Times* column), I adopted Joshua's technique as well, which does not call for massaging the kale but rather for a fine shave. When I am not serving this salad alongside pizza, olive oil–toasted bread crumbs are a wonderful addition. And if you wanted to add them here, I'd never fault you.

Remove the stems and midribs from the kale leaves and thinly slice the leaves into very fine ribbons. (You can do this by stacking leaves on top of each other, rolling the stack into a tight coil, then slicing crosswise.)

Place the kale in a large bowl. Season with a pinch of sea salt. Add the lemon zest, pepper flakes, Parmigiano, and black pepper to taste. Toss to combine. Add the lemon vinaigrette and toss again to distribute.

Taste and adjust with more salt and/or black pepper. Add more dressing if necessary. Using a Microplane grater, finely shave the Parmigiano over the top of the salad until it's blanketed with a layer of white.

Roasted Broccoli Pizza with Tomato "Butter" and Olives

Makes one 12-inch pizza

1 ball Neapolitanish Pizza Dough (page 22)

All-purpose flour, for dusting

1 small head of broccoli (about 8 ounces)

1 tablespoon extra-virgin olive oil, plus more for drizzling

Kosher salt

Semolina flour, rice flour, or all-purpose flour, for the peel

3 tablespoons Roasted Tomato "Butter" (page 36)

2 tablespoons chopped kalamata olives

3 ounces low-moisture whole-milk mozzarella cheese, pulled into ½-inch pieces (about ¾ cup)

Flaky sea salt

In its September 2020 issue, *Food & Wine* published a recipe from Philadelphia chef Greg Vernick for roasted broccoli steaks with tomato butter and olive tapenade, and I found the combination irresistible. This pizza captures all of those flavors: charred earthy broccoli, sweet fresh tomato, salty briny olives. The roasted tomato "butter" is a revelation: It's one of the simplest, tastiest tomato sauce recipes I make.

Prepare the dough: Transfer the dough from its storage container to a roomier, lightly floured, covered container (see Dough containers, page 16) and allow it to proof at room temperature for 1½ to 2 hours.

Roast the broccoli: Preheat the oven to 475°F. Trim off the end of the broccoli stem and discard or compost. Peel the stem to remove the tough outer layer. Cut the head into small florets and the stem into ¼-inch-thick coins. Transfer to a sheet pan. Toss with the olive oil and a pinch of kosher salt. Taste a floret. It should be nicely seasoned. Add more salt if needed.

Roast until the broccoli is beginning to char at the edges, 20 to 25 minutes. Remove from the oven and set aside.

Prepare the oven and pizza peel: About 1 hour before you want to bake the pizza, place a baking steel in the top third of the oven and preheat it to 550°F convection roast (or as high as it will go). Dust a pizza peel lightly with semolina flour or top with parchment paper.

Stretch the dough: Lightly dust a work surface with flour. Using lightly floured hands, pat the dough gently to flatten it, then stretch it into a 10- to 11-inch round by laying it on the back of your hands and gently rotating it, taking care not to depress the beautiful air pockets in the dough. If the dough begins resisting, set it down on the work surface to rest for 5 to 10 minutes, then continue stretching. Transfer the stretched dough to the prepared peel and give it a shake to ensure it's not sticking.

Top the pizza: Spread the tomato butter over the dough, leaving a ½-inch border. Scatter the olives, roasted broccoli florets, and mozzarella evenly over the top. Drizzle with olive oil. Season with a pinch of flaky sea salt. Stretch the dough one last time by pulling outward on the edges. Redistribute the toppings as needed, then give the peel one last shake to ensure the dough is not sticking.

Bake the pizza: Shimmy the pizza (still on the parchment if using) onto the steel and bake until the cheese is melted and the edges are beginning to char, 5 to 6 minutes. (This may take 8 to 10 minutes, depending on your oven.)

Using the peel, transfer the pizza to a cutting board (discard the parchment paper). Cut and serve.

Classic Chopped Salad

Serves 4

1 head romaine lettuce, finely sliced

1½ cups cooked or canned chickpeas (from a 16-ounce can), drained and rinsed

2 ounces salami, cut into ¼-inch-thick slices

1 small red onion, finely sliced

1 cup halved cherry tomatoes

1 red bell pepper, cut into 1-inch pieces (about 1 cup)

1 cucumber, peeled and roughly chopped (about 1 cup)

½ cup cubed provolone cheese (2 to 3 ounces)

½ cup wrinkly black oil-cured olives or olive of choice

⅓ cup Italian Dressing (page 39), plus more to taste

Freshly ground black pepper

Flaky sea salt

This salad is a meal unto itself, one I do in fact serve for dinner when it's not pizza night. Loaded with all of my favorite things—cured meats, sharp cheese, briny olives, and loads of vegetables—it's satisfying and filling and endlessly adaptable to what you have on hand.

In a large bowl, combine the romaine, chickpeas, salami, onion, tomatoes, bell pepper, cucumber, provolone, and olives. Add the dressing and season with black pepper to taste. Toss to combine. Taste and add more dressing, a pinch of sea salt if necessary, and more pepper to taste.

Caramelized Leek and Potato Pizza with Chive Cream

Makes one 13-inch pizza

1 ball Thin-Crust Pizza Dough (page 26)

All-purpose flour, for dusting

2 leeks, white and light-green parts only, thinly sliced

Extra-virgin olive oil

Kosher salt

1 teaspoon white balsamic vinegar

2 tablespoons heavy cream

2 tablespoons thinly sliced fresh chives

1 small Yukon Gold potato (3 to 4 ounces), very thinly sliced (ideally on a mandoline)

Semolina flour, rice flour, or all-purpose flour, for the peel

4 ounces Gruyère cheese, grated (about 1 cup)

Flaky sea salt

Every fall, when the leeks and potatoes begin arriving together in the farm share, I immediately make a pot of potato-leek soup, which I garnish with herby, olive oil–toasted bread crumbs. And when I've had my fill of soup, I make this pizza. Here, you'll sauté leeks and scatter them atop the dough, which has been spread with whipped heavy cream flavored with chives. Gruyère will follow along with a layer of partially baked, thinly sliced potatoes, which is the key to getting the timing right with this pizza: Without the parbake, the potatoes will not crisp up before the dough cooks. The parbake is brief, just 3 to 4 minutes, or until you see the faintest hint of brown around the edges.

Prepare the dough: Transfer the dough from its storage container to a roomier, lightly floured, covered container (see Dough containers, page 16) and allow it to proof at room temperature for 1½ to 2 hours.

Prepare the oven: About 1 hour before you want to bake the pizza, place a baking steel in the top third of the oven and preheat it to 550°F convection roast (or as high as it will go).

Place the sliced leeks in a bowl of cold water and let stand for 5 minutes to allow the dirt to settle. Scoop the leeks out and transfer to a colander to drain. Place the leeks in a large skillet over medium heat—it's okay if they're wet. Stir the leeks for about a minute, or until the water evaporates, then add 1 tablespoon olive oil and a pinch of kosher salt. Cook, stirring occasionally, until the leeks begin to sizzle in the oil, then immediately reduce the heat to low, cover, and cook for 5 minutes, or until the leeks are browned at the edges. Uncover, stir in the vinegar, and remove the pan from the heat. Transfer the leeks to a bowl to cool. Taste and add a pinch of kosher salt if necessary.

In a small bowl, using a fork or small flat-bottomed whisk, beat the cream until it thickens and forms soft peaks. Stir in the chives and a pinch of kosher salt.

Line a sheet pan with parchment paper. Place the potatoes in a pile in the center of the pan. Drizzle with 1 teaspoon olive oil and season with kosher salt. Toss to coat, then spread the potatoes in an even layer. Transfer the pan to the oven (on top of the baking steel if you are using one) and cook just until the edges of the potatoes show any sign of browning, 3 to 4 minutes—watch it very closely from the 3-minute mark on and remove the pan from the oven as soon as you see any edges beginning to take on color.

Recipe continues

Prepare the peel: Dust a pizza peel lightly with semolina flour or top with parchment paper.

Roll the dough: Lightly dust a work surface and the dough ball with flour. With lightly floured hands, pinch the outermost edge of the dough to flatten and depress the air from the edges. Flip the ball and repeat the pinching at the edges. Using a lightly dusted rolling pin, roll the dough into a 13-inch round, flipping the dough every few strokes and using flour as needed. Transfer the stretched dough to the prepared peel and give it a shake to ensure it's not sticking.

Top the pizza: Spread the chive cream over the dough all the way to the edges. Scatter the leeks evenly over the top, followed by the Gruyère, again spreading both all the way to the edges. Layer the partially baked potatoes over the top in a single layer, again spreading them all the way to the edges. Drizzle with some olive oil. Season with a pinch of flaky sea salt.

Bake the pizza: Shimmy the pizza (still on the parchment if using) onto the steel and bake until the cheese is melted and the edges are beginning to char, 4 to 5 minutes. (This may take 8 to 10 minutes, depending on your oven.)

Using the peel, transfer the pizza to a cutting board (discard the parchment paper). Cut and serve.

Mixed Greens Salad
with Plums, Blue Cheese, and Candied Walnuts

Serves 4

10 ounces mixed greens

6 to 8 Italian black plums, pitted and quartered (see Note)

4 ounces blue cheese, crumbled

1 cup Candied Walnuts (recipe follows)

⅓ cup Apple Cider Vinaigrette (page 37), plus more to taste

Flaky sea salt and freshly ground black pepper

One Saturday afternoon in late September, finding myself in Saratoga Springs, New York, with some time to kill between my children's soccer games, I went to Healthy Living, an independent local market, whose aisles make my heart sing. On this particular day, I stumbled upon a display of Valor plums, a variety I had never heard of but that reminded me of the small Italian prune plums everyone goes crazy over during the late summer. I picked up 6 pints with the intention of making Marion Burros's famous torte, but in the end never got there. I ate one pint in my car before heading back to the fields, then took the remainder home, where they were quickly demolished by the family. What remained, I threw in a salad, where, as you can imagine, they shined, their sweet, juicy flesh such a nice complement to the nutty, sharp, and creamy elements.

In a large bowl, combine the greens, plums, cheese, walnuts, and dressing and toss. Add salt, pepper, and more dressing to taste if necessary.

Candied Walnuts

Makes 1½ cups

1 cup walnuts (4 ounces)

¼ cup sugar

Flaky sea salt

In a large skillet, toast the walnuts over medium heat, stirring occasionally, until they turn light brown and begin to smell fragrant, 5 to 6 minutes. Transfer to a plate to cool. Line a sheet pan with parchment paper.

In the same skillet, heat the sugar without stirring—shake the pan if necessary to distribute the sugar in an even layer. When it turns evenly golden or amber, remove the pan from the heat, and add the toasted walnuts and a pinch of sea salt. Using a heatproof spatula, stir to combine. When the walnuts are nicely coated in the sugar syrup, transfer them to the prepared sheet pan.

Once cool enough to handle, break the walnuts into pieces. Store the walnuts at room temperature in an airtight container for weeks.

NOTE
If you can't find Italian black plums, standard plums will work. You'll need 3 to 4, and you'll want to dice them into ¾-inch pieces.

Greek Pizza
with Spinach, Cherry Tomatoes, Kalamata Olives, and Feta

1 ball Neapolitanish Pizza Dough (page 22)

All-purpose flour, for dusting

Toppings

Extra-virgin olive oil

2 to 3 cups baby spinach (about 2½ ounces)

Kosher salt

1 cup halved cherry tomatoes, quartered if large

⅓ cup thinly sliced red onion

1 small garlic clove, finely minced

¼ teaspoon dried oregano

Assembly

Semolina flour, rice flour, or all-purpose flour, for the peel

3 ounces low-moisture whole-milk mozzarella cheese, pulled into ½-inch pieces (about ¾ cup)

10 kalamata olives, pitted and halved

¼ cup pickled banana peppers (about 1½ ounces)

⅓ cup crumbled feta cheese (about 1 ounce)

Extra-virgin olive oil

Flaky sea salt

Whenever I talk to my friend Christine, I ask her what her father, a former chef, has cooked for her lately. Her tales of homemade blynai, Lithuanian pancakes, topped with blueberries for breakfast and double-stuffed potatoes alongside marinated grilled steaks for dinner always make me hungry. But Christine's favorite is his Greek pizza, a layering of quickly sautéed spinach, herb-marinated tomatoes, kalamata olives, banana peppers, and feta. Upon hearing about it, I made it for my family immediately, and one bite left me smitten, the combination evoking a warm Greek salad, a refreshing mix of vegetables punctuated by lots of bright, briny bites.

Prepare the dough: Transfer the dough from its storage container to a roomier, lightly floured, covered container (see Dough containers, page 16) and allow it to proof at room temperature for 1½ to 2 hours.

Prepare the toppings: In a large skillet, heat 2 teaspoons olive oil over high heat until it shimmers. Add some of the spinach and a pinch of kosher salt. Stir the greens to help them wilt down, adding more greens as they do. When nearly all of the greens have wilted, after 30 to 60 seconds, transfer them to a plate to cool.

In a medium bowl, combine the tomatoes, onion, garlic, and oregano. Season with a pinch of kosher salt and drizzle with 1 tablespoon olive oil. Toss to combine.

Prepare the oven and pizza peel: About 1 hour before you want to bake the pizza, place a baking steel in the top third of the oven and preheat it to 550°F convection roast (or as high as it will go). Dust a pizza peel lightly with semolina flour or top with parchment paper.

Stretch the dough: Lightly dust a work surface with flour. Using lightly floured hands, pat the dough gently to flatten it, then stretch it into a 10- to 11-inch round by laying it on the back of your hands and gently rotating it, taking care not to depress the beautiful air pockets in the dough. If the dough begins resisting, set it down on the work surface to rest for 5 to 10 minutes, then continue stretching. Transfer the stretched dough to the prepared peel and give it a shake to ensure it's not sticking.

Assemble the pizza: Sprinkle the mozzarella over the dough, leaving a ½-inch border. Spread the spinach evenly over the top. Top with the cherry tomato/onion mixture, leaving any juices in the bowl behind. Sprinkle the olives and banana peppers evenly over the top, followed by the feta. Drizzle with olive oil. Season with a pinch of flaky sea salt. Stretch the dough one last time by pulling outward on the edges. Redistribute the toppings as needed, then give the peel one last shake to ensure the dough is not sticking.

Recipe continues

Bake the pizza: Shimmy the pizza (still on the parchment if using) onto the steel and bake until the cheese is melted and the edges are beginning to char, 5 to 6 minutes. (This may take 8 to 10 minutes, depending on your oven.)

Using the peel, transfer the pizza to a cutting board (discard the parchment paper). Cut and serve.

Chicories alla Romana

Serves 4

1 head radicchio (6 to 8 ounces total)

2 heads Belgian endive (6 to 8 ounces total)

½ head escarole (4 to 6 ounces total)

2 garlic cloves, peeled

6 anchovy fillets

¼ cup white balsamic vinegar, plus more to taste

⅓ cup extra-virgin olive oil, plus more to taste

Flaky sea salt and freshly ground black pepper

When I read in Andrew Janjigian's wonderful newsletter, *Wordloaf*, that puntarelle alla romana is a salad he often serves alongside pizza, I had to learn more. Puntarelle is a member of the chicory family and looks like a cross between frisée and a head of celery. It's so ubiquitous in Italy that there is a specific tool, taglia puntarelle, that cuts (*tagliare*) the green into thin strips. Unfortunately, as Andrew notes, puntarelle is "tragically hard to find in the US." In all of my various farmers' market visits, I have never stumbled upon it, and until I do, I'll continue doing what works very well, which is to substitute the readily available chicories sold nearly everywhere: endive, radicchio, and escarole. The dressing of a classic puntarelle alla romana is garlic, anchovies, olive oil, and vinegar, which evokes Caesar dressing but is less creamy. I actually prefer the punchiness of this dressing and find the salad completely irresistible, especially alongside pizza.

Slice the radicchio, endive, and escarole into thin slivers and place in a large bowl.

In a food processor or blender, combine the garlic, anchovies, and vinegar and puree. With the machine running, stream in the olive oil until emulsified. Taste and adjust with a pinch of sea salt if needed and more vinegar or oil.

Pour ⅓ cup of the dressing over the greens, season with pepper, and toss. Taste and adjust with more dressing, pepper, and/or salt.

Brussels Sprouts Pizza
with Pancetta, Balsamic, and Ricotta

Makes one 12-inch pizza

1 ball Neapolitanish Pizza Dough (page 22)

All-purpose flour, for dusting

Toppings

2 ounces thin-sliced pancetta rounds (8 to 10 slices)

2 cups packed Brussels sprouts leaves (4 or 5 large sprouts; about 4 ounces)

1 tablespoon extra-virgin olive oil

1½ teaspoons white balsamic vinegar

Flaky sea salt

2 tablespoons heavy cream

1 small garlic clove, peeled

Assembly

Semolina flour, rice flour, or all-purpose flour, for the peel

¼ cup Whipped Ricotta (page 41)

Good syrupy aged balsamic vinegar or Homemade Balsamic Syrup (recipe follows)

My introduction to the failsafe pairing of Brussels sprouts and pancetta came by way of Ina Garten and a recipe in her book *Foolproof*. In Ina's recipe, the sprouts and the pancetta roast together, crisping up in unison, the fat from the meat flavoring the sprouts. Here, pancetta rounds are crisped stovetop before being transferred to the pizza dough. In the oven, the Brussels sprout leaves, tossed with both olive oil and vinegar, sweeten, charring at the edges, ultimately nestling into the pancetta and whipped garlicky cream beneath them. Out of the oven, a little splash of aged balsamic vinegar provides a welcome bite that makes Brussels sprouts sing.

Prepare the dough: Transfer the dough from its storage container to a roomier, lightly floured, covered container (see Dough containers, page 16) and allow it to proof at room temperature for 1½ to 2 hours.

Prepare the toppings: In a large skillet, heat the pancetta rounds over medium heat. (It's okay to cram the slices in, because once they start rendering their fat, they'll make more space.) Cook just until the pancetta is beginning to crisp, 8 to 10 minutes—you don't want it completely crisp. Transfer to a plate to cool.

In a large bowl, toss the Brussels sprout leaves with the olive oil, white balsamic vinegar, and pinch of flaky salt. Taste a leaf. It should taste seasoned. Add more salt if needed.

In a small bowl, using a fork or small flat-bottomed whisk, beat the cream until it thickens and forms soft peaks. Grate the garlic on a Microplane directly into the bowl (or finely mince

it by hand). Season with a pinch of sea salt and stir to combine. Store in the fridge until you are ready to assemble your pizza.

Prepare the oven and pizza peel: About 1 hour before you want to bake the pizza, place a baking steel in the top third of the oven and preheat it to 550°F convection roast (or as high as it will go). Dust a pizza peel lightly with semolina flour or top with parchment paper.

Stretch the dough: Lightly dust a work surface with flour. Using lightly floured hands, pat the dough gently to flatten it, then stretch it into a 10- to 11-inch round by laying it on the back of your hands and gently rotating it, taking care not to depress the beautiful air pockets in the dough. If the dough begins resisting, set it down on the work surface to rest for 5 to 10 minutes, then continue stretching. Transfer the stretched dough to the prepared peel and give it a shake to ensure it's not sticking.

Recipe continues

Assemble the pizza: Spread the garlic cream over the dough, leaving a ½-inch border. Top with the pancetta rounds, spacing them evenly. Spread the Brussels sprouts over the top. Stretch the dough one last time by pulling outward on the edges. Redistribute the toppings as needed, then give the peel one last shake to ensure the dough is not sticking.

Bake the pizza: Shimmy the pizza (still on the parchment if using) onto the steel and bake until the edges are beginning to char, 5 to 6 minutes. (This may take 8 to 10 minutes, depending on your oven.)

Using the peel, transfer the pizza to a cutting board (discard the parchment paper). Drop spoonfuls of the ricotta over the dough. Drizzle lightly with the aged balsamic. Cut and serve.

Homemade Balsamic Syrup

Makes ½ cup

1 cup balsamic vinegar

This makes a small batch, but you can easily use this same method to make as much as you want.

In a small saucepan over medium heat, simmer the balsamic vinegar until reduced by half and thick enough to coat the back of a spoon. Remove from the heat immediately and transfer to a small storage jar. Store at room temperature for months.

Fall Wedge Salad with Bacon, Pear, and Blue Cheese Dressing

Serves 4

2 ounces bacon, finely diced

⅓ cup pine nuts

1 head iceberg lettuce
(1¼ to 1½ pounds), cut into
8 wedges

Flaky sea salt or kosher salt

1 pear, diced

½ cup Blue Cheese Dressing
(page 40), plus more to taste

Freshly ground black pepper

¼ cup minced fresh chives

Growing up as a faculty child (affectionately known as "fac-brat") on a boarding school campus meant I had my fair share of dining hall meals. It wasn't all bad. I have fond memories of the black-bottom cupcakes, yogurt and granola, and the salad bar with its dizzying number of toppings, the bacon bits being my favorite. The lettuce option—iceberg exclusively—dressed with bottled Italian dressing, did, however, leave much to be desired and turned me off the anemic-looking green for decades. So when the wedge salad began enjoying a resurgence several years ago, I was skeptical: Could any amount of dressing make that watery backbone of a salad palatable? It turns out yes. Today, I love a wedge salad with all sorts of dressings, but the classic blue cheese dressing is hard to beat. Here, diced pear, crispy (*homemade*) bacon bits, and pine nuts toasted in the rendered bacon fat join the fun. Tip: Don't hold back on the dressing and pass more on the side.

In a small skillet, cook the bacon over medium heat until the fat is rendered and the meat is crisp, 5 to 10 minutes. Transfer the crispy bacon bits to a plate, leaving the fat in the skillet.

Add the pine nuts to the skillet and cook, stirring frequently, over low heat until evenly golden—they'll brown up very quickly, so do not walk away. Leaving the fat in the skillet, transfer the pine nuts to the plate with bacon.

Set the iceberg wedges on a large platter and season them on both sides with some salt. Arrange them wedge-edge up. Scatter the crisped bacon, toasted pine nuts, and diced pears over the wedges. Drizzle the dressing evenly over the top, being sure to dress each wedge generously—use more dressing as needed. Season with pepper to taste. Scatter the chives over the top. Serve, passing more dressing on the side.

Mashed Potato and Bacon Pizza

Makes one 13-inch pizza

1 ball Thin-Crust Pizza Dough
(page 26)

All-purpose flour, for dusting

3 ounces bacon, cut into ½-inch
pieces

1½ tablespoons extra-virgin olive
oil, plus more for drizzling

1 garlic clove, peeled

Semolina flour, rice flour, or
all-purpose flour, for the peel

2 tablespoons finely grated
Pecorino Romano or parmesan
cheese (see page 19)

½ cup Mashed Potatoes (recipe
follows)

4 ounces low-moisture whole-milk
mozzarella cheese, pulled into
½-inch pieces (about 1 cup)

Flaky sea salt

Pinch of dried oregano

NOTE
The mashed potato recipe that
follows will yield enough for a nice
meal (or many pizzas). But this
pizza is great for leftover mashed
potatoes, so use whatever mashed
potatoes you have on hand.

Whenever I have leftover mashed potatoes on hand, I make this mashed potato and bacon pizza, a combination I've loved ever since first trying it at Bar, the New Haven restaurant that's famous for it. Understandably, you may be wary of the idea, but I can assure you mashed potatoes on pizza is just one of those sounds-weird-until-you-try-it toppings. It's surprisingly not heavy and incredibly delicious—so delicious in fact, you may find yourself making mashed potatoes just to make this pizza, or, at the very least, squirreling some away before serving to ensure you have some on hand for pizza night. The keys to success here are twofold: First, do not spread the mashed potatoes in an even layer but rather dollop or crumble them on. Second, parcook the bacon to ensure it crisps fully in the oven. One bite, I have no doubt, will make you a mashed potato-on-pizza believer. Maybe even an evangelist.

Prepare the dough: Transfer the dough from its storage container to a roomier, lightly floured, covered container (see Dough containers, page 16) and allow it to proof at room temperature for 1½ to 2 hours.

Prepare the toppings: Place the bacon in a large skillet and set over high heat. As soon as the bacon begins sizzling, reduce the heat to medium and cook until the bacon has rendered some fat but is not yet crisp, 3 to 5 minutes. Transfer the bacon to a plate, leaving the fat in the pan.

Place the olive oil in a small bowl. Grate the garlic on a Microplane directly into the olive oil (or finely mince by hand) and stir together.

Prepare the oven and pizza peel: About 1 hour before you want to bake the pizza, place a baking steel in the top third of the oven and preheat it to 550°F convection roast (or as high as it will go). Dust a pizza peel lightly with

semolina flour or top with parchment paper.

Roll the dough: Lightly dust a work surface and the dough ball with flour. With lightly floured hands, pinch the outermost edge of the dough to flatten and depress the air from the edges. Flip the ball and repeat the pinching at the edges. Using a lightly dusted rolling pin, roll the dough into a 13-inch round, flipping the dough every few strokes and using flour as needed. If the dough begins resisting, let rest for 5 to 10 minutes, then continue rolling. Transfer the stretched dough to the prepared peel and give it a shake to ensure it's not sticking.

Assemble the pizza: Spread the garlic oil over the dough all the way to the edges. Scatter the pecorino over the top. For freshly made mashed potatoes, drop small spoonfuls over the dough; for leftover potatoes cold from the fridge, crumble them over the top. Scatter the mozzarella evenly over

Recipe continues

the top spreading it all the way to the edges. Scatter the bacon over the top. Drizzle lightly with oil and season with a pinch of flaky sea salt and oregano.

Bake the pizza: Shimmy the pizza (still on the parchment if using) onto the steel and bake until the cheese is melted and the edges are beginning to char, 4 to 5 minutes. (This may take 8 to 10 minutes, depending on your oven.)

Using the peel, transfer the pizza to a cutting board (discard the parchment paper). Cut and serve.

Mashed Potatoes

Makes 1 quart (enough for eight 13-inch pizzas)

1¾ pounds Yukon Gold potatoes, peeled and cut into 2-inch chunks

2 teaspoons kosher salt

¾ cup buttermilk, at room temperature

Freshly ground black pepper

Flaky sea salt

1 tablespoon unsalted butter, plus more to taste

In a medium saucepan, combine the potatoes, kosher salt, and enough water to cover. Bring to a boil over high heat. Reduce the heat to medium and simmer until the potatoes are tender when pierced with a fork, about 45 minutes.

Reserving at least 1 cup of the cooking liquid, drain the potatoes. Return the potatoes to the pan and set over low heat, uncovered, for about 5 minutes, stirring occasionally, to let the potatoes dry out a little.

Add the buttermilk, ¼ cup of the reserved cooking liquid, pepper to taste, and a pinch of flaky sea salt. Mash the potatoes with a potato masher until you have a coarse puree. Add the butter and mash again. Once the potatoes are as mashed up as possible you can switch to a wooden spoon or spatula and beat them further. Taste and add more sea salt, pepper, or butter to taste. Thin with more reserved cooking liquid if desired. Store in the fridge for up to 1 week or in the freezer for up to 3 months.

Bar's Mixed Greens Salad with Candied Pecans, Blue Cheese, and Pear

Serves 4

10 ounces mixed greens

2 pears, finely diced

¾ cup Candied Pecans (recipe follows)

4 ounces blue cheese, crumbled (about 1 cup)

⅓ cup Red Wine Vinaigrette (page 39), plus more to taste

Flaky sea salt and freshly ground black pepper

Of all the salads in this book, this one is most near and dear to my heart. It's inspired by the sole salad offered at Bar, my favorite of all the renowned New Haven pizzerias, where, as I noted earlier in the book, I fell in love. It's a simple mixed greens salad dressed in a red wine vinaigrette, but it includes that classic nut/fruit/cheese trifecta that never fails to be completely irresistible. My favorite thing about this salad, however, is its consistency, how it hasn't changed a single bit since the first time I tasted it, how it always arrives in an unassuming stainless steel bowl with a pair of tongs nestled inside. Simple as it may be, its role is paramount, a necessary acidic counter to the two pizzas I love at Bar so very much: Clam Pizza with Garlic, Olive Oil, and Pecorino (page 143) and the accompanying Mashed Potato and Bacon Pizza (page 124). Without this salad by their sides, I have no doubt neither of those pizzas would be quite so delicious.

In a large bowl, combine the greens, pears, pecans, and blue cheese. Toss with the dressing. Taste and season with salt and pepper if needed and add more dressing to taste.

Candied Pecans

Makes 1½ cups

1 cup pecans (4 ounces)

¼ cup sugar

Flaky sea salt

In a large skillet, toast the pecans over medium heat, stirring occasionally, until they turn light brown and begin to smell fragrant, about 5 minutes. Transfer to a plate to cool.

Line a sheet pan with parchment paper. In the same skillet, heat the sugar without stirring—shake the pan if necessary to distribute the sugar in an even layer. When it turns evenly golden or amber, remove from the heat, add the toasted pecans and a pinch of sea salt. Using a heatproof spatula, stir to combine. When the pecans are nicely coated in the sugar syrup, transfer them to the lined pan.

Once cool enough to handle, break the pecans into pieces. Store the pecans at room temperature in an airtight container for weeks.

Cast-Iron Skillet Meatball Pizza with Caramelized Onions and Mozzarella

Makes one 10-inch pizza

1 tablespoon unsalted butter, at room temperature

1 teaspoon extra-virgin olive oil, plus more as needed

One 260-gram ball Pan Pizza Dough (page 30)

¼ cup Simple Tomato Sauce (page 34) or your favorite jarred sauce

5 ounces low-moisture whole-milk mozzarella cheese, pulled into ½-inch pieces (about 1¼ cups)

¼ cup Caramelized Onions (page 138; see Note)

7 to 8 Homemade Meatballs (recipe follows), halved

Extra-virgin olive oil

Flaky sea salt

Parmigiano-Reggiano or Pecorino Romano cheese (optional), for finishing

Crushed red pepper flakes (optional), for serving

NOTE

If you're pressed for time, you can use ½ cup thinly sliced raw onions in place of the caramelized ones. You can also use a 12-inch cast-iron skillet, which will produce a thinner but equally delicious pizza.

Though the origin of meatball pizza is unknown, it likely was created to prevent wasting leftovers, making it the ultimate example of economy cooking, an upcycled creation whose star ingredient was born of thrift itself. Origin aside, it's no surprise meatball pizza is anything but delicious: sauce, cheese, meatballs—the trio has been dressing pasta and filling hoagie rolls for millennia, winning the hearts and minds of all who delight. I am a huge fan, especially when caramelized onions join the party along with a generous showering of Parmigiano-Reggiano out of the oven. Here I've used the pan pizza dough and baked it in a cast-iron skillet, but I love this combination with the Neapolitanish Pizza Dough (page 22), too.

Prepare the dough: Grease a 10-inch cast-iron skillet with the softened butter. Pour the olive oil into the center of the pan. Place the dough ball in the oil and turn to coat.

Let the dough rest in the skillet uncovered for 1 hour. Lightly oil your hands and use your fingertips to dimple and stretch the dough to fit the pan. When the dough resists, let it rest for 10 minutes, then stretch it again using the same technique. Once the dough fits the pan, let rest for 1 more hour.

Prepare the oven: Preheat the oven to 500°F.

Parbake the dough: Using oiled hands, dimple the dough one last time taking care to not dimple the perimeter, which will help the dough bake more evenly.

Transfer the pan to the oven for 5 to 6 minutes — the dough will be puffed and slightly bubbly, but still very pale. Remove the pan from oven but leave the oven on and reduce the temperature to 475°F.

Top the pizza: Spoon the tomato sauce over the dough, using the back of a spoon to spread it. Sprinkle the mozzarella evenly over the top, spreading it to the edges. Scatter the caramelized onions evenly over the cheese. Top with the meatball halves, cut-side down, spacing them evenly. Drizzle with olive oil. Season with a pinch of flaky sea salt.

Return the pan to the oven and bake until the cheese has melted and blistered slightly, about 10 minutes.

Set the skillet on the stovetop. Use an offset spatula to peek at the underside of the dough. If the crust looks pale, set the skillet over medium-high heat and cook, watching closely, until the crust is lightly golden, 1 to 2 minutes.

Carefully remove the entire pizza from the pan and transfer it to a cutting board. If desired, shave Parmigiano or Pecorino over the top to taste. Cut and serve with red pepper flakes on the side.

Recipe continues

Homemade Meatballs

Makes 24 to 26 meatballs

3 tablespoons milk

2 slices stale bread (about 1 ounce each), crumbled (about 1 cup)

1 pound ground beef (80% lean, 20% fat)

Kosher salt

¼ cup diced onion

½ cup grated Parmigiano-Reggiano cheese

1 garlic clove, finely minced

1 large egg, beaten

4 tablespoons extra-virgin olive oil, for frying

In a large bowl, pour the milk over the bread crumbs and let stand for 10 minutes for the bread to absorb the liquid. Add the beef and season with 1 teaspoon kosher salt. Add the onion, Parmigiano, garlic, and egg and mix well with your hands until thoroughly combined.

Using a #50 scoop or a 1-tablespoon measure, shape the meat mixture into balls the size of Ping-Pong balls; if using a tablespoon measure, it will be a heaping tablespoon. Transfer to a small tray.

In a large skillet, heat 2 tablespoons of the oil over high heat until it begins to shimmer. Immediately reduce the heat to low and add half of the meatballs. Season with kosher salt. Cook until the underside is golden, 2 to 3 minutes. Use two forks to flip the meatballs over and brown the other side for another 2 to 3 minutes or until cooked through. Transfer the meatballs to a plate. Wipe out the skillet and repeat with the remaining meatballs and 2 tablespoons oil.

Fall Caesar Salad with Shaved Brussels Sprouts

Serves 4

1 pound Brussels sprouts, ends trimmed

½ teaspoon kosher salt

1 head romaine lettuce, thinly sliced

½ to 1 cup grated Parmigiano-Reggiano cheese (2 to 3 ounces)

Freshly ground black pepper

½ cup Caesar Dressing (page 39), plus more to taste

Flaky sea salt

As with the classic raw kale salad recipe, the key to making a good raw Brussels sprouts salad lies in the fine shave. I use my food processor fitted with the shredder or slicer attachment, which makes the process go incredibly quickly. If you are a patient person, you of course can use your knife. If you are not, I'd ditch the sprouts altogether and go for a classic Caesar salad (see Spring Caesar Salad à la Speedy Romeo, page 236) made with trusty ol' romaine lettuce. I love the addition of romaine here anyway because it lightens the mix a bit, making it feel less slaw-like and more salad-y.

Thinly slice the Brussels sprouts on the shredder disc in a food processor (or use a knife). Place the shaved Brussels sprouts in a large bowl, toss with the kosher salt, and let sit for 15 minutes.

Add the romaine and ½ cup of the Parmigiano, pepper to taste, and the dressing. Toss to combine. Taste and add a pinch of sea salt if needed, more dressing to taste, and the remaining Parmigiano, if desired.

Kale Pizza
with Butternut Squash Sauce and Mozzarella

Makes one 13-inch pizza

1 ball Thin-Crust Pizza Dough
(page 26)

All-purpose flour, for dusting

Kale

1 tablespoon extra-virgin olive oil

4 cups coarsely chopped lacinato
(Tuscan) kale leaves, stems and
midribs removed (from about
8 ounces untrimmed)

Kosher salt

2 teaspoons white balsamic
vinegar

Assembly

Semolina flour, rice flour, or
all-purpose flour, for the peel

¼ cup Butternut Squash Sauce
(page 36)

4 ounces low-moisture whole-milk
mozzarella cheese, pulled into
½-inch pieces (about 1 cup)

Extra-virgin olive oil

Flaky sea salt

Parmigiano-Reggiano or Pecorino
Romano cheese (optional), for
finishing

Crushed red pepper flakes, for
serving

Featured in the "10-Minute Main" column of an old issue of *Gourmet* magazine, a recipe for penne with butternut squash sauce promised to be fast and tasty, and it was: Nearly twenty years later, I'm still making it, and it continues to be one of my children's most requested meals throughout the fall and winter. Over the years I've layered the sauce in lasagna with sautéed Swiss chard and stirred it into risotto with wilted kale. Incredibly, without cream or butter, the sauce lends a richness, earthiness, and sweetness to anything it slicks, including pizza dough. Butternut squash pairs well with all sorts of greens, and while I particularly love it with lacinato (Tuscan) kale, feel free to swap in your favorite.

Prepare the dough: Transfer the dough from its storage container to a roomier, lightly floured, covered container (see Dough containers, page 16) and allow it to proof at room temperature for 1½ to 2 hours.

Prepare the kale: In a large skillet, heat the olive oil over high heat until it shimmers. Add the kale and a pinch of kosher salt and sauté for 1 to 2 minutes, using tongs to rearrange the greens frequently, until they wilt down. Stir in the vinegar and transfer the greens to a plate to cool. Taste and add more salt if needed.

Prepare the oven and pizza peel: About 1 hour before you want to bake the pizza, place a baking steel in the top third of the oven and preheat it to 550°F convection roast (or as high as it will go). Dust a pizza peel lightly with semolina flour or top with parchment paper.

Roll the dough: Lightly dust a work surface and the dough ball with flour. With lightly floured hands, pinch the outermost edge of the dough to flatten and depress the air from the edges. Flip the ball and repeat the pinching at the edges. Using a lightly dusted rolling pin, roll the dough into a 13-inch round, flipping the dough every few strokes and using flour as needed. Transfer the stretched dough to the prepared peel and give it a shake to ensure it's not sticking.

Assemble the pizza: Spread the butternut sauce over the dough all the way to the edges. Scatter the mozzarella evenly over the top. Top with the kale, spreading it all the way to the edges. Drizzle with olive oil. Season with a pinch of flaky sea salt.

Bake the pizza: Shimmy the pizza (still on the parchment if using) onto the steel and bake until the cheese is melted and the edges are beginning to char, 4 to 5 minutes. (This may take 8 to 10 minutes, depending on your oven.)

Using the peel, transfer the pizza to a cutting board (discard the parchment paper). If desired, shave Parmigiano or Romano over the top to taste. Cut and serve with pepper flakes on the side.

Beets and Mixed Greens Salad with Golden Raisins and Pistachios

Serves 4

1 cup kosher salt

4 medium golden beets (1¼ to 1½ pounds total; see Note)

Flaky sea salt

2 tablespoons plus ¼ cup Apple Cider Vinaigrette (page 37), plus more to taste

¼ cup golden raisins

2 tablespoons white balsamic vinegar or other vinegar

5 ounces mixed greens

Freshly ground black pepper

⅓ cup pistachios, coarsely chopped

2 to 3 ounces goat cheese or feta cheese (optional)

If I were given the task of converting a beet hater into a lover, I would start with golden beets, whose flavor is sweeter and less earthy than the red variety. As with red beets, I like to dress the freshly roasted beets with sea salt and a small amount of the vinaigrette to ensure they are nicely seasoned before combining them with the other elements, which here include golden raisins, soaked briefly in vinegar, and coarsely chopped pistachios. This salad does not demand cheese, but I do love goat cheese or feta with beet varieties of all kinds.

Preheat the oven to 425°F.

Pour the kosher salt into an 8- or 9-inch square baking pan. (See Note for an alternative cooking method.) Place the beets on the salt bed. Cover the pan tightly with foil and place in the oven until the beets are knife-tender, about 1 hour. Uncover and let them stand until cool enough to handle, about 15 minutes. Discard the salt.

Trim off the rough (stem) end, then use your hands or paper towels to rub off the skins and discard. If the skin is being stubborn, remove with a paring knife. Cut each beet into 6 or 8 wedges, then cut each wedge in half crosswise. Transfer to a bowl. Season with flaky sea salt and 2 tablespoons of the vinaigrette. Toss, taste, and adjust with salt to taste.

In a small bowl, combine the raisins and balsamic and let stand for 10 minutes.

Place the greens in a large shallow serving bowl. Drizzle with the remaining ¼ cup vinaigrette. Season lightly with salt and pepper and toss gently. Taste and adjust with more salt, pepper, and dressing to taste. Add the beets. Sprinkle the pistachios and the soaked raisins with the vinegar over the top. If using, crumble the goat cheese or feta over the top. Season with more pepper to taste. Toss gently and serve.

NOTES

If you can't find golden beets, you can use red beets.

If you'd rather not use the salt-roasted method, you can simply boil the beets until they are knife tender, 60 to 90 minutes.

Broccoli Rabe and Smoked Mozzarella Pizza

Makes one 12-inch pizza

1 ball Neapolitanish Pizza Dough
(page 22)

All-purpose flour, for dusting

Broccoli rabe

1 bundle of broccoli rabe (about
½ pound), ends trimmed

1 tablespoon extra-virgin olive oil

1 garlic clove, minced

Pinch of crushed red pepper flakes

Kosher salt

½ lemon

Assembly

Semolina flour, rice flour, or
all-purpose flour, for the peel

3 tablespoons Roasted Tomato
"Butter" (page 36) or Simple
Tomato Sauce (page 34)

3 ounces smoked mozzarella
or low-moisture whole-milk
mozzarella cheese, pulled into
½-inch pieces (about ¾ cup)

Extra-virgin olive oil

Flaky sea salt

For the past few years, starting in late May and going through the end of November, I send out a newsletter, *The Farm Share Newsletter*, with tips and recipes geared toward managing a weekly delivery of vegetables. Often when I'm short on ideas for certain vegetables, I reach out to readers for suggestions. Though broccoli rabe is not as unfamiliar to me as some (namely kohlrabi and Tokyo bekana), it is not a vegetable I cook with often, and when I solicited ideas for what to do with it, someone suggested I use it to make a pizza paired with smoked mozzarella. As it turns out, that someone was Domenica Marchetti, prolific cookbook writer and author of *Buona Domenica*, a Substack newsletter all about Italian cooking. No surprise, Domenica's suggestion was brilliant, a wonderful use for a small bundle of broccoli rabe, its slight bitterness a perfect complement to the sweet roasted tomato sauce and smoky, melty cheese.

Prepare the dough: Transfer the dough from its storage container to a roomier, lightly floured, covered container (see Dough containers, page 16) and allow it to proof at room temperature for 1½ to 2 hours.

Prepare the broccoli rabe: Cut the broccoli rabe into 1-inch segments. In a large skillet, heat the oil, garlic, and pepper flakes over medium-high heat just until the garlic begins to shimmer and take on the slightest amount of color, 1 to 2 minutes. Add the broccoli rabe, season with ½ teaspoon kosher salt, and cook, stirring and rearranging frequently with tongs, until wilted, about 2 minutes. Add 2 tablespoons water, cover, and cook for 2 minutes more. Remove the cover and squeeze lightly with the lemon. Stir, taste, and adjust with more salt or lemon to taste.

Prepare the oven and peel: About 1 hour before you want to bake the pizza, place a baking steel in the top third of the oven and preheat it to 550°F convection roast (or as high as it will go). Dust a pizza peel lightly with semolina flour or top with parchment paper.

Stretch the dough: Lightly dust a work surface with flour. Using lightly floured hands, pat the dough gently to flatten it, then stretch it into a 10- to 11-inch round by laying it on the back of your hands and gently rotating it, taking care not to depress the beautiful air pockets in the dough. If the dough begins resisting, set it down on the work surface to rest for 5 to 10 minutes, then continue stretching. Transfer the stretched dough to the prepared peel and give it a shake to ensure it's not sticking.

Assemble the pizza: Spread the tomato butter or sauce over the dough, leaving a ½-inch border. Scatter ½ cup of the broccoli rabe evenly over the top followed by the smoked mozzarella. (Store the remaining broccoli rabe in the fridge

Recipe continues

for up to 1 week or in the freezer for up to 3 months.) Drizzle lightly with olive oil. Season with a pinch of flaky sea salt. Stretch the dough one last time by pulling outward on the edges. Redistribute the toppings as needed, then give the peel one last shake to ensure the dough is not sticking.

Bake the pizza: Shimmy the pizza (still on the parchment if using) onto the steel and bake until the cheese is melted and the edges are beginning to char, 5 to 6 minutes. (This may take 8 to 10 minutes, depending on your oven.)

Using the peel, transfer the pizza to a cutting board (discard the parchment paper). Cut and serve.

Farm Share Harvest Slaw

Serves 4

8 radishes, trimmed

5 small turnips, trimmed

5 medium carrots, trimmed

½ head napa cabbage (about 9 ounces)

4 scallions, whites and light-green parts only, thinly sliced

⅓ cup Apple Cider Vinaigrette (page 37), plus more to taste

Flaky sea salt

If you belong to a farm share or other community-supported agriculture system, this is a handy template to have in your back pocket: shredded raw roots + shredded cabbage + apple cider vinaigrette. If you don't belong to a weekly vegetable share, you might find the formula helpful anyway, a framework for cleaning out your vegetable bins. You can use any combination of raw vegetables here, including raw beets, and you can use other herbs as well, such as cilantro, parsley, basil, or chives. Due to the quantity of scallions we receive every week, they almost always make an appearance, and I love both the color and flavor they provide. In the fall, I most often dress the vegetables with the apple cider vinaigrette, but I also love it with the Lemon Vinaigrette (page 37) and Creamy Cashew Dressing (page 40).

Grate the radishes, turnips, carrots, and cabbage on the shredding disc of a food processor (or use a box grater or a mandoline). Transfer to a large bowl and add the scallions and dressing. Toss together. Taste and adjust with some flaky sea salt and/or more dressing.

Roasted Cauliflower Pizza
with Caramelized Onions and Pickled Cherry Peppers

Makes one 13-inch pizza

1 ball Thin-Crust Pizza Dough
(page 26)

All-purpose flour, for dusting

Semolina flour, rice flour, or
all-purpose flour, for the peel

¼ cup No-Cook Tomato Sauce
(page 34)

¼ cup Caramelized Onions (recipe
follows)

1½ cups Roasted Cauliflower
(recipe follows)

¼ cup finely chopped pickled hot
cherry peppers

4 ounces low-moisture whole-milk
mozzarella cheese, pulled into
½-inch pieces (about 1 cup)

Extra-virgin olive oil

Flaky sea salt

From late fall until early spring, I make one recipe on repeat: roasted cauliflower and onions, a dish that comes together in no time and never fails to please, the florets emerging tender and golden, tangled in a web of sweet caramelized onions. That combination is captured here along with pickled hot cherry peppers, which, just to warn you, may turn into an addiction: Once you start topping pizzas with pickled chiles, it's hard *not* to add them to every pizza for the bright, acidic pops of flavor they provide. Depending on the other ingredients at play on a pizza, I'll use spicy or mild chiles, but here, to balance the sweetness of the roasted vegetables, I like extra-hot cherry peppers. If you don't love heat, pickled banana peppers work well in their place.

Prepare the dough: Transfer the dough from its storage container to a roomier, lightly floured, covered container (see Dough containers, page 16) and allow it to proof at room temperature for 1½ to 2 hours.

Prepare the oven and peel: About 1 hour before you want to bake the pizza, place a baking steel in the top third of the oven and preheat it to 550°F convection roast (or as high as it will go). Dust a pizza peel lightly with semolina flour or top with parchment paper.

Roll the dough: Lightly dust a work surface and the dough ball with flour. With lightly floured hands, pinch the outermost edge of the dough to flatten and depress the air from the edges. Flip the ball and repeat the pinching at the edges. Using a lightly dusted rolling pin, roll the dough into a 13-inch round, flipping the dough every few strokes and using flour as needed. Transfer the stretched dough to the prepared peel and give it a shake to ensure it's not sticking.

Recipe continues

Assemble the pizza: Spread the tomato sauce over the dough all the way to the edges. Top the pizza evenly in this order: caramelized onions, roasted cauliflower, chopped cherry peppers, and mozzarella. Drizzle with olive oil. Season with a pinch of flaky sea salt.

Bake the pizza: Shimmy the pizza (still on the parchment if using) onto the steel and bake until the cheese is melted and the edges are beginning to char, 4 to 5 minutes. (This may take 8 to 10 minutes, depending on your oven.)

Using the peel, transfer the pizza to a cutting board (discard the parchment paper). Cut and serve.

Roasted Cauliflower

Serves 3 or 4 as a side dish

1 large head cauliflower (about 2 pounds), cut into 1-inch pieces

¼ cup extra-virgin olive oil

Kosher salt

Preheat the oven to 425°F. Line a sheet pan with parchment paper.

Arrange the cauliflower on the lined pan and toss with the olive oil and a big pinch of kosher salt. Spread into an even layer and roast until the cauliflower is knife-tender and browned at the edges, 25 to 30 minutes.

If serving as a side dish, serve hot. If making for a pizza topping, transfer the cauliflower to a plate to cool. Store in the fridge for up to 1 week or in the freezer for up to 3 months.

Caramelized Onions

Makes ½ cup (enough for two 13-inch pizzas)

2 tablespoons extra-virgin olive oil

4 cups thinly sliced white or yellow onions

Kosher salt

½ teaspoon sugar

½ teaspoon vinegar, any kind

In a large skillet, heat the olive oil over high heat until it shimmers. Add the onions and a pinch of salt. Cover, immediately reduce the heat to low, and cook, stirring every few minutes, until the onions are lightly golden, about 20 minutes.

Uncover and let any water caught in the lid drip back into the skillet. Sprinkle the sugar over the onions and cook, stirring frequently, until the onions have turned a deep brown, 10 to 15 minutes (or longer: be patient and rely on the visual cues before proceeding).

Pour in the vinegar, remove from the heat, and scrape the bottom of the pan with a wooden spoon or spatula to remove any browned bits. Transfer the onions to a bowl to cool. Store in the fridge for up to 1 week or in the freezer for up to 3 months.

Collard Greens Salad with Pepitas, Persimmons, and Manchego

Serves 4

½ cup pumpkin seeds

1½ pounds collard greens, thick midribs removed

Kosher salt

¼ teaspoon sugar

⅓ cup dried cranberries

1 Fuyu persimmon, peeled and thinly sliced, or 10 dried slices

½ cup shaved Manchego cheese (about 1 ounce)

⅓ cup Lemon Vinaigrette (page 37), plus more to taste

Flaky sea salt and freshly ground black pepper

For years I associated collard greens with braising, an hours-long process requiring bacon, onions, and apple cider vinegar. So when I read about serving collard greens raw in Ronna Welsh's *The Nimble Cook*, I was intrigued. Ronna's method calls for tossing thinly sliced collard greens with a little bit of salt and sugar, then letting them stand for 15 minutes. Using salt as a way to tenderize and draw out moisture made sense, but the sugar surprised me, so I emailed Ronna to learn more. "I use a pinch of sugar with collards," she wrote me back, "because they tend to lean a bit bitter." This technique serves another purpose, too: Whereas massaged raw greens can sometimes get too soft, "a light toss," Ronna notes, "leaves them crisp." Ronna suggests dressing the greens with a sharp vinaigrette, and the lemon vinaigrette called for in this festive fall salad is just that. The Apple Cider Vinaigrette (page 37) also works well here.

In a large skillet, toast the pumpkin seeds over medium heat until fragrant and just starting to color, 3 to 5 minutes. Check often and stir frequently. Transfer the seeds to a plate to cool.

Stack a few of the collard green leaves on top of one another, roll into a tight coil, then cut the roll crosswise to create thin ribbons. Place the greens in a large bowl and toss with a pinch of kosher salt and the sugar. Set aside for 15 minutes.

Add the cranberries, persimmon, toasted pumpkin seeds, and shaved Manchego to the bowl of greens. Toss with the dressing. Season with flaky sea salt and pepper to taste. Add more dressing if desired.

NOTE
Pumpkin seeds are also called pepitas.

Winter

Snow. Ice. Cold. Sledding. Skating. Fires. Holidays. Cookies. Carols. Cocoa. Winter: It's the time of year to embrace the chilly temperatures or hide from them. For me, it's the latter. If I'm not at a hockey rink or out walking the dog, I'm home, with my hat and slippers on, trying to stay warm. I hate being cold, and I hate winter, which frankly is just too long in Upstate New York. My Minnesotan husband loves to remind me there is no such thing as bad weather, only bad clothes, and over the years I have come to accept this mantra. Except in May, when it's still too cold to break out the flip-flops and I don't dare leave home without my heated vest.

For those of us who like to hibernate, we have our ovens to keep us warm, especially on pizza night as it makes its way up to 550°F, heating the whole kitchen in the process. In the winter, rarely do I fire up my outdoor oven, which is usually covered with half a foot of snow anyway. Instead, I rely mostly on my Neapolitanish Pizza Dough (page 22) and my favorite Pan Pizza Dough (page 30) recipes, which are wonderful for feeding the hungry masses gathered around the TV cheering on their favorite team—see Detroit-Style Pizza for a Crowd with Pepperoni, Pickled Jalapeños, and Hot Honey (page 159) and Sicilian-Style Pizza for a Crowd with "The Works" (page 174). I love bringing a parbaked Sicilian or Detroit-style pizza to a Super Bowl or March Madness party, finishing it on-site, plopping it down on the buffet, and watching how quickly it disappears.

To accompany these wintry pies, you'll find salads composed of vibrant storage roots—watermelon radishes, turnips, carrots, and beets—both in raw and cooked forms. Mixed with chicories and other sturdy greens, along with dried fruits, nuts, and cheese, these winter salads are often united by bright citrus-forward vinaigrettes but sometimes rich and creamy dressings as in the Winter Wedge Salad with Roasted Savoy Cabbage, Blue Cheese, and Walnuts (page 173) and the Charred Endive Salad with Caesar Dressing (page 176).

Clam Pizza
with Garlic, Olive Oil, and Pecorino

Makes one 13-inch pizza

1 ball Thin-Crust Pizza Dough (page 26)

All-purpose flour, for dusting

Semolina flour, rice flour, or all-purpose flour, for the peel

2 pounds littleneck clams (about 18)

1 tablespoon extra-virgin olive oil, plus more for drizzling

1 garlic clove

Flaky sea salt

¼ teaspoon dried oregano

2 tablespoons finely grated Pecorino Romano or parmesan cheese (see page 19)

Fresh oregano leaves, optional

Lemon wedges, for serving

NOTE
Clams, unlike oysters, are opened from the front as opposed to the back. I always watch a quick YouTube video on how to open clams prior to making this recipe. Some clams are more stubborn than others, but once you get the hang of it, the process moves along quickly.

I have always loved clams. When I was five, my mother found me at the raw bar at my uncle's wedding slurping down littlenecks and cherrystones. In my teens, anytime I found myself at the counter of a seafood shack, I faced the difficult decision of choosing between fried clams with lemon or steamers with drawn butter, but invariably I chose the latter, the juicy orbs, plump with the flavors of the sea, too hard to resist. Clam pizza has been my favorite since the first time I tasted it at a local spot in my hometown, where they blanketed the dough with the chopped meat, nearly unrecognizable as clam, but delicious briny rubble nonetheless. In my twenties, I discovered the wonder of New Haven clam pizza, where the large thin pies are topped with a generous amount of garlic, olive oil, Pecorino Romano, and freshly shucked clams, the nectar of which permeates every slice. When you're assembling this pizza, you'll be tempted to throw in some mozzarella or other cheese, but I encourage you to refrain. This is a less-is-more pizza, an exercise in restraint, a perfect union of ingredients that needs nothing more than a squeeze of lemon when it emerges from the oven in all its glory. I hope you'll agree.

Prepare the dough: Transfer the dough from its storage container to a roomier, lightly floured, covered container (see Dough containers, page 16) and allow it to proof at room temperature for 1½ to 2 hours.

Prepare the oven and peel: About 1 hour before you want to bake the pizza, place a baking steel in the top third of the oven and preheat it to 550°F convection roast (or as high as it will go). Dust a pizza peel lightly with semolina flour or top with parchment paper.

Using a clam or oyster knife, carefully open the clams (see Note), remove the meats, and place them in a colander as you work. You should have roughly 4 ounces of meat.

Place the olive oil in a small bowl. Grate the garlic on a Microplane directly into the olive oil (or finely mince it by hand). Stir together the oil and garlic.

Roll the dough: Lightly dust a work surface and the dough ball with flour. With lightly floured hands, pinch the outermost edge of the dough to flatten and depress the air from the edges. Flip the ball and repeat the pinching at the edges. Using a lightly dusted rolling pin, roll the dough into a 13-inch round, flipping the dough every few strokes and using flour as needed. Transfer the stretched dough to the prepared peel and give it a shake to ensure it's not sticking.

Top the pizza: Brush the garlic oil evenly over the dough. Scatter the clam meats evenly over the top. Season with flaky sea salt and the dried oregano. Sprinkle the Romano over the top. Drizzle lightly with olive oil.

Recipe continues

Bake the pizza: Shimmy the pizza (still on the parchment if using) onto the steel and bake until the cheese is melted and the edges are beginning to char, 4 to 5 minutes. (This may take 8 to 10 minutes, depending on your oven.)

Using the peel, transfer the pizza to a cutting board (discard the parchment paper). Sprinkle with fresh oregano leaves to taste, if using. Cut and serve with lemon wedges on the side.

Watermelon Radish and Turnip Salad with Citrus, Chives, and Pistachios

Serves 4

3 oranges

3 tablespoons white balsamic vinegar

¼ cup minced shallot (1 or 2 small shallots)

Flaky sea salt

3 watermelon radishes (about 1 pound total)

2 medium or 6 small turnips (about 8 ounces total)

2 tablespoons extra-virgin olive oil

⅓ cup pistachios, coarsely chopped

2 tablespoons finely sliced fresh chives

2 ounces goat cheese

During our first winter in Upstate New York, I signed up for a winter farm share, a daunting commitment to three forty-pound deliveries of root vegetables. Over those three months, we lived on roasted parsnips, cabbage soup, oven fries, and this watermelon radish salad, a dish that materialized after I cut one of those unassuming bulbs in half to reveal a magenta-hued disk webbed with a starlike motif, like nature's charcuterie. The key when using watermelon radishes in a salad is to slice them thinly and to salt them briefly, which makes them more pliable and more receptive to absorbing the dressing. Here, turnips enter the mix along with quick-pickled shallots, chopped pistachios, and chives. I find goat cheese adds a lovely creaminess to this otherwise crisp salad, but feta or ricotta salata would work well here, too.

Slice off the ends of each orange. Squeeze the juice out of those ends into a small bowl, then discard the ends. Stand each orange on one of its cut sides. Run a knife down the side of each orange to remove the peel, pith, and membrane and expose the fruit. Squeeze the juice out of those peels into the bowl, then discard.

Turn the oranges on their sides and remove the orange segments by running a knife down the side of each membrane and slicing the segment out. Once all of the segments are removed, squeeze what's left of the orange into the bowl to extract the juice. You should get 2 to 3 tablespoons of juice total.

Add the vinegar, shallots, and a pinch of sea salt to the bowl of orange juice.

Slice the radishes as thinly as possible on a mandoline (or with a knife). Transfer to a large bowl, season with a pinch of sea salt, and toss gently. Slice the turnips as thinly as possible on the mandoline (or with a knife) and transfer to the bowl with the radishes. Season with another pinch of sea salt and toss gently. Let stand for 5 minutes. Toss again, taste, and adjust with more salt to taste.

Arrange the radishes and turnips on a serving platter. Scatter the orange segments over the top. Pour the pickled shallots and their juices over everything and drizzle with the olive oil. Scatter the pistachios and chives on top. Finally, crumble the goat cheese over the top.

'Nduja and Pickled Pepper Pizza with Burrata

Makes one 12-inch pizza

1 ball Neapolitanish Pizza Dough (page 22)

All-purpose flour, for dusting

Semolina flour, rice flour, or all-purpose flour, for the peel

3 tablespoons Homemade Vodka Sauce (page 34)

2 ounces 'nduja (see Note)

¼ cup pickled banana peppers (about 1½ ounces)

Extra-virgin olive oil

Flaky sea salt

3 ounces burrata, at room temperature (about ¾ cup)

A handful of fresh basil leaves (optional), torn if large

'Nduja can be hard to find. Markets such as Whole Foods typically carry it and online retailers such as La Quercia sell it as well.

My friend Colu Henry, author of *Back Pocket Pasta*, makes her vodka sauce with 'nduja, a spreadable salami from Calabria. The sauce comes together incredibly quickly but tastes complex thanks to the 'nduja, which lends both spicy and smoky notes. As pasta combinations often translate well to pizza, I suspected the two ingredients would pair well on a pie, but I didn't anticipate how much I would love it—this is one of my favorites, a combination that has forced me to have a tube of 'nduja, which keeps for months in the fridge, on hand at all times. Here, rather than infuse the vodka sauce with the 'nduja, I'm topping the sauce with it, leaving it exposed to brown and caramelize, allowing its flavor to shine even more. Pickled banana peppers, which are not spicy, provide a welcomed bite and tang, and burrata, added post bake, brings the richness: cool, creamy dollops, unadulterated by the blazing hot oven, melting into every bight.

Prepare the dough: Transfer the dough from its storage container to a roomier, lightly floured, covered container (see Dough containers, page 16) and allow it to proof at room temperature for 1½ to 2 hours.

Prepare the oven and pizza peel: About 1 hour before you want to bake the pizza, place a baking steel in the top third of the oven and preheat it to 550°F convection roast (or as high as it will go). Dust a pizza peel lightly with semolina flour or top with parchment paper.

Stretch the dough: Lightly dust a work surface with flour. Using lightly floured hands, pat the dough gently to flatten it, then stretch it into a 10- to 11-inch round by laying it on the back of your hands and gently rotating it, taking care not to depress the beautiful air pockets in the dough. If the dough begins resisting, set it down on the work surface to rest for 5 to 10 minutes, then continue stretching. Transfer the stretched dough to the prepared peel and give it a shake to ensure it's not sticking.

Top the pizza: Spread the vodka sauce evenly over the dough, leaving a ½-inch border. Top with the 'nduja, breaking it into small pieces as you scatter it evenly over the dough. Scatter the peppers evenly over the top. Drizzle with olive oil. Sprinkle with sea salt. Stretch the dough one last time by pulling outward on the edges. Redistribute the toppings as needed, then give the peel one last shake to ensure the dough is not sticking.

Bake the pizza: Shimmy the pizza (still on the parchment if using) onto the steel and bake until the edges are beginning to char, 5 to 6 minutes. (This may take 8 to 10 minutes, depending on your oven.)

Using the peel, transfer the pizza to a cutting board (discard the parchment paper). Top with the burrata, breaking it into pieces as you spread it over the dough. Scatter the fresh basil, if using, over the top. Cut and serve.

Winter Kale Salad
with Roasted Delicata Squash, Dates, and Almonds

Serves 4

1 small delicata squash (about 12 ounces), halved, seeded, and cut into ¾-inch cubes

½ teaspoon kosher salt

1 tablespoon extra-virgin olive oil

⅓ cup sliced almonds

8 ounces lacinato (Tuscan) kale, stemmed, or 6 ounces baby kale

Flaky sea salt

3 ounces aged Gouda or cheddar cheese, cut into ¾-inch cubes

½ cup finely chopped pitted Medjool dates (3 or 4 dates)

⅓ cup Apple Cider Vinaigrette (page 37), plus more to taste

Freshly ground black pepper

When delicata squash came onto the scene several years ago, it quickly became my favorite of all the winter squashes. Why? For so many reasons, but namely, for its soft skin, which is not only easy to cut through but also delicious and beautiful. Its small size furthermore makes it less daunting, something easy to tackle if you're, say, wanting to bulk up a kale salad with some sort of wintry element, as here. This combination of roasted squash, aged Gouda, and dates is irresistible, a perfect medley to brighten up a pile of kale. Many dressings could work here, but I love the bite and sweetness offered by the apple cider vinaigrette in particular.

Preheat the oven to 425°F. Line a sheet pan with parchment paper.

Toss the cubed squash with the kosher salt and olive oil on the sheet pan, then spread it into an even layer. Roast until the squash is caramelized at the edges, 18 to 20 minutes. Let the squash cool on the sheet pan.

In a small skillet, toast the almonds over medium heat until they smell toasty and are beginning to brown, 5 to 7 minutes. Transfer to a plate to cool.

If using the large kale, stack 3 or 4 leaves on top of one another, roll into a tight coil, and cut crosswise to create thin ribbons. Place the kale ribbons in a large serving bowl. If using baby kale, simply place it in a serving bowl. Season with a pinch of sea salt and toss gently.

Add the toasted almonds, Gouda, dates, and cooled squash to the kale and toss gently. Add ⅓ cup of the vinaigrette and toss again. Taste and adjust with more dressing and/or sea salt. Season with pepper to taste.

Sautéed Radicchio Pizza with Fig Jam and Gorgonzola

Makes one 13-inch pizza

1 ball Thin-Crust Pizza Dough (page 26)

All-purpose flour, for dusting

Radicchio

1 tablespoon extra-virgin olive oil

1 head radicchio (6 to 7 ounces), cored and roughly chopped

Flaky sea salt

2 teaspoons white balsamic vinegar

Assembly

Semolina flour, rice flour, or all-purpose flour, for the peel

3 tablespoons crème fraîche, at room temperature

2 tablespoons fig jam

⅓ cup crumbled Gorgonzola cheese (about 1½ ounces)

Flaky sea salt

Good syrupy aged balsamic vinegar or Homemade Balsamic Syrup (page 120), for drizzling

Without an abundance of fresh fruits and vegetables on hand during the winter months, a well-stocked pantry pays dividends on pizza night. Here, fig jam stands in for fresh figs in the classic pairing with Gorgonzola, both of which complement the star here, sautéed radicchio, whose bitterness softens in the skillet, and whose purple leaves emerge from the oven glistening like scalloped seashells. I love finishing this one with a drizzle of syrupy balsamic vinegar, which you can make yourself quickly if you don't have any on hand, see Homemade Balsamic Syrup (page 120). And while the toppings here can be used on any pizza dough you like, I prefer this one with the Thin-Crust Pizza Dough, which remains crisp and sturdy even under the weight of a layer of crème fraîche and sautéed greens. Hot honey, in place of the syrupy balsamic vinegar, also works well here.

Prepare the dough: Transfer the dough from its storage container to a roomier, lightly floured, covered container (see Dough containers, page 16) and allow it to proof at room temperature for 1½ to 2 hours.

Sauté the radicchio: In a large skillet, heat the olive oil over high heat until it shimmers. Add the radicchio, season with a pinch of sea salt, and let sit undisturbed for 30 seconds. Then stir constantly using tongs to rearrange the radicchio until it wilts down, another 30 seconds. Stir in the vinegar and transfer the radicchio to a plate to cool.

Prepare the oven and pizza peel: About 1 hour before you want to bake the pizza, place a baking steel in the top third of the oven and preheat it to 550°F convection roast (or as high as it will go). Dust a pizza peel lightly with semolina flour or top with parchment paper.

Roll the dough: Lightly dust a work surface and the dough ball with flour. With lightly floured hands, pinch the outermost edge of the dough to flatten and depress the air from the edges. Flip the ball and repeat the pinching at the edges. Using a lightly dusted rolling pin, roll the dough into a 13-inch round, flipping the dough every few strokes and using flour as needed. Transfer the stretched dough to the prepared peel and give it a shake to ensure it's not sticking.

Assemble the pizza: Spread the crème fraîche evenly over the dough all the way to the edges. Drop small spoonfuls of the fig jam evenly over the top, then use the back of a spoon to lightly spread them out. Spread the radicchio over the top all the way to the edges. Finally, sprinkle the Gorgonzola evenly over the top. Season with a pinch of flaky sea salt.

Recipe continues

Bake the pizza: Shimmy the pizza (still on the parchment if using) onto the steel and bake until the cheese is melted and the edges are beginning to char, 4 to 5 minutes. (This may take 8 to 10 minutes, depending on your oven.)

Using the peel, transfer the pizza to a cutting board (discard the parchment paper). Drizzle with the syrupy balsamic to taste. Cut and serve.

Escarole Salad with Apples and Walnuts

Serves 4

½ cup walnuts

1 head escarole (1 to 1¼ pounds), roughly chopped

1 sweet apple, such as Honeycrisp, unpeeled and thinly sliced

¾ cup crumbled blue cheese (3 to 4 ounces)

½ cup chopped scallions

½ cup Apple Cider Vinaigrette (page 37), plus more to taste

Flaky sea salt and freshly ground black pepper

Escarole is my favorite green to wilt into soups or stir into beany broths, and I love it sautéed, too (see Garlicky, Spicy Sautéed Escarole with Olives, Pine Nuts, and Currants, page 186). But it's also lovely raw, its slight bitter flavor and crisp texture so nice for pairing with sweet fruits and citrusy vinaigrettes. You'll need one medium head of escarole for this salad, which might seem like not enough at the grocery store, but which will magically multiply once you find it on your cutting board. If you bought extra to be safe, lucky you: You can make this salad two nights in a row, and with the vinaigrette already made, it will come together in no time.

In a small skillet, toast the walnuts slowly over low heat. When the walnuts are lightly golden and smell toasty, transfer them to a cutting board and coarsely chop.

If the escarole is dirty, place it in a large bowl, cover with cold water, swoosh it around a bit to jostle the dirt, and let it sit for 5 to 10 minutes, or until the dirt settles. Scoop the escarole out of the bowl and dry it in a salad spinner or a large towel.

Transfer the escarole to a large serving bowl. Add the apple, blue cheese, scallions, and chopped nuts. Pour the dressing on and toss to combine. Taste. If the leaves are nicely coated but the salad tastes underseasoned, add a pinch of flaky sea salt. If it needs more dressing, add more to taste. Season with pepper to taste and serve.

Winter White Pizza with Garlic and Herbs

Makes one 12-inch pizza

1 ball Neapolitanish Pizza Dough (page 22)

All-purpose flour, for dusting

Garlic/herb oil

1 tablespoon extra-virgin olive oil

1 large garlic clove, thinly sliced (about 1 tablespoon)

1 teaspoon finely chopped fresh thyme

1 teaspoon finely chopped fresh rosemary

¼ teaspoon crushed red pepper flakes

Assembly

Semolina flour, rice flour, or all-purpose flour, for the peel

2 tablespoons crème fraîche, at room temperature

3 ounces fontina cheese, pulled into ½-inch pieces (about ¾ cup)

1 ounce Gruyère cheese, pulled into ½-inch pieces (about ¼ cup)

Flaky sea salt

One January evening, after a day of skiing with my aunt and uncle in Vermont, my aunt Marcy presented us with the most inviting appetizer: a piping-hot skillet filled with garlicky, herby bubbling fontina cheese. No sooner had Marcy set it down was the skillet wiped clean, every morsel of melty cheese mopped up by eager hands wielding baguette slices. The recipe came from Ina Garten's *How Easy Is That?* and it had become Marcy's new favorite party trick. It soon became mine. This white pizza captures all of the flavors of Ina's baked fontina ensemble, cheese and bread melding together, the flavors of rosemary, thyme, and garlic permeating every slice.

Prepare the dough: Transfer the dough from its storage container to a roomier, lightly floured, covered container (see Dough containers, page 16) and allow it to proof at room temperature for 1½ to 2 hours.

Make the garlic/herb oil: In a small skillet, combine the olive oil, garlic, thyme, rosemary, and pepper flakes and set over medium heat. The herbs and garlic will begin sizzling in the oil. As soon as the garlic begins taking on color at the edges, remove from the heat and transfer the oil to a small bowl.

Prepare the oven and pizza peel: About 1 hour before you want to bake the pizza, place a baking steel in the top third of the oven and preheat it to 550°F convection roast (or as high as it will go). Dust a pizza peel lightly with semolina flour or top with parchment paper.

Stretch the dough: Lightly dust a work surface with flour. Using lightly floured hands, pat the dough gently to flatten it, then stretch it into a 10- to 11-inch round by laying it on the back of your hands and gently rotating it, taking care not to depress the beautiful air pockets in the dough. If the dough begins resisting, set it down on the work surface to rest for 5 to 10 minutes, then continue stretching. Transfer the stretched dough to the prepared peel and give it a shake to ensure it's not sticking.

Assemble the pizza: Spread the crème fraîche evenly over the dough, leaving a ½-inch border. Drizzle the garlic/herb oil over the top, brushing it on to distribute it evenly. Spread both cheeses over the dough. Season with a pinch of sea salt. Stretch the dough one last time by pulling outward on the edges. Redistribute the toppings as needed, then give the peel one last shake to ensure the dough is not sticking.

Bake the pizza: Shimmy the pizza (still on the parchment if using) onto the steel and bake until the cheese is melted and the edges are beginning to char, 5 to 6 minutes. (This may take 8 to 10 minutes, depending on your oven.)

Using the peel, transfer the pizza to a cutting board (discard the parchment paper). Cut and serve.

Salt-Roasted Beet Salad with Walnuts, Goat Cheese, and Chives

Serves 4

1 cup kosher salt, plus more as
    needed

4 medium beets (1¼ to 1½ pounds
    total)

½ cup walnuts

6 tablespoons Citrus-Shallot
    Vinaigrette (page 39), plus more
    to taste

5 ounces mixed greens

Freshly ground black pepper

3 ounces goat cheese

¼ cup finely chopped fresh chives

I learned this method for cooking beets from the chef of the café where I waitressed for several years when I lived in California. One of his signature dishes was a "salt-roasted" beet salad, which he made by baking beets on a thin layer of salt in a foil-covered baking dish. I always thought his beets tasted particularly good, and what struck me when I tried the method at home was the absence of any liquid in the pan when I removed the foil. Having only ever steam-roasted beets, I was accustomed to finding lots of red liquid in the pan at the end of the cooking process. The salt-roasted experiment made me wonder if flavor (and nutrients) seep from the beets when steam-roasted and if the salt-roasting better preserves them. Though I'm not sure how I would do in a blind taste test, I find the salt-roasted method concentrates the beets' flavor without making them the least bit salty. This salad combines a classic grouping—beets, goat cheese, and walnuts—along with a citrus-shallot vinaigrette. While this is not a fast salad, pretty much everything can be prepared ahead of time, which will make for a swift last-minute assembly.

Preheat the oven to 425°F.

Pour the kosher salt into an 8- or 9-inch square baking pan. (See Note for an alternative cooking method.) Place the beets on the salt bed. Cover the pan tightly with foil and roast until the beets are knife-tender, about 1 hour. Remove the beets but leave the oven on, reducing the temperature to 375°F.

Uncover the beets and let stand until cool enough to handle, about 15 minutes. Discard the salt.

Meanwhile, place the walnuts on a sheet pan and toast in the oven until they begin to turn light brown and smell toasty, 8 to 10 minutes. Transfer the walnuts to a cutting board and chop coarsely.

Trim off the rough (stem) end of the beets and use your hands or paper towels to rub off the skins and discard. Cut the beets into 6 or 8 wedges, then cut each wedge in half crosswise.

Transfer the beets to a bowl. Toss with 2 tablespoons of the vinaigrette. Taste and adjust with salt if needed.

Arrange the greens in a large shallow serving bowl. Drizzle with the remaining 4 tablespoons vinaigrette. Season lightly with salt and pepper and toss gently. Taste and adjust with more salt, pepper, and/or vinaigrette. Scatter the dressed beets over the greens and sprinkle with the walnuts. Crumble the goat cheese over the top. Sprinkle with chives and season with pepper to taste. Resist the urge to toss—the beets will turn the salad into a big red mess. As you serve, the elements of the salad will all come together.

NOTE
If you'd rather not use the salt-roasted method, you can simply boil the beets until they are knife tender, 60 to 90 minutes.

Roasted Wild Mushroom Pizza with Garlic, Thyme, and Fontina

Makes one 12-inch pizza

1 ball Neapolitanish Pizza Dough (page 22)

All-purpose flour, for dusting

Toppings

1 pound wild mushrooms, roughly chopped or torn into 1-inch pieces

Kosher salt

3 tablespoons extra-virgin olive oil

1 garlic clove

1 teaspoon minced fresh thyme

¼ teaspoon crushed red pepper flakes

Assembly

Semolina flour, rice flour, or all-purpose flour, for the peel

3 tablespoons heavy cream

½ cup grated fontina cheese (about 2 ounces)

Flaky sea salt

Fresh thyme leaves, optional

On our honeymoon, Ben and I spent three nights in New York City, living from meal to meal: oysters at Balthazar, burgers at Gramercy Tavern, bagels and lox at Russ & Daughters, and most memorably, the mushrooms on toast at Craft. I still dream of those morels, my first ever taste of one, the honeycomb spears bathing in a creamy, garlicky sauce, spilling off a thick slice of olive oil–toasted bread. It was heaven, and for me far more thrilling than the steak (which was also delicious) that arrived next. Although there are no morels on this pizza—unless, of course, you can find them—the flavors of that toast are all here, and while any mushrooms will work, this pizza is especially delicious with an assortment of wild mushrooms. Many supermarkets carry mixes of oyster, trumpet, and enoki mushrooms, and winter farmers' markets abound with them.

Prepare the dough: Transfer the dough from its storage container to a roomier, lightly floured, covered container (see Dough containers, page 16) and allow it to proof at room temperature for 1½ to 2 hours.

Prepare the toppings: Preheat the oven to 550°F.

Arrange the mushrooms on a sheet pan. Season generously with kosher salt and toss with 2 tablespoons of the olive oil. Roast until the mushrooms are just beginning to brown at the edges, 10 to 12 minutes. Let the mushrooms cool. Taste and season the mushrooms with more kosher salt if necessary. You need about 1 cup of mushrooms for this pizza. Store the remainder in the fridge for up to 1 week or in the freezer for 3 months.

Place the remaining 1 tablespoon olive oil in a small skillet. Grate the garlic on a Microplane directly into the olive oil (or finely mince it by hand). Add the thyme and pepper flakes. Set the skillet over medium heat. As soon as the garlic,

pepper flakes, and thyme begin to sizzle, remove the pan from the heat.

Prepare the oven and pizza peel: About 1 hour before you want to bake the pizza, place a baking steel in the top third of the oven and preheat it to 550°F convection roast (or as high as it will go). Dust a pizza peel lightly with semolina flour or top with parchment paper.

Stretch the dough: Lightly dust a work surface with flour. Using lightly floured hands, pat the dough gently to flatten it, then stretch it into a 10- to 11-inch round by laying it on the back of your hands and gently rotating it, taking care not to depress the beautiful air pockets in the dough. If the dough begins resisting, set it down on the work surface to rest for 5 to 10 minutes, then continue stretching. Transfer the stretched dough to the prepared peel and give it a shake to ensure it's not sticking.

Assemble the pizza: Brush the dough with the garlic/thyme oil. Spoon the cream over the top. Top with about 1 cup

Recipe continues

of the sautéed mushrooms. Scatter the fontina evenly over the top. Season with flaky sea salt. Stretch the dough one last time by pulling outward on the edges. Redistribute the toppings as needed, then give the peel one last shake to ensure the dough is not sticking.

Bake the pizza: Shimmy the pizza (still on the parchment if using) onto the steel and bake until the cheese is melted and the edges are beginning to char, 5 to 6 minutes. (This may take 8 to 10 minutes, depending on your oven.)

Using the peel, transfer the pizza to a cutting board (discard the parchment paper). Sprinkle with fresh thyme leaves to taste, if using. Cut and serve.

Orange and Avocado Salad with Citrus-Shallot Vinaigrette

Serves 4

½ red onion, thinly sliced (about 1 cup)

1 tablespoon white balsamic vinegar

Flaky sea salt

6 oranges, a mix of navel, Cara Cara, and/or others

1 avocado, diced

¼ cup Citrus-Shallot Vinaigrette (page 39)

Handful of arugula (about 1 ounce)

Extra-virgin olive oil

Freshly ground black pepper

When I lived in California and had access to good citrus and avocados year-round, I made this salad often. These days, I save it for the winter, when I can count on a few solid months of excellent citrus and good avocados here and there. When I find them, I make this salad, using a mix of orange varieties, namely Cara Cara for their pinky-red hue and sweet flavor. One bite of this salad in the dead of February never fails to wash away the winter blues, transporting me to sunnier lands, with ocean breezes passing through my apartment's open front doors.

Place the onion in a small bowl and toss with the vinegar and a pinch of sea salt. Let stand for 15 minutes.

Slice off the ends of each orange. Stand each orange up on one of its cut sides. Run a knife down the side of each orange to remove the peel, pith, and membrane to expose the fruit. Turn each orange onto its side and cut it crosswise into ¼-inch-thick rounds.

Arrange the orange slices on a serving platter. Season all over with sea salt. Scatter the onion slices and vinegar over the oranges as well as the avocado and season with another pinch of sea salt. Pour the dressing over the top. Scatter the arugula over everything. Drizzle lightly with olive oil and season to taste with freshly ground pepper.

Detroit-Style Pizza for a Crowd with Pepperoni, Pickled Jalapeños, and Hot Honey

Makes one 10 × 14-inch pizza

2 tablespoons unsalted butter, at room temperature

Extra-virgin olive oil

One 525-gram ball Pan Pizza Dough (page 30)

1 cup preshredded cheddar cheese (4 ounces; see Note)

½ cup preshredded low-moisture whole-milk mozzarella cheese (2 ounces)

1½ cups cubed cheese (6 ounces), such as Wisconsin brick, low-moisture whole-milk mozzarella, or a mix of Monterey Jack, cheddar, and mozzarella

Heaping ½ cup Homemade Vodka Sauce (page 34)

2 to 3 ounces pepperoni (depending on thickness of slices)

½ cup Pickled Jalapeños (page 88)

Hot honey, for serving (optional)

NOTE
Preshredded cheese is best for forming a frico crust because the starches in it prevent it from clumping and melting too quickly.

One Friday evening at the height of the 2020 lockdown, longing to eat something from beyond my five-mile radius, I splurged on a trio of pizzas from Brooklyn's Emmy Squared via Goldbelly (a gourmet food delivery service). The rectangular pies, topped with all sorts of pickled chiles and various cheeses and each accompanied by tiny tubs of side sauces and dressings, transported us to what felt like a faraway land. It was a blast, and the experience introduced me to the virtues of large pan pizzas, namely their ability to feed a crowd and to be so crowd-pleasing: They're thick and cheesy with an irresistible frico crust (see Detroit-Style Pizza, page 161). The toppings here—pickled jalapeños plus pepperoni—are inspired entirely by Emmy Squared's pizza called The Colony. I love to make it with a vodka sauce, the creaminess of which pairs so well with the spicy, salty toppings.

Prepare the dough: Grease a 10 × 14-inch Detroit-style pizza pan or a 9 × 13-inch baking pan with the softened butter. Pour 1 teaspoon olive oil into the center of the pan. Place the dough ball in the oil and turn to coat. Let rest uncovered until the dough has doubled in volume, 3 to 4 hours.

Stretch the dough: Lightly oil your hands and use your fingertips to dimple and stretch the dough to fit the pan. When the dough resists, let it rest for 30 minutes, then stretch it again using the same technique. Repeat this stretching and resting until the dough fits the pan.

Prepare the oven: If you have a baking steel, place it on a rack in the middle or lower third of the oven and preheat the oven to 500°F.

Parbake the dough: Dimple the dough one last time with lightly oiled hands, taking care not to dimple the perimeter. Transfer the pan to the oven and bake until the dough has puffed, released ever so slightly from the edges, and is just beginning to brown in spots, about 8 minutes. Remove the pan from the oven and, using an offset spatula, carefully transfer the parbaked crust to a wire rack.

Let the parbaked dough cool upside down on the rack for 20 minutes. Do not wash the pan. (At this point, once the dough is cooled, you can transfer it to an airtight storage bag for 1 to 2 days at room temperature or up to 3 months in the freezer.)

Leave the oven on and reduce the temperature to 475°F.

Top the pizza: In a medium bowl, combine the shredded cheddar and mozzarella. Return the parbaked crust to the pan, bottom-side down. To make the "frico crust," spread the shredded cheese mixture around

Recipe continues

Detroit-style pizza (DSP) refers to
pan pizza originating from Detroit,
specifically from a restaurant called
Buddy's Pizza. As the story goes, the
original owner of Buddy's started
baking his mother-in-law's Sicilian
pizza dough in rectangular blue steel
pans, which were scrap pans from the
nearby auto plants. The crust of
DSP is light and airy, not unlike
focaccia, and on traditional DSP,
the toppings go on in reverse order:
pepperoni, cheese, sauce. One of the
defining characteristics of a DSP is
its cheese frico crust, created by
the generous amount of cheese spread
edge to edge, which, during the
baking, melts and seeps between the
pan's edge and the dough, frying the
crust in the process. It's delicious,
and it can be visually striking, too:
tall and lacy, crisp and caramelized.

the perimeter of the parbaked crust pressing it against the sides of the pan. Sprinkle the cubed cheese over the surface of the crust inside the shredded cheese perimeter. Spread the sauce evenly over the cheese in the pan. Spread the pepperoni and pickled jalapeños evenly over the sauce.

Bake the pizza: Transfer the pan to the oven (and place on the baking steel, if using) and bake until the edges are caramelized to your liking, about 10 minutes.

Remove the pan from the oven and let the pizza rest for 1 to 2 minutes in the pan. Run a thin metal spatula around the pan's edges to release the cheese frico crust from the sides of the pan. Carefully remove the entire pizza from the pan, transferring it to a cutting board. Drizzle with hot honey, if using, to taste. Cut into 8 to 12 squares and serve.

Winter Chopped Salad with Radicchio and Endive

Serves 4

1 head radicchio (about 10 ounces),
  cored and cut into 1-inch pieces

2 heads Belgian endive, halved and
  sliced into 1-inch pieces

1½ cups cooked or canned
  chickpeas (from a 16-ounce can),
  drained and rinsed

2 ounces salami, cut into ¼-inch-
  thick slices

1 small red onion, finely sliced

¼ cup oil-packed sun-dried
  tomatoes, drained

½ cup cubed provolone cheese

4 pepperoncini, thinly sliced

½ cup Italian Dressing (page 39),
  plus more to taste

Freshly ground black pepper and
  flaky sea salt

In this winter version of the Classic Chopped Salad (page 111), chicories replace the more commonly found romaine and iceberg lettuces, and sun-dried tomatoes replace fresh. But all of the other critical players are here: pickled peppers, cured meat, sharp cheese, sweet onions, and more. A deconstructed Italian deli sandwich in salad form: What's not to love?

In a large bowl, combine the radicchio, endive, chickpeas, salami, onion, sun-dried tomatoes, provolone, and pepperoncini. Add the dressing and season with pepper to taste. Toss to combine. Add more dressing to taste. Taste and season with a pinch of sea salt if needed and more pepper to taste.

Kale and Sun-Dried Tomato Pesto Pizza with Mozzarella

Makes one 12-inch pizza

1 ball Neapolitanish Pizza Dough
(page 22)

All-purpose flour, for dusting

Kale

2 teaspoons extra-virgin olive oil

4 ounces lacinato (Tuscan) kale,
stems and midribs removed,
coarsely chopped (about 2 cups)

Kosher salt

Assembly

Semolina flour, rice flour, or
all-purpose flour, for the peel

3 tablespoons Sun-Dried Tomato
Pesto (page 37)

2 ounces low-moisture whole-milk
mozzarella cheese, pulled into
½-inch pieces (about ½ cup)

⅓ cup crumbled feta cheese
(about 1½ ounces)

Extra-virgin olive oil

Flaky sea salt

During the winter, I often have a vat of homemade sun-dried tomato pesto in the fridge. It's a super-flavorful spread made with mostly pantry items and spinach (as opposed to basil) that's wonderful on its own smeared across crostini but also a secret-weapon flavor bomb, there to brighten up your morning omelet or afternoon grilled cheese or evening pasta one spoonful at a time. As it turns out, it makes a fantastic base sauce for pizza. Here I've topped it with sautéed kale and a mix of mozzarella and feta, but countless combinations of greens and cheese can be used in their place, such as broccoli rabe and provolone or spinach and Gruyère.

Prepare the dough: Transfer the dough from its storage container to a roomier, lightly floured, covered container (see Dough containers, page 16) and allow it to proof at room temperature for 1½ to 2 hours.

Prepare the kale: In a large skillet, heat the olive oil over high heat until it shimmers. Add the kale and a pinch of kosher salt. Sauté for 1 to 2 minutes, using tongs to rearrange the greens frequently, until they wilt down. Transfer the greens to a plate to cool. Taste and adjust with more salt if needed.

Prepare the oven and pizza peel: About 1 hour before you want to bake the pizza, place a baking steel in the top third of the oven and preheat it to 550°F convection roast (or as high as it will go). Dust a pizza peel lightly with semolina flour or top with parchment paper.

Stretch the dough: Lightly dust a work surface with flour. Using lightly floured hands, pat the dough gently to flatten it, then stretch it into a 10- to 11-inch round by laying it on the back of your hands and gently rotating

it, taking care not to depress the beautiful air pockets in the dough. If the dough begins resisting, set it down on the work surface to rest for 5 to 10 minutes, then continue stretching. Transfer the stretched dough to the prepared peel and give it a shake to ensure it's not sticking.

Assemble the pizza: Spread the sun-dried tomato pesto evenly over the dough, leaving a ½-inch border. Top with the sautéed kale. Scatter both cheeses evenly over the top. Drizzle lightly with olive oil. Season with flaky sea salt. Stretch the dough one last time by pulling outward on the edges. Redistribute the toppings as needed, then give the peel one last shake to ensure the dough is not sticking.

Bake the pizza: Shimmy the pizza (still on the parchment if using) onto the steel and bake until the cheese is melted and the edges are beginning to char, 5 to 6 minutes. (This may take 8 to 10 minutes, depending on your oven.)

Using the peel, transfer the pizza to a cutting board (discard the parchment paper). Cut and serve.

Citrus Salad
with Blood Oranges, Shallots, and Olives

Serves 4

1 small shallot, thinly sliced crosswise into rings

2 tablespoons white balsamic vinegar

Flaky sea salt

5 blood oranges or other varieties

¼ cup wrinkly oil-cured black olives, pitted

3 tablespoons extra-virgin olive oil

A block of Pecorino Romano cheese, for shaving

Freshly ground black pepper

Handful of fresh basil leaves, torn if large (optional)

With orange and olive groves thriving together throughout the Mediterranean, it's no wonder the two ingredients have long been paired together in dishes from this region. This is a dead-easy salad and incredibly tasty, one of those assemblies that tastes like far more than the sum of its parts. I love adding shaved pecorino here and a generous amount of it, too, along with lots of freshly ground pepper. And while blood oranges are especially striking in this salad, any orange variety will do, as will any type of olive.

In a small bowl, toss together the shallot rings, vinegar, and a pinch of sea salt. Let stand for 15 minutes.

Slice off the ends of each orange. Stand each orange up on one of its cut sides. Run a knife down the side of each orange to remove the peel, pith, and membrane to expose the fruit. Turn each orange onto its side and cut it crosswise into ¼-inch-thick rounds.

Arrange the orange slices on a serving platter. Season all over with sea salt. Scatter the shallots and vinegar over the oranges along with the olives. Drizzle the olive oil over the top. Use a peeler to shave pecorino over the salad. Season with pepper to taste. Scatter the basil, if using, over the top.

Spinach-Artichoke Dip Pizza

Makes one 12-inch pizza

1 ball Neapolitanish Pizza Dough (page 22)

All-purpose flour, for dusting

Semolina flour, rice flour, or all-purpose flour, for the peel

1 cup Spinach/Artichoke Pizza Topping (recipe follows)

3 ounces low-moisture whole-milk mozzarella cheese, pulled into ½-inch pieces (about ¾ cup)

Extra-virgin olive oil

Flaky sea salt

Upon having leftover spinach-artichoke dip from one New Year's Eve celebration, I spread the mixture over pizza dough, topped it with some grated mozzarella, and popped it in the oven. The pizza was surprisingly well received, prompting several requests for a repeat performance the following evening. Without any more dip on hand, however, I had to start from scratch, which gave me the opportunity to tinker: Rather than make a full-fledged dip laden with cream cheese and heavy cream, I sautéed chopped artichoke hearts with a sliced shallot, added a heap of spinach, a splash of vinegar, and a handful of parmesan cheese. It took no time to throw together and yielded the perfect amount of toppings for two pizzas, both of which disappeared quickly. If you have spinach-artichoke dip on hand, simply spread a heaping 1 cup of it over the dough and top with mozzarella. If you don't, use the recipe that follows.

Prepare the dough: Transfer the dough from its storage container to a roomier, lightly floured, covered container (see Dough containers, page 16) and allow it to proof at room temperature for 1½ to 2 hours.

Prepare the oven and pizza peel: About 1 hour before you want to bake the pizza, place a baking steel in the top third of the oven and preheat it to 550°F convection roast (or as high as it will go). Dust a pizza peel lightly with semolina flour or top with parchment paper.

Stretch the dough: Lightly dust a work surface with flour. Using lightly floured hands, pat the dough gently to flatten it, then stretch it into a 10- to 11-inch round by laying it on the back of your hands and gently rotating it, taking care not to depress the beautiful air pockets in the dough. If the dough begins resisting, set it down on the work surface to rest for 5 to 10 minutes, then continue stretching.

Transfer the stretched dough to the prepared peel and give it a shake to ensure it's not sticking.

Top the pizza: Spread the spinach/artichoke mixture over the dough, leaving a ½-inch border. Scatter the mozzarella evenly over the top. Drizzle lightly with olive oil. Season with flaky sea salt. Stretch the dough one last time by pulling outward on the edges. Redistribute the toppings as needed, then give the peel one last shake to ensure the dough is not sticking.

Bake the pizza: Shimmy the pizza (still on the parchment if using) onto the steel and bake until the cheese is melted and the edges are beginning to char, 5 to 6 minutes. (This may take 8 to 10 minutes, depending on your oven.)

Using the peel, transfer the pizza to a cutting board (discard the parchment paper). Cut and serve.

Spinach/Artichoke Pizza Topping

Makes about 2 cups (enough for two 12-inch pizzas)

1 tablespoon olive oil

½ cup finely sliced shallots

Kosher salt

5 ounces canned artichoke hearts, drained (about 1 cup)

Pinch of crushed red pepper flakes

5 ounces baby spinach (about 5 cups)

1 teaspoon white balsamic, white wine, or apple cider vinegar

¼ cup grated Parmigiano-Reggiano cheese (¾ ounce)

In a large skillet, heat the oil and shallots over high heat. Season with a pinch of salt. As soon as the oil and shallots begin to sizzle, give them a stir, reduce the heat to low, cover, and cook for 5 minutes.

Meanwhile, finely chop the artichoke hearts.

Uncover the skillet, increase the heat to medium, add the pepper flakes and artichoke hearts, and cook for 30 seconds.

Add all of the spinach and season with a pinch of salt. Let the spinach stand undisturbed for about 60 seconds, then add the vinegar and remove from the heat. Use tongs to stir and rearrange the spinach, just until it has all wilted down. Stir in the Parmigiano and transfer the mixture immediately to a plate to cool. Taste and adjust with salt if needed. Store in the fridge for 1 week or the freezer for up to 3 months.

Grapefruit, Endive, and Apple Salad

Serves 4

2 grapefruits

⅓ cup white balsamic vinegar, plus more to taste

2 teaspoons honey or maple syrup, plus more to taste

½ teaspoon kosher salt, plus more to taste

¾ cup extra-virgin olive oil

2 heads Belgian endive

1 apple, such as Honeycrisp, unpeeled

Flaky sea salt

2 ounces arugula

A small block of Manchego cheese, for shaving

Freshly ground black pepper

Every year for my grapefruit-loving husband's birthday, which falls at the end of December, I order a dozen Ruby Red grapefruits from the Orange Shop. I always feel a bit like Homer Simpson giving Marge a bowling ball when the box arrives, as I perhaps derive as much pleasure from having those hefty, floral, fragrant juice bombs in the fridge. Throughout January, I make this salad—a mix of sweet apples, bitter endive, and tart grapefruit—and in the wake of the weeks-long season of indulgences, never does it taste so refreshing.

Slice off the ends of each grapefruit. Squeeze the juice out of those ends into a small bowl, then discard the ends. Stand up each grapefruit on one of its cut sides. Run a knife down the side of each grapefruit to remove the peel, pith, and membranes to expose the fruits. Squeeze any juice out of those peels into the bowl, then discard.

Turn each grapefruit onto its side and remove the segments by running a knife down the side of each membrane and slicing the segment out. Once all of the segments are removed, squeeze what's left of the grapefruit into the bowl to extract the juice. Measure out ⅓ cup juice and place it in a bowl. If you have less than ⅓ cup juice, make up the difference with any vinegar you have on hand (ideally white balsamic, white wine, or apple cider vinegar).

Add the balsamic vinegar, honey, and kosher salt to the bowl and whisk to combine. Stream in the olive oil while whisking constantly. Taste and adjust with more kosher salt, vinegar, and/or honey.

Separate the endive heads into leaves. Slice the apple thinly. In a serving bowl, toss together the endives, apple, and grapefruit segments. Season with a pinch of sea salt and toss with ¼ cup of the grapefruit dressing. Add the arugula and toss lightly.

Using a peeler, shave Manchego to taste over the top. Season with black pepper. Store the remaining dressing, covered, in the fridge for up to 2 weeks.

Buffalo Cauliflower Pizza with Scallion Crème Fraîche

Makes one 12-inch pizza

1 ball Neapolitanish Pizza Dough (page 22)

All-purpose flour, for dusting

Toppings

1 tablespoon extra-virgin olive oil

3 tablespoons thinly sliced scallions

2 tablespoons crème fraîche, at room temperature

1 stalk celery, sliced thinly on the bias

Pinch of flaky sea salt

1 teaspoon white balsamic vinegar

Assembly

Semolina flour, rice flour, or all-purpose flour, for the peel

1 cup (about 4 ounces) Buffalo Cauliflower (recipe follows)

3 ounces low-moisture whole-milk mozzarella cheese, pulled into ½-inch pieces (about ¾ cup)

Extra-virgin olive oil

Flaky sea salt

Blue Cheese Dressing (page 40) or Herby Ranch Dressing (page 41), for serving

Though I grew up in a family that loved sports of all kinds, football was not one of them, and "game day" was not something we celebrated. I never watched a football game in its entirety before meeting my husband, Ben, and when we attended our first game-day potluck together, I made roasted red peppers sprinkled with feta and lots of freshly ground pepper. When I set my platter on the buffet next to the Crock-Pot of queso and platter of 7-layer taco dip, I wanted to hide, like the lone person who shows up in costume to the "costume" party. As the years passed, I became better versed in what passes as acceptable game-day fare, namely bread bowls filled with creamy spreads and anything that includes the word *Buffalo*: wings, dips, nachos. One of my favorites is Buffalo cauliflower, which requires three ingredients—cauliflower, melted butter, and Frank's RedHot sauce—and roughly 30 minutes in the oven. With a vat of tangy dressing by its side, I find those spicy, caramelized florets irresistible. It turns out that Buffalo cauliflower also makes a great pizza topping. Here, it's paired with a scallion crème fraîche, and out of the oven it's finished with quick-pickled celery. A side of blue cheese dressing or homemade ranch is nonnegotiable.

Prepare the dough: Transfer the dough from its storage container to a roomier, lightly floured, covered container (see Dough containers, page 16) and allow it to proof at room temperature for 1½ to 2 hours.

Prepare the toppings: In a small skillet, heat the oil and 2 tablespoons of the scallions over high heat. As soon as the scallions are evenly sizzling, remove the skillet from the heat and allow the oil to cool, 5 to 10 minutes. Stir in the crème fraîche.

In a small bowl, sprinkle the celery with the salt and vinegar. Toss and let stand for 5 minutes. Add the remaining 1 tablespoon scallions and toss to combine.

Prepare the oven and pizza peel: About 1 hour before you want to bake the pizza, place a baking steel in the top third of the oven and preheat it to 550°F convection roast (or as high as it will go). Dust a pizza peel lightly with semolina flour or top with parchment paper.

Stretch the dough: Lightly dust a work surface with flour. Using lightly floured hands, pat the dough gently to flatten it, then stretch it into a 10- to 11-inch round by laying it on the back of your hands and gently rotating it, taking care not to depress the beautiful air pockets in the dough. If the dough begins resisting, set it down on the work surface to rest for 5 to 10 minutes, then continue stretching. Transfer the stretched dough to the prepared peel and give it a shake to ensure it's not sticking.

Recipe continues

Assemble the pizza: Spread the scallion/crème fraîche mixture over the dough, leaving a ½-inch border. Top with the Buffalo cauliflower. Scatter the mozzarella evenly over the top. Drizzle lightly with olive oil. Season with a pinch of salt. Stretch the dough one last time by pulling outward on the edges. Redistribute the toppings as needed, then give the peel one last shake to ensure the dough is not sticking.

Bake the pizza: Shimmy the pizza (still on the parchment if using) onto the steel and bake until the cheese is melted and the edges are beginning to char, 5 to 6 minutes. (This may take 8 to 10 minutes, depending on your oven.)

Using the peel, transfer the pizza to a cutting board (discard the parchment paper). Scatter the celery pickle over the top. Cut and serve. Serve with the blue cheese dressing on the side.

Buffalo Cauliflower

Makes about 3 cups (enough for three 12-inch pizzas)

¼ cup hot sauce, such as Frank's RedHot

2 tablespoons unsalted butter, melted

1 head cauliflower, cut into 1- to 2-inch pieces (about 1 pound florets)

Preheat the oven to 425°F. Line a sheet pan with parchment paper.

In a large bowl, whisk together the hot sauce and melted butter. Add the cauliflower florets and toss to combine. (Do not season with salt, as brands such as Frank's RedHot already contain salt.)

Spread the cauliflower in a single layer on the prepared sheet pan. Transfer to the oven and roast until the cauliflower is knife-tender and browned around the edges, about 30 minutes. Store in the fridge for up to 1 week or in the freezer for up to 3 months.

Winter Wedge Salad
with Roasted Savoy Cabbage, Blue Cheese, and Walnuts

Serves 4

1 head savoy cabbage (2½ to 3 pounds), cut through the core into roughly 8 wedges

¼ cup extra-virgin olive oil

Kosher salt

¾ cup walnuts

2 tablespoons dried currants

1 tablespoon white balsamic vinegar

1 tablespoon hot water

½ cup Blue Cheese Dressing (page 40), plus more to taste

½ cup crumbled blue cheese

¼ cup finely chopped fresh chives

Freshly ground black pepper

As a farm share subscriber, discovering that cabbage takes well to roasting was the gift of the century—with crispy, caramelized edges needing little more than a splash of vinegar and a pinch of sea salt, never again did I wonder what to do with the many green and purple heads arriving in my weekly vegetable box. Here, roasted savoy cabbage wedges meet creamy blue cheese dressing and a sprinkling of toasted walnuts, currants, and more blue cheese for good measure, all of which bring the humble head to a whole new level. As with all of the wedge salad recipes in this book, be sure to pass more dressing on the side.

Preheat the oven to 450°F convection roast (if possible). Line a sheet pan with parchment paper.

Place the cabbage wedges on the sheet pan, toss with the olive oil and a generous pinch of salt, and spread into an even layer. Roast until the cabbage is beginning to char at the edges, about 20 minutes. Transfer to a serving platter.

In a large skillet, toast the walnuts over medium heat until they turn light brown and begin to smell fragrant.

Transfer to a plate to cool, then roughly chop.

In a small bowl, combine the currants, vinegar, and hot water. Let stand for 5 minutes, then drain.

Spoon the blue cheese dressing over the cabbage wedges, being sure to dress each wedge generously—use more dressing as needed. Top with the chopped walnuts, currants, and blue cheese. Scatter the chives over the top and season with pepper to taste. Serve, passing more dressing on the side.

Sicilian-Style Pizza for a Crowd with "The Works"

Makes 1 sheet pan pizza

2 tablespoons unsalted butter, at room temperature

1 tablespoon extra-virgin olive oil, plus more as needed

One 1,050-gram ball Pan Pizza Dough (page 30)

Toppings

3 tablespoons extra-virgin olive oil

8 ounces mushrooms, sliced

Kosher salt

1 bell pepper (any color), diced

1 cup thinly sliced red onion

Heaping 1 cup Simple Tomato Sauce (page 34) or your favorite jarred sauce

3 cups grated cheese (12 ounces), such as low-moisture whole-milk mozzarella or a mix of Monterey Jack, cheddar, and mozzarella

6 ounces pepperoni

6 ounces hot Italian sausage, in bulk or links with casings removed

Whenever I hear someone lamenting the exhausting process of making pizza at home—from the assembly process to the cleaning—I suggest they give making Sicilian-style pizza a go. Sicilian pizza crust, like Detroit-style pizza, can be parbaked days in advance and topped as desired on pizza night. Moreover, because Sicilian-style pizza is baked on a sheet pan, which yields roughly 20 pieces, you'll potentially have to make only one pizza. Loaded with veggies, sausage, pepperoni, and cheese, this one is a favorite to make during the winter, especially for the many occasions—New Year's Eve, Super Bowl, March Madness—demanding heartwarming, crowd-pleasing creations.

Prepare the dough: Grease a 12 × 16-inch grandma-style pan or a 13 × 18-inch sheet pan with the softened butter. Pour the olive oil into the center of the pan. Place the dough ball in the oil and turn to coat. Let rest uncovered until the dough has doubled in volume, 3 to 4 hours.

Stretch the dough: Lightly oil your hands and use your fingertips to dimple and stretch the dough to fit the pan. When the dough resists, let it rest for 30 minutes, then stretch it again using the same technique. Repeat this stretching and resting until the dough fits the pan.

Prepare the oven: If you have a baking steel, place it on a rack in the middle or lower third of the oven and preheat the oven to 500°F.

Parbake the dough: Using oiled hands, dimple the dough one last time, taking care not to dimple the

perimeter, which will help the dough bake more evenly.

Transfer the pan to the oven (and place on the baking steel if using) and bake until evenly golden, 10 to 12 minutes. Remove the pan from the oven but leave the oven on and reduce the temperature to 475°F.

Prepare the toppings: In a large skillet, heat 2 tablespoons of the olive oil over high heat until it shimmers. Add the mushrooms and let cook undisturbed for about a minute. Season with salt, then stir and cook until the mushrooms are beginning to brown, 3 to 5 minutes. Transfer to a bowl.

Add the remaining 1 tablespoon olive oil to the skillet, then add the bell pepper and onions and cook until slightly softened, 1 to 3 minutes. Season with salt, then transfer to the bowl with the mushrooms. Toss to combine. Taste and adjust with salt if needed.

Recipe continues

SICILIAN PIZZA

For many people, Sicilian pizza is synonymous with grandma pizza, but some distinguish the two as follows: Sicilian pizza is parbaked before the toppings are added, whereas grandma pizza is baked once with toppings and all. For others, it's the opposite. And for others still, it's the height of the slice and the length of the fermentation that matter. In this book, the Sicilian-style pizza is parbaked and the crust closely resembles that of focaccia. While the definition of Sicilian pizza is debatable, its indisputable origin is something called sfincione, a focaccia-like dough topped with onions, bread crumbs, and caciocavallo cheese.

Assemble the pizza: Spread the sauce evenly over the parbaked dough all the way to the edges. Top with the grated cheese. Spread the sautéed veggies evenly over the dough. Spread the pepperoni evenly on top. Finally, pinch the sausage into small pieces and scatter them evenly over the dough.

Bake the pizza: Return the pan to the oven and bake until the cheese is melted and just beginning to brown in spots, 10 to 12 minutes. Remove the pan from the oven and let the pizza rest for 5 minutes in the pan.

Run a knife or spatula around the pan's edges. Carefully remove the entire pizza from the pan, transferring it to a cutting board. Cut the pizza into roughly 20 squares.

Charred Endive Salad with Caesar Dressing

Serves 4

8 heads Belgian endive (about 2 pounds total), ends trimmed, halved lengthwise

2 tablespoons extra-virgin olive oil

Kosher salt

¼ cup Caesar Dressing (page 39), plus more for serving

A block of Pecorino Romano cheese, for shaving

Freshly ground black pepper

I learned this hot-salad technique from Joshua McFadden's *Six Seasons*, which includes a recipe for roasted radicchio and arugula with provolone. In the recipe, the greens broil with the cheese for just one minute, during which time the greens wilt ever so slightly, losing their chill. Here I broil the endive halves without cheese, which allows their surfaces to brown, then, out of the oven, I shave Pecorino Romano over them. This is a very simple preparation, but broiling the endive not only brings an element of warmth but also a layer of caramelization that plays so well with the salty Romano and lemony Caesar dressing.

Place an oven rack 6 inches from the broiler and preheat it for 15 minutes. Line a sheet pan with foil.

In a large bowl, toss the endive halves with the olive oil and season with a big pinch of salt. Arrange the endive on the prepared sheet pan cut-side down. Broil until the edges are just beginning to char, about 5 minutes. Flip the endive over and broil until the endive are nicely charred, another 5 minutes. Transfer the endive to a platter.

Spoon the Caesar dressing over the endive. Using a peeler, shave lots of pecorino over the top. Season generously with pepper or to taste. Serve, passing more Caesar dressing on the side.

Grandma-Style Pizza with Potato and Rosemary

Makes 1 sheet pan pizza

2 tablespoons unsalted butter, at room temperature

1 tablespoon extra-virgin olive oil, plus more as needed

One 525-gram ball Pan Pizza Dough (page 30)

Toppings

Kosher salt

4 cups hot tap water

1 pound Yukon Gold potatoes

4 tablespoons extra-virgin olive oil

1 tablespoon fresh rosemary

Flaky sea salt

8 ounces low-moisture whole-milk mozzarella cheese, pulled into ½-inch pieces (about 2 cups)

During the three days my husband and I spent in Rome one August, we, like many, fell in love with the *pizza al taglio*—"pizza by the cut"—offered at Forno Campo di Fiori, a grab-and-go bakery in the heart of the city. During our visit, we tried nearly all of the various offerings from the simple but perfect olive oil and salt (pizza bianca) to the fresh tomato (pizza con pomodoro) to the shredded zucchini (pizza di zucca) to the potato and rosemary (pizza con patate), my favorite. Cut, folded in half, and wrapped in paper, one of these breakfast "slices" was all the fuel we needed to start the day, a style of pizza I had read about in many books but did not fully understand until I held it in my hand. When I think of those folded rectangles, my heart aches, so filled with a longing to return. When this happens, I make this grandma-style pizza con patate, not an exact likeness, but similar enough to soothe my soul and quell my wanderlust. While some versions of pizza con patate contain no cheese, Forno Campo di Fiori's does, a light sprinkling of mozzarella, which I've included in the recipe here. You'll add the cheese during the final minutes of baking, which allows the potatoes to cook and crisp and gives the cheese just enough time to gently melt but not blister and bubble.

Prepare the dough: Grease a 12 × 16-inch grandma-style pan or a 13 × 18-inch sheet pan with the softened butter. Pour the olive oil into the center of the pan. Place the dough ball in the oil and turn to coat. Let rest uncovered until the dough has doubled in volume, 3 to 4 hours.

Stretch the dough: Lightly oil your hands and use your fingertips to dimple and stretch the dough to fit the pan. When the dough resists, let it rest for 30 minutes, then stretch it again using the same technique. Repeat this stretching and resting until the dough fits the pan.

Prepare the toppings: In a large bowl, dissolve 2 tablespoons kosher salt in the hot tap water. Use a mandoline to cut the potatoes into thin slices (roughly the thickness of a quarter). Transfer to the bowl of salty water as you slice. Let stand for 30 minutes (or as long as 2 hours).

Prepare the oven: If you have a baking steel, place it on a rack in the middle or lower third of the oven and preheat the oven to 450°F.

Top the pizza: Using lightly oiled hands, stretch the dough one final time to fit the pan. Brush 2 tablespoons of the olive oil over the dough. Drain the potatoes and transfer them to a large towel to pat dry as best as possible. Dry the used bowl, return the potatoes to the bowl, and toss with the remaining 2 tablespoons olive oil and ½ teaspoon kosher salt.

Recipe continues

Spread the potatoes over the surface of the dough—I do this by grabbing big handfuls of the potatoes and spreading them as evenly as possible. There is no need to arrange them in an organized, equally distributed scalloped pattern unless you have the time and/or desire. Scatter the rosemary over the top. Sprinkle generously with sea salt.

Bake the pizza: Transfer the pan to the oven and bake for 18 to 20 minutes or until you see the potatoes beginning to brown at the edges—be patient here: wait until you see the potatoes browning before proceeding. Scatter the mozzarella over the top and return to the oven until the edges look very caramelized, another 7 to 10 minutes.

Remove the pan from the oven and transfer the pizza to a cutting board. Cut into 12 to 16 pieces.

Vegan Kale Caesar Salad with Pickled Onions

Serves 4

½ red onion, thinly sliced (about 1 cup)

2 tablespoons white balsamic vinegar

Flaky sea salt

½ cup pumpkin seeds

1 pound lacinato (Tuscan) kale, stemmed

½ cup Creamy Cashew Dressing (page 40), plus more to taste

Freshly ground black pepper

One December morning at the Honest Weight Food Coop in Albany, I bumped into my friend Vicki at my favorite spot: the prepared-food aisle, stacked floor to ceiling with grain salads and vegetable slaws, tofu curries and beany salsas, each clamshell as enticing as the next. Before I began my usual browsing, Vicki handed me a tub of the vegan kale Caesar, telling me to look no further. When I got home, I discovered why: In addition to being delicious, the kale itself was extremely soft and tender. And there was something else, too—something grainy and cheese-like coating every leaf. A call to Honest Weight provided answers, namely that the grainy, cheesy element was pureed pumpkin seeds, that they use curly kale and massage it, and finally that they soak the red onions in vinegar, the longer the better. Here, I use lacinato (Tuscan) kale—I prefer it to curly—and my own creamy cashew dressing that includes a few tablespoons of nutritional yeast, which ups the cheesiness factor even more.

In a small bowl, toss together the onion, vinegar, and a pinch of sea salt. Let stand for 10 minutes.

In a large sauté pan, toast the pumpkin seeds over medium heat until fragrant and just starting to color, 5 to 7 minutes. Check often and stir frequently. Transfer the seeds to a plate to cool. Once cool, puree in a food processor until finely ground.

To prep the kale, stack 3 or 4 leaves on top of one another, roll into a tight coil, then cut crosswise to create thin ribbons. Place the kale ribbons in a large serving bowl. Season with a pinch of sea salt and toss gently.

Add the onions and vinegar to the kale and toss to coat. Add the ground pumpkin seeds and toss again. Toss with the cashew dressing. Taste and adjust with salt, pepper, and/or more dressing.

Hot Italian Sausage and Giardiniera Pizza with Mozzarella

Makes one 13-inch pizza

1 ball Thin-Crust Pizza Dough (page 26)

All-purpose flour, for dusting

Semolina flour, rice flour, or all-purpose flour, for the peel

Toppings

¼ cup No-Cook Tomato Sauce (page 34) or Simple Tomato Sauce (page 34)

4 ounces low-moisture whole-milk mozzarella cheese, pulled into ½-inch pieces (about 1 cup)

1 cup (4 ounces) drained Chicago-style giardiniera (see Note)

3 ounces raw hot Italian sausage (not in casing)

Extra-virgin olive oil

Flaky sea salt

NOTE
Before making this pizza, it is worth the effort of mail-ordering a jar or two of authentic Chicago-style giardiniera—unless, of course, you are able to find it locally. I love both the hot and mild versions of each of these brands: Caruso's, Marconi, and Hank's Giardiniera.

Upon discovering Steve Dolinsky's *Pizza City* podcast, I became a loyal listener. If you are someone who likes to know the intimate details of hydration percentages, fermentation times, flour types, and oven temperatures, you will love listening to Steve's conversations with pizza makers from across the country and beyond. In addition to dough and baking matters, I've loved learning about various regional pizza styles, like true Chicago-style pizza—thin and crispy as opposed to deep-dish—and topping combinations I've never considered, like raw bulk sausage and giardiniera, a pickled vegetable condiment. This classic Chicago pizza is one of Steve's favorites, and to make it you'll need a jar of Chicago-style giardiniera, which is made with vegetables that are pickled in a vinegar brine first, then marinated in olive oil (see Note). It's different from the giardiniera I can find locally, and it makes a difference: When made with the right giardiniera, this iconic Windy City pie is outstanding and no doubt will give giardiniera a permanent spot in your pantry. It has in mine.

Prepare the dough: Transfer the dough from its storage container to a roomier, lightly floured, covered container (see Dough containers, page 16) and allow it to proof at room temperature for 1½ to 2 hours.

Prepare the oven and pizza peel: About 1 hour before you want to bake the pizza, place a baking steel in the top third of the oven and preheat it to 550°F convection roast (or as high as it will go). Dust a pizza peel lightly with semolina flour or top with parchment paper.

Roll the dough: Lightly dust a work surface and the dough ball with flour. With lightly floured hands, pinch the outermost edge of the dough to flatten and depress the air from the edges. Flip the ball and repeat the pinching at the edges. Using a lightly dusted rolling pin, roll the dough into a 13-inch round, flipping the dough every few strokes and using flour as

needed. Transfer the stretched dough to the prepared peel and give it a shake to ensure it's not sticking.

Assemble the pizza: Spread the tomato sauce evenly over the dough all the way to the edges. Sprinkle the cheese evenly over the top, followed by the giardiniera. Finally, pinch the sausage into dime-sized pieces and distribute evenly over the top. Drizzle lightly with olive oil. Sprinkle with sea salt.

Bake the pizza: Shimmy the pizza (still on the parchment if using) onto the steel and bake until the cheese is melted and the edges are beginning to char, 4 to 5 minutes. (This may take 8 to 10 minutes, depending on your oven.)

Using the peel, transfer the pizza to a cutting board (discard the parchment paper). Cut and serve.

Shaved Fennel Salad with Parmesan and Pomegranate

Serves 4

3 or 4 bulbs fennel, (about 2½ pounds total), trimmed

½ teaspoon kosher salt, plus more to taste

¼ cup Lemon Vinaigrette (page 37), plus more to taste

½ cup shaved Parmigiano-Reggiano cheese (about 1 ounce)

Freshly ground black pepper

½ cup pomegranate arils

2 ounces arugula

Many years ago when I worked at Fork, a restaurant located in Old City, Philadelphia, the first Friday evening of every month was an occasion: The local art galleries opened their doors, providing wine and nibbles for nominal fees, and we did similarly, offering a reasonably priced family-style spread. One of my favorite First Friday menus was Italian-themed, and we went all out, curing fresh sardines in orange and lime juices, making trays of arancini, marinating vats of olives, boiling and peeling pounds of onions for cipollini agrodolce, and slicing fennel for this simple, classic salad. The evening was a success, this crisp salad being a highlight, a refreshing palate cleanser to balance the cheese-stuffed fried rice balls, oily fish, and buttery olives. As it turns out, the salad is a great pizza-palate cleanser, too.

Shave the fennel bulbs thinly on a mandoline (or slice as thinly as possible with a knife). Place the shaved fennel in a large bowl and toss with the salt. Let sit for 15 minutes.

Add the lemon vinaigrette and toss. Taste and adjust with more salt and/or dressing. Add the shaved Parmigiano, pepper to taste, pomegranate arils, and arugula. Toss gently to combine.

Caramelized Onion and Speck Pizza with Mozzarella

Makes one 12-inch pizza

1 ball Neapolitanish Pizza Dough (page 22)

All-purpose flour, for dusting

Semolina flour, rice flour, or all-purpose flour, for the peel

3 tablespoons No-Cook Tomato Sauce (page 34)

¼ cup Caramelized Onions (page 138)

3 ounces low-moisture whole-milk mozzarella cheese, pulled into ½-inch pieces (about ¾ cup)

2 ounces thinly sliced speck

Extra-virgin olive oil

The first time I had speck was at Nancy Silverton's Pizzeria Mozza, where it was combined with pineapple and jalapeño, Nancy's take on a "Hawaiian" pizza. Speck, like prosciutto, is a dry-cured ham, but unlike prosciutto, it gets smoked, too. It's delicious raw, but it is spectacular as a pizza topping, where it crisps slightly, its fat melting into the ingredients beneath it. It's especially good paired with something sweet (like pineapple) or, as here, caramelized onions, which will require roughly 40 minutes of slow cooking on the stovetop, a task you can complete while your oven gets up to temperature. Overall, this is a very simple combination—onions, sauce, cheese, meat—but it tastes far more complex thanks to the speck, which imparts salty, smoky notes into every bite.

Prepare the dough: Transfer the dough from its storage container to a roomier, lightly floured, covered container (see Dough containers, page 16) and allow it to proof at room temperature for 1½ to 2 hours.

Prepare the oven and pizza peel: About 1 hour before you want to bake the pizza, place a baking steel in the top third of the oven and preheat it to 550°F convection roast (or as high as it will go). Dust a pizza peel lightly with semolina flour or top with parchment paper.

Stretch the dough: Lightly dust a work surface with flour. Using lightly floured hands, pat the dough gently to flatten it, then stretch it into a 10- to 11-inch round by laying it on the back of your hands and gently rotating it, taking care not to depress the beautiful air pockets in the dough. If the dough begins resisting, set it down on the work surface to rest for 5 to 10 minutes, then continue stretching. Transfer the stretched dough to the prepared peel and give it a shake to ensure it's not sticking.

Top the pizza: Spread the tomato sauce evenly over the dough, leaving a ½-inch border. Scatter the caramelized onions evenly over the top. Top with the mozzarella, then lay the speck evenly over the top. Drizzle lightly with olive oil. Stretch the dough one last time by pulling outward on the edges. Redistribute the toppings as needed, then give the peel one last shake to ensure the dough is not sticking.

Bake the pizza: Shimmy the pizza (still on the parchment if using) onto the steel and bake until the cheese is melted and the edges are beginning to char, 5 to 6 minutes. (This may take 8 to 10 minutes, depending on your oven.)

Using the peel, transfer the pizza to a cutting board (discard the parchment paper). Cut and serve.

Garlicky, Spicy Sautéed Escarole with Olives, Pine Nuts, and Currants

Serves 4

¼ cup pine nuts

2 heads escarole (about 2 pounds total)

2 tablespoons extra-virgin olive oil

3 garlic cloves, thinly sliced

Pinch of crushed red pepper flakes

Kosher salt

¼ cup white wine

¼ cup olives, any variety, pitted and halved

3 tablespoons dried currants

In nearly every Italian cookbook I own (and in some non-Italian cookbooks as well), there exists some variation of this simple sauté. I have never made a variation I haven't liked, and the reason for this is simple: When you cook escarole quickly in a hot skillet with olive oil, it becomes meltingly tender and its bitterness softens. And when you add to those silky, garlicky greens toasted pine nuts, olives, and currants, well, only good things can happen. This is such a fast, simple dish, and every time I make it, I wonder why I don't make it more often. If you don't want to use wine, use 3 tablespoons water and 1 tablespoon white vinegar (such as white wine, white balsamic, or rice vinegar) in its place.

In a small skillet, toast the pine nuts over low heat, watching closely, until golden, 5 to 7 minutes. Set aside.

Trim away the stem end of the escarole, then chop the leaves roughly into 2-inch pieces. If it's dirty, place it in a large bowl, cover with cold water, and let it sit for 10 minutes to allow the dirt to settle. Scoop out the escarole and transfer it to a large towel or a colander to drain. The escarole does not have to be completely dry.

In a large skillet, combine the oil, garlic, and pepper flakes. Cook over medium heat until the garlic is sizzling, about 1 minute. At the first sign of the garlic starting to color, add the greens, increase the heat to medium-high, and season with a pinch of salt. Use tongs to rearrange the greens in the skillet and help them wilt down. After 1 minute, add the wine, olives, currants, and pine nuts. Cook for another minute, until the escarole has wilted completely down.

Remove the skillet from the heat. Let the greens cool briefly. Taste for salt and adjust as needed. Transfer to a serving platter.

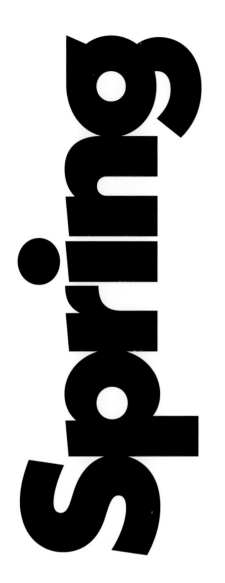

Spring

Rain. Mud. Clouds. Cold. Wind. Snow. Sun. Spring: In Upstate New York, spring feels mostly like a continuation of winter, a less chilly three months, but a far cry from the lush, verdant transition the mention of the season evokes for most. When I visit my local farmers' markets at the end of March or early April, none of the highly anticipated harbingers of the season—asparagus, rhubarb, fresh peas, fiddlehead ferns, ramps—are anywhere to be found. Tables abound, rather, with mushrooms and potatoes of all kinds as well as radishes, carrots, and other roots.

Sprinkled among all the hardy storage vegetables, however, are heaps of the first lettuces of the season, baby varieties of kale, spinach, Asian greens, bok choy, mustard greens, and more. After months of roasting, braising, and stewing, these tender greens are as thrilling to see as that first ripe summer tomato, and in this chapter, you'll find them blanketing several of the pizzas and starring in many of the salads.

And to be clear: Just because I can't find *local* asparagus does not mean I don't cook it. As soon as it sniffs of asparagus season, I seek out the fattest spears I can find and shave them into ribbons for Asparagus Pizza with Crème Fraîche and Whipped Ricotta (page 190) and Asparagus and Prosciutto Slab Pizza (page 207). And if they're not going *on* my pizza, they're going beside it, often in the form of Raw Asparagus Salad with Anchovies, Garlic, and Parmesan (page 224).

With spring being a season where many congregate at the brunch hour celebrating graduates, mothers, fathers, and others, in this chapter you'll also find egg-topped pizzas (see Breakfast Pizza with Sausage, Eggs, and Pickled Banana Peppers on page 223) and Spanakopita-Inspired Spinach and Feta Pizza (page 214), as well as a pizza inspired by bagels and lox: Smoked Salmon and Cream Cheese Pizza for a Crowd (page 199).

Asparagus Pizza
with Crème Fraîche and Whipped Ricotta

Makes one 12-inch pizza

1 ball Neapolitanish Pizza Dough
(page 22)

All-purpose flour, for dusting

Asparagus

8 ounces fat asparagus spears
(about 6 spears), tough ends
trimmed

Kosher salt

1 tablespoon extra-virgin olive oil

Assembly

Semolina flour, rice flour, or
all-purpose flour, for the peel

3 tablespoons crème fraîche, at
room temperature

¼ cup grated Parmigiano-
Reggiano cheese

1 lemon

¼ cup Whipped Ricotta
(page 41)

Flaky sea salt

I usually prefer thin asparagus for roasting, but for this pizza I suggest using fat spears for ease of prep. I'd go so far, in fact, to encourage you to hold off on making this one until you find a bundle of fat spears—you'll go mad trying to shave thin asparagus into ribbons. This pizza is topped minimally, but the simplicity, I think, is why it's so good: It allows the asparagus to really shine. If you are serving this one to a meat lover, a layer of salami or soppressata above the crème fraîche works well here.

Prepare the dough: Transfer the dough from its storage container to a roomier, lightly floured, covered container (see Dough containers, page 16) and allow it to proof at room temperature for 1½ to 2 hours.

Prepare the asparagus: Using a peeler, peel the asparagus into long, thin ribbons. When the asparagus get too hard to peel, slice what remains as thinly as possible. Place the asparagus in a large bowl, season with a pinch of kosher salt, and toss with the olive oil. Taste. It should taste nicely seasoned. Add another pinch of kosher salt if it doesn't.

Prepare the oven and peel: About 1 hour before you want to bake the pizza, place a baking steel in the top third of the oven and preheat it to 550°F convection roast (or as high as it will go). Dust a pizza peel lightly with semolina flour or top with parchment paper.

Stretch the dough: Lightly dust a work surface with flour. Using lightly floured hands, pat the dough gently to flatten it, then stretch it into a 10- to 11-inch round by laying it on the back of your hands and gently rotating it, taking care not to depress the

beautiful air pockets in the dough. If the dough begins resisting, set it down on the work surface to rest for 5 to 10 minutes, then continue stretching. Transfer the stretched dough to the prepared peel and give it a shake to ensure it's not sticking.

Assemble the pizza: Spread the crème fraîche over the dough, leaving a ½-inch border. Sprinkle the Parmigiano over the top. Spread the asparagus evenly over the top. Stretch the dough one last time by pulling outward on the edges. Redistribute the toppings as needed, then give the peel one last shake to ensure the dough is not sticking.

Bake the pizza: Shimmy the pizza (still on the parchment if using) onto the steel and bake until the cheese is melted and the edges are beginning to char, 5 to 6 minutes. (This may take 8 to 10 minutes, depending on your oven.)

Meanwhile, in a small bowl, zest half the lemon (1 teaspoon) into the whipped ricotta and stir to combine. Using the peel, transfer the pizza to a cutting board (discard the parchment paper). Drop the whipped ricotta in small spoonfuls over the top. Season with a pinch of flaky sea salt. Cut and serve.

Fennel Salad
with Citrus, Olives, and Parmesan

Serves 4

2 bulbs fennel (about 1½ pounds total), trimmed

½ teaspoon kosher salt, plus more to taste

¼ cup Lemon Vinaigrette (page 37) or Mimosa Vinaigrette (page 40), plus more to taste

2 navel oranges

½ cup wrinkly black oil-cured olives or other olives, pitted (see Note)

1½ ounces Parmigiano-Reggiano cheese, shaved (about ½ cup lightly packed)

Freshly ground black pepper

NOTE
To easily pit the olives, use the side of a chef's knife to gently crush each olive, then pull out the pit with your hands.

Every time I make this salad, I am reminded of Sunday lunches at my friend Laureen Conigliaro's house. Laureen's parents, Sicilian immigrants, ran a pizza restaurant in my hometown and every Sunday hosted lunch for their extended family. These lunches spanned hours, beginning around noon and ending in the early evening, and I loved them. In addition to introducing me to foods I had never seen, they gave me a glimpse into the life of a real Italian family: barely a word of English spoken, a soccer game never not on the TV always with a crowd before it, yelling and gesticulating, the room filled with cigarette smoke. It was magical. This salad, a classic Sicilian ensemble and a staple on the Conigliaros' lunch table, was my introduction to fennel, which I fell for immediately—sweet and crunchy, bright with that anise flavor you either love or don't. I'm using navel oranges here and wrinkly oil-cured black olives, but know that many a citrus-olive pairing will work here—Cara Cara oranges with kalamata olives, for example, or grapefruit with Castelvetrano olives. Traditionally this salad is dressed simply with fresh lemon juice and olive oil, but I prefer it with a slightly sweetened dressing such as the lemon vinaigrette or mimosa vinaigrette suggested here.

Shave the fennel bulbs thinly (but not paper thin) on a mandoline (or thinly slice them with a knife). Place the shaved fennel in a large bowl and toss with the salt. Let sit for 15 minutes.

Add the dressing and toss. Taste and adjust with more salt—fennel can handle it—and/or more dressing.

Slice off the ends of each orange. Stand each orange up on one of its cut sides. Run a knife down the side of each orange to remove the peel, pith, and membrane to expose the fruit. Turn each orange onto its side and slice into ¼-inch-thick rounds. Slice each round into quarters.

Add the oranges, olives, and Parmigiano to the bowl with the fennel. Season with pepper to taste and toss. Taste and adjust with more salt and/or pepper.

Sautéed Mushroom Pizza with Roasted Red Peppers, Scallions, and Cashew Cream

Makes one 12-inch pizza

1 ball Neapolitanish Pizza Dough (page 22)

All-purpose flour, for dusting

Mushrooms

2 tablespoons extra-virgin olive oil

12 ounces wild mushrooms, roughly chopped or torn into 1-inch pieces

Flaky sea salt or kosher salt

1 garlic clove, minced

¼ to ½ teaspoon crushed red pepper flakes, to taste

½ cup finely sliced scallions

Assembly

Semolina flour, rice flour, or all-purpose flour, for the peel

¼ cup Fresh Tomato Sauce (page 34)

½ cup sliced Roasted Red Peppers (recipe follows)

Extra-virgin olive oil

Flaky sea salt

¼ cup Cashew Cream (page 37), plus more for serving

Whenever my friend Gena Hamshaw comes to visit, I prepare by soaking mounds of cashews in water. Gena is the author of four vegan cookbooks and the vegan blog The Full Helping, and she introduced me to the wonder of the cashew and its ability to morph into many a form, from "parmesan" to "ranch" dressing. My favorite form is cashew "cream," a sour cream–like sauce that lends a richness and tang to anything it dresses, rendering cheese unnecessary. Having been underwhelmed by many vegan cheeses, especially on pizza, this sauce was a revelation. Here, it's drizzled over the pizza post bake, and while it's particularly good on this pizza topped with sautéed wild mushrooms, roasted red peppers, and scallions, it would work well on many others in this book should you need a dairy-free option. In no way does it taste like a compromise.

Prepare the dough: Transfer the dough from its storage container to a roomier, lightly floured, covered container (see Dough containers, page 16) and allow it to proof at room temperature for 1½ to 2 hours.

Sauté the mushrooms: In a large skillet, heat the olive oil over high heat until it shimmers. Add the mushrooms and spread into a single layer. (If your mushrooms don't fit in a single layer, cook them in two batches.) Let cook undisturbed for 1 minute, then stir and season with a pinch of salt. Cook until the mushrooms are evenly golden and beginning to brown at the edges, another 4 to 5 minutes. Add the garlic and pepper flakes and cook for 1 minute more. Stir in the scallions and transfer the mixture to a plate to cool. Taste and adjust with salt if needed. The mushrooms should taste nicely seasoned.

Prepare the oven and pizza peel: About 1 hour before you want to bake the pizza, place a baking steel in the top third of the oven and preheat it to 550°F convection roast (or as high as it will go). Dust a pizza peel lightly with semolina flour or top with parchment paper.

Stretch the dough: Lightly dust a work surface with flour. Using lightly floured hands, pat the dough gently to flatten it, then stretch it into a 10- to 11-inch round by laying it on the back of your hands and gently rotating it, taking care not to depress the beautiful air pockets in the dough. If the dough begins resisting, set it down on the work surface to rest for 5 to 10 minutes, then continue stretching. Transfer the stretched dough to the prepared peel and give it a shake to ensure it's not sticking.

Assemble the pizza: Spread the tomato sauce over the dough, leaving a ½-inch border. Top with the sautéed mushrooms and roasted red peppers. Drizzle lightly with olive oil and season

Recipe continues

with a pinch of flaky sea salt. Stretch the dough one last time by pulling outward on the edges. Redistribute the toppings as needed, then give the peel one last shake to ensure the dough is not sticking.

Bake the pizza: Shimmy the pizza (still on the parchment if using) onto the steel and bake until the edges are beginning to char, 5 to 6 minutes. (This may take 8 to 10 minutes, depending on your oven.)

Using the peel, transfer the pizza to a cutting board (discard the parchment). Drizzle the cashew cream evenly over the pizza. Cut and serve with more cashew cream on the side.

Roasted Red Peppers

Makes 1 cup (enough for two 12-inch pizzas)

Extra-virgin olive oil (optional)

3 red bell peppers, halved and seeded (see Note)

Preheat the oven to 450°F. Line a sheet pan with parchment paper (or rub with a small amount of olive oil).

Place the peppers cut-side down on the lined pan. Roast until the skin is blistery and charred, 30 to 40 minutes. Don't be impatient here: If the skin isn't blistery enough, the peppers will be difficult to peel.

Place the peppers in a large bowl and cover with a plate or a kitchen towel. Let rest for at least 20 minutes and up to 5 hours. Remove the skin and discard. Store the peppers in their juices in the fridge for up to 1 week or freeze for 3 months.

NOTE
This method works well for all sorts of bell peppers (green, yellow, orange) as well as poblano peppers.

Raw Snap Pea Salad with Radishes and Mint

Serves 4

1 pound snap peas (2½ to 3 cups)

Flaky sea salt

10 radishes

⅔ cup packed fresh mint leaves (about ½ ounce), torn if large

A block of Pecorino Romano cheese, for shaving

Freshly ground black pepper

⅓ cup Lemon Vinaigrette (page 37), plus more to taste

Sweet and crisp, snap peas are a great snack and, when diced into small pieces, are a wonderful addition to any salad. As much as I love them, I never considered giving them more of a starring role before spotting a photo of a salad in *Bon Appétit* featuring sliced-on-the-bias snap peas mounded atop a creamy yogurt schmear drizzled with olive oil. It was so striking, I made it immediately. Since then, I've made many a snap pea salad with various dressings and seasonings, and this one, with radishes and mint, is one of my favorites. There is no need to remove the stringy membrane from each snap pea here, because the slicing process removes it. And although the cutting takes some time, one bite of this salad will remove any doubts about the value of your efforts.

Slice the snap peas thinly on the bias and transfer to a large serving bowl. Season with a pinch of salt and toss to coat. Thinly slice the radishes using a mandoline or a knife. Add to the bowl along with the mint leaves and toss to coat. Using a peeler, shave lots of pecorino directly into the bowl. Season with pepper to taste. Add the dressing and toss. Taste and adjust with more salt, pepper, and/or dressing.

Smoked Salmon and Cream Cheese Pizza for a Crowd

Makes 1 sheet pan pizza

2 tablespoons unsalted butter, at room temperature

1 tablespoon extra-virgin olive oil, plus more as needed

One 525-gram ball Pan Pizza Dough (page 30)

Chive cream cheese

⅓ cup cream cheese, at room temperature

⅓ cup crème fraîche, at room temperature

¼ cup finely minced fresh chives

Assembly

1½ tablespoons extra-virgin olive oil

2 tablespoons everything bagel seasoning

16 ounces thinly sliced smoked salmon

½ cup sliced red onion

4 tablespoons drained capers

A small bunch of fresh dill

½ lemon, for finishing, plus more lemon wedges for serving

Sometimes pizza night becomes pizza morning or pizza brunch, an occasion that welcomes egg bakes, big-crumbed coffee cakes, piles of bacon, and this thin-crust focaccia topped with all of your favorite bagels-and-lox fixin's: chive cream cheese, smoked salmon, red onion, capers, and fresh dill. Because the dough bakes with only a slick of olive oil and the seedy seasoning, it stays crisp, becoming a sturdy base to cradle the many toppings added post bake. I love serving this one as part of a brunch buffet, but if you're planning an all-out "pizza morning," two others from this chapter would complete the party: Breakfast Pizza with Sausage, Eggs, and Pickled Banana Peppers (page 223) and Spanakopita-Inspired Spinach and Feta Pizza (page 214).

Prepare the dough: Grease a 12 × 16-inch grandma-style pan or a 13 × 18-inch sheet pan with the softened butter. Pour 1 tablespoon olive oil into the center of the pan. Place the dough ball in the oil and turn to coat. Let rest uncovered until the dough has doubled in volume, 3 to 4 hours.

Stretch the dough: Lightly oil your hands and use your fingertips to dimple and stretch the dough to fit the pan. When the dough resists, let it rest for 30 minutes, then stretch it again using the same technique. Repeat this stretching and resting until the dough fits the pan.

Make the chive cream cheese: In a medium bowl, stir together the cream cheese, crème fraîche, and chives. Store in the fridge until needed.

Prepare the oven: If you have a baking steel, place it on a rack in the middle or lower third of the oven and preheat the oven to 450°F.

Assemble the pizza: Using lightly oiled hands, stretch the dough one final time to fit the pan. Brush 1½ tablespoons olive oil evenly over the dough all the way to the edges. Sprinkle the everything bagel seasoning evenly over the top.

Bake the pizza: Transfer pan to the oven and bake until the surface is lightly golden, 12 to 15 minutes. The dough will shrink from the sides of the pan. This is okay. Remove the pan from the oven and use an offset spatula to transfer the pizza from the pan to a cooling rack. Let cool for 5 minutes.

Finish the pizza: Transfer the pizza to a cutting board. Spread the chive cream cheese over the dough all the way to the edges. Lay the smoked salmon over the top, spreading it all the way to the edges. Scatter with the red onion and then the capers. Use scissors to snip dill, to taste, over the top. Squeeze the ½ lemon over everything to taste. Cut and serve with more lemon wedges on the side.

Baby Spinach Salad with Apple, Pine Nuts, and Goat Cheese

Serves 4

½ cup pine nuts

10 ounces baby spinach or a mix of other tender greens such as baby romaine or baby kale

4 ounces goat cheese, crumbled

2 apples, such as Honeycrisp, thinly sliced

⅓ cup Apple Cider Vinaigrette (page 37), plus more to taste

Flaky sea salt and freshly ground black pepper

Having lived in Upstate New York for over a decade now, I have learned to manage my expectations at the spring farmers' markets. While much of the country is already celebrating asparagus, peas, and rhubarb, we're still roasting root after root (and some of us might be sitting in front of our SAD lights scrolling Southern California Zillow listings). But it's not all doom and gloom; come mid-March at my local farmers' market, I can always find bags of the tastiest baby spinach, the sight of which instantly lifts my bluesy spirits. I could eat these tender greens on their own, but they're especially good tossed with a simple vinaigrette and matched with some of their best pals: toasted pine nuts, tangy goat cheese, and crisp sweet apples.

In a small skillet, toast the pine nuts slowly, stirring occasionally, over low heat until golden brown and fragrant, about 5 minutes.

In a large bowl, combine the greens, goat cheese, apples, and toasted pine nuts. Toss with the dressing. Taste and season with salt and pepper and more dressing if needed.

Roasted Artichoke Pizza
with Castelvetrano Olives, Lemon, and Ricotta

Makes one 12-inch pizza

1 ball Neapolitanish Pizza Dough
(page 22)

All-purpose flour, for dusting

Roasted artichokes

1 (14-ounce) can water-packed
artichoke hearts, drained, or
12 ounces frozen artichoke
hearts

2 tablespoons extra-virgin olive oil,
plus more for drizzling

Kosher salt

10 Castelvetrano olives or other
olives, pitted and coarsely
chopped (about ⅓ cup)

1 small garlic clove, finely minced
or grated on a Microplane

Grated zest of 1 lemon

Pinch of crushed red pepper flakes
(optional)

Flaky sea salt

Assembly

Semolina flour, rice flour, or
all-purpose flour, for the peel

3 ounces low-moisture whole-milk
mozzarella cheese, pulled into
½-inch pieces (about ¾ cup)

Extra-virgin olive oil

Flaky sea salt

¼ cup Whipped Ricotta
(page 41)

Here, frozen or canned artichokes, roasted with olive oil and salt at high heat until their edges caramelize, meet a mix of Castelvetrano olives, lemon, and crushed red pepper flakes. And to finish the pizza—inspired by a memorable artichoke pie served at Pepe in Grani in Caiazzo, Italy—whipped ricotta is added post bake, which preserves its freshness and provides a welcomed cool contrast to the melty mozzarella beneath.

Prepare the dough: Transfer the dough from its storage container to a roomier, lightly floured, covered container (see Dough containers, page 16) and allow it to proof at room temperature for 1½ to 2 hours.

Roast the artichokes: Preheat the oven to 550°F convection roast (or as high as it will go). Line a sheet pan with parchment paper.

If the artichokes are whole, quarter them. Spread the artichokes on the lined pan. Drizzle with 1 tablespoon of the olive oil, season with a pinch of kosher salt, and toss to combine. Roast until the artichokes begin to brown and caramelize at the edges, 10 to 15 minutes. Transfer artichokes to a plate to cool.

In a medium bowl, combine the artichokes, olives, garlic, lemon zest, and pepper flakes (if using). Drizzle with the remaining 1 tablespoon olive oil, season with a pinch of sea salt, and toss to combine. Taste and adjust with more sea salt if needed.

Prepare the oven and pizza peel: About 1 hour before you want to bake

the pizza, place a baking steel in the top third of the oven and preheat it to 550°F convection roast (or as high as it will go). Dust a pizza peel lightly with semolina flour or top with parchment paper.

Stretch the dough: Lightly dust a work surface with flour. Using lightly floured hands, pat the dough gently to flatten it, then stretch it into a 10- to 11-inch round by laying it on the back of your hands and gently rotating it, taking care not to depress the beautiful air pockets in the dough. If the dough begins resisting, set it down on the work surface to rest for 5 to 10 minutes, then continue stretching. Transfer the stretched dough to the prepared peel and give it a shake to ensure it's not sticking.

Assemble the pizza: Scatter the mozzarella over the dough, leaving a ½-inch border. Top with the roasted artichoke mixture. Drizzle lightly with olive oil. Season with sea salt. Stretch the dough one last time by pulling outward on the edges. Redistribute the toppings as needed, then give the peel one last shake to ensure the dough is not sticking.

Recipe continues

Bake the pizza: Shimmy the pizza (still on the parchment if using) onto the steel and bake until the cheese is melted and the edges are beginning to char, 5 to 6 minutes. (This may take 8 to 10 minutes, depending on your oven.)

Using the peel, transfer the pizza to a cutting board (discard the parchment paper). Drop spoonfuls of the whipped ricotta over the dough. Cut and serve.

Arugula Salad
with Prosciutto and Parmesan

Serves 4

8 ounces arugula

Flaky sea salt or kosher salt

¼ cup Lemon Vinaigrette (page 37), plus more to taste

8 slices Prosciutto di Parma

Parmigiano-Reggiano cheese, for shaving

Freshly ground black pepper

One of the things I missed most about Philadelphia upon moving away was the wonderful BYOB restaurant scene, the small, reasonably priced bistros serving dishes I rarely made at home—pillowy potato gnocchi, crispy skinned striped bass, fresh fig gelato—as well as salads composed entirely of produce from local farms. My favorite of all was Melograno, located at the corner of 22nd and Spruce, a gem of a spot run by a husband-and-wife team. I ordered the same meal every time: the arugula and prosciutto salad, the pappardelle tartufato, and tiramisu. Melograno has since moved from its original location, but my Philly friends tell me the menu still features many of their beloved dishes, including their arugula salad. This is a plated salad, meaning you'll dress the greens and divvy them up among four plates, each of which has been lined with a few slices of Prosciutto di Parma. It looks dramatic—a mound of arugula topped generously with shavings of Parmigiano-Reggiano and freshly ground pepper—and you'll want to serve it with a knife and fork to ensure bits of prosciutto are included in every bite. A nice vegetarian alternative here is to line the plates with thinly sliced melon or persimmon.

Place the arugula in a large bowl. Season with a pinch of sea salt. Add the dressing and toss gently. I like to use my hands here as arugula is so delicate. Taste and adjust with more salt and/or dressing.

Lay 2 slices of prosciutto on each of four salad plates. Mound the salad on top—using your hands here will allow you to make nice tall mounds. Use a peeler to shave lots of Parmigiano over the top of each salad mound. Crack pepper to taste over the top of each mound. Serve the salad with a knife and fork.

White Pizza with Arugula, Pistachios, and Honey

Makes one 12-inch pizza

1 ball Neapolitanish Pizza Dough (page 22)

All-purpose flour, for dusting

Semolina flour, rice flour, or all-purpose flour, for the peel

2 tablespoons heavy cream

Flaky sea salt

3 tablespoons grated Parmigiano-Reggiano cheese

3 ounces Brie or Camembert cheese, pulled into ½-inch pieces (about ¾ cup)

Extra-virgin olive oil

1 tablespoon honey, plus more for serving

2 tablespoons coarsely chopped pistachios

Handful of arugula (about 1½ cups)

Upon seeing pistachios, hazelnuts, and walnuts used as pizza toppings in a few of my favorite pizza cookbooks, I had to give them a try, starting with pistachios, my favorite of all and one I always have on hand for snacking. Inspired by a recipe in *Emily: The Cookbook*, which pairs the pistachios with honey and truffled cheese, I made a white pizza topped with whipped heavy cream, Parmigiano-Reggiano, and Brie cheese, and out of the oven I drizzled it, as in the *Emily* pizza, with honey and chopped pistachios. To balance the sweetness of the honey, I added a handful of fresh arugula, drizzled it with olive oil, and sprinkled it with flaky sea salt. Upon tasting this cheese plate meets salad meets pizza, all I could think was *Where have you been all my life?*

Prepare the dough: Transfer the dough from its storage container to a roomier, lightly floured, covered container (see Dough containers, page 16) and allow it to proof at room temperature for 1½ to 2 hours.

Prepare the oven and pizza peel: About 1 hour before you want to bake the pizza, place a baking steel in the top third of the oven and preheat it to 550°F convection roast (or as high as it will go). Dust a pizza peel lightly with semolina flour or top with parchment paper.

Stretch the dough: Lightly dust a work surface with flour. Using lightly floured hands, pat the dough gently to flatten it, then stretch it into a 10- to 11-inch round by laying it on the back of your hands and gently rotating it, taking care not to depress the beautiful air pockets in the dough. If the dough begins resisting, set it down on the work surface to rest for 5 to 10 minutes, then continue stretching. Transfer the stretched dough to the prepared peel and give it a shake to ensure it's not sticking.

Assemble the pizza: In a small bowl, beat the heavy cream with a fork or small flat-bottomed whisk until it thickens and forms soft peaks. Season with a pinch of sea salt. Spread the whipped cream over the dough, leaving a ½-inch border. Sprinkle the Parmigiano and Brie over the top. Drizzle lightly with olive oil and season with a pinch of salt. Stretch the dough one last time by pulling outward on the edges. Redistribute the toppings as needed, then give the peel one last shake to ensure the dough is not sticking.

Bake the pizza: Shimmy the pizza (still on the parchment if using) onto the steel and bake until the cheese is melted and the edges are beginning to char, 4 to 6 minutes, keeping a close watch—this pizza browns more quickly than others. (This may take 8 to 10 minutes, depending on your oven.)

Using the peel, transfer the pizza to a cutting board (discard the parchment paper). Drizzle the honey evenly over the pizza. Sprinkle the pistachios over top, followed by the arugula. Drizzle lightly with olive oil. Season with one more pinch of flaky salt. Cut and serve, with more honey on the side.

Celery, Endive, and Apple Salad with Walnuts, Blue Cheese, and Dates

Serves 4

½ cup walnuts

2 heads Belgian endive, halved lengthwise and thinly sliced on the bias

6 stalks celery with leaves, thinly sliced on the bias

Flaky sea salt or kosher salt

1 sweet apple, such as Honeycrisp, thinly sliced

⅓ cup crumbled blue cheese, plus more to taste

4 Medjool dates, pitted and finely diced

⅓ cup Lemon Vinaigrette (page 37), plus more to taste

Freshly ground black pepper

For years, I did not understand the enthusiasm for celery. Beyond the things where I find it an essential ingredient—tuna and egg salads, stuffings, chicken noodle soup, and stocks and broths of all kinds—I've felt indifferent to its existence. But upon watching Ina Garten make a celery and parmesan salad on the Food Network one day, I wondered if I had too long consigned celery to a supporting role. I made the salad immediately and discovered I had. Ina's celery salad opened the door for many a celery salad to come, and this is one of my favorites, a combination of apples and blue cheese—two of celery's best friends—along with endive for heft and walnuts and dates for additional crunch and sweetness respectively. I do think it's important to slice the celery on the bias for this application, which will create long, flat, thin slices, and I prefer using a sharp, bright dressing here as opposed to a creamy one.

In a small skillet, toast the walnuts, stirring occasionally, over medium-low heat until they are lightly golden and smell toasty, 8 to 10 minutes. Transfer to a cutting board and chop coarsely.

In a large bowl, toss together the endive, celery, and a pinch of sea salt. Add the apple, walnuts, blue cheese, dates, dressing, and pepper to taste and toss to combine. Taste and adjust with more salt, pepper, cheese, and/or dressing.

Asparagus and Prosciutto Slab Pizza

Makes 1 sheet pan pizza

2 tablespoons unsalted butter, at room temperature

3 tablespoons extra-virgin olive oil, plus more as needed

One 525-gram ball Pan Pizza Dough (page 30)

1 pound fat asparagus spears (about 12), tough ends trimmed

Flaky sea salt

8 ounces Taleggio, Camembert, or Robiola cheese, thinly sliced (see Note)

4 ounces Prosciutto di Parma, thinly sliced

Topping the list of the thirty-plus pizzerias I hoped my husband, Ben, and I could get to during our five days in Italy was Gabriele Bonci's Pizzarium, a renowned shop selling Roman-style *pizza al taglio* ("pizza by the slice"). So, after a three-hour guided tour of the Vatican and the Sistine Chapel, Ben and I walked to Pizzarium for lunch and, with grumbling tummies, joined a very long queue. We passed the time reflecting on the awe-inspiring art we had just taken in. . . . I'm kidding, we pored over Bonci's Instagram feed to be sure we ordered the right slice when our time came. And when it did, well, we ordered it all—nothing like a museum trip to build up an appetite! I loved every bite, but what I loved more than anything was the whole concept: the light and airy focaccia-like base, a canvas for countless toppings from squash blossoms and melted mozzarella to roasted eggplant and fresh ricotta to crispy potatoes and paper-thin slices of cured meats. For this Bonci-inspired slab pizza, I use a thinner dough and bake it without any toppings. Out of the oven, it's topped with Taleggio, a tangle of raw asparagus ribbons, and slices of Prosciutto di Parma. The ensemble looks like a work of art, an edible masterpiece to make Bonci (or Michelangelo) proud.

Prepare the dough: Grease a 12 × 16-inch grandma-style pan or a 13 × 18-inch sheet pan with the softened butter. Pour 1 tablespoon of the olive oil into the center of the pan. Place the dough ball in the oil and turn to coat. Let rest uncovered until the dough has doubled in volume, 3 to 4 hours.

Stretch the dough: Lightly oil your hands and use your fingertips to dimple and stretch the dough to fit the pan. When the dough resists, let it rest for 30 minutes, then stretch it again using the same technique. Repeat this stretching and resting until the dough fits the pan.

Prepare the oven: If you have a baking steel, place it on a rack in the middle or lower third of the oven and preheat the oven to 450°F.

Meanwhile, using a peeler, peel the asparagus into long, thin ribbons. When the asparagus get too hard to peel, slice what remains as thinly as possible. Place the asparagus in a large bowl, season with a pinch of salt, and toss with 1 tablespoon of the olive oil. Taste. It should be nicely seasoned. Add another pinch of salt if it doesn't.

Bake the pizza: Brush the dough with the remaining 1 tablespoon olive oil. Using lightly oiled hands, stretch the dough one final time to fit the pan. Transfer the pan to the oven and bake until the surface is lightly golden, 12 to 15 minutes. The dough will shrink from the sides of the pan. This is okay.

Finish the pizza: Remove the pan from the oven and use an offset spatula to transfer the pizza from the pan to a cutting board. Top the dough with the sliced cheese. Mound the asparagus over the top, spreading it to cover. Nestle the prosciutto slices, evenly spaced, in the asparagus tangles. Cut into 16 to 20 squares.

NOTE
Keeping the cheese chilled before slicing it will make the slicing process easier.

Butter Lettuce Salad with Pea Shoots, Dill, Chives, and Tarragon

Serves 4

2 heads butter lettuce
(8 ounces each)

2 ounces pea shoots or
microgreens

¼ cup fresh tarragon leaves

¼ cup chopped fresh chives

Small bunch of fresh dill
(about ¼ cup)

Flaky sea salt and freshly ground
black pepper

⅓ cup Lemon Vinaigrette
(page 37)

The beauty of this salad is its simplicity—there is no cheese, there are no nuts, there are no additional fruits or vegetables. It's just greens and herbs, and its success therefore lies in the freshness of those greens and herbs. I find the inclusion of tarragon, the most potent (and polarizing) of the three herbs used here, to be essential, but if you are not fond of anise flavor, simply omit it or replace it with another herb such as parsley or basil. Adding herbs like basil and fresh mint to tomato, cucumber, and other vegetable-based salads is common. Less so is adding herbs to green salads, and if you've never done so, this will be a revelation.

Remove the root end from each head of lettuce, then separate the leaves. Place the leaves in a large serving bowl. Add the pea shoots, tarragon, and chives. Use scissors to snip the dill into the bowl. Season with a pinch of sea salt and pepper to taste. Dress with the lemon vinaigrette and toss lightly. Taste and adjust with more salt and/or pepper. Serve the salad with a knife and fork.

Kale Pizza
with Sizzling Scallions and Crème Fraîche

Makes one 13-inch pizza

1 ball Thin-Crust Pizza Dough (page 26)

All-purpose flour, for dusting

4 tablespoons extra-virgin olive oil

½ cup finely sliced scallions or ramps

¼ to ½ teaspoon crushed red pepper flakes, to taste

Semolina flour, rice flour, or all-purpose flour, for the peel

4 ounces roughly chopped lacinato (Tuscan) kale leaves (about 4 cups)

Flaky sea salt

¼ cup crème fraîche, at room temperature

¼ cup grated Parmigiano-Reggiano cheese

I never considered using uncooked greens like kale or spinach on pizza until a photo in the cookbook *Tartine Bread* caught my attention. Atop a round of pizza dough sat a heap of nettle leaves, which I had never seen before. I tried the recipe using a pile of raw kale instead, and the combination with crème fraîche and parmesan became an instant spring favorite for pizza night. This version, which includes a sizzling spicy scallion or ramp oil drizzled over post bake, is an invention of my mother's. It's completely irresistible and a great way to eat your greens to boot.

Prepare the dough: Transfer the dough from its storage container to a roomier, lightly floured, covered container (see Dough containers, page 16) and allow it to proof at room temperature for 1½ to 2 hours.

In a small skillet, combine 3 tablespoons of the olive oil, the scallions, and pepper flakes. Set it on the stovetop, but don't turn on a burner just yet.

In a medium bowl, toss the kale leaves with the remaining 1 tablespoon olive oil and season with a pinch of sea salt. The leaves should be nicely coated.

Prepare the oven and pizza peel: About 1 hour before you want to bake the pizza, place a baking steel in the top third of the oven and preheat it to 550°F convection roast (or as high as it will go). Dust a pizza peel lightly with semolina flour or top with parchment paper.

Roll the dough: Lightly dust a work surface and the dough ball with flour. With lightly floured hands, pinch the outermost edge of the dough to flatten and depress the air from the edges. Flip the ball and repeat the pinching at the edges. Using a lightly dusted rolling pin, roll the dough into

a 13-inch round, flipping the dough every few strokes and using flour as needed. Transfer the stretched dough to the prepared peel and give it a shake to ensure it's not sticking.

Set the skillet of scallion oil over high heat. When the scallions begin sizzling, give them a stir, then immediately reduce the heat to low. Keep the skillet over low heat while the pizza bakes.

Assemble the pizza: Spread the crème fraîche over the dough all the way to the edges. Sprinkle the Parmigiano over the top. Spread the kale over the top all the way to the edges.

Bake the pizza: Shimmy the pizza (still on the parchment if using) onto the steel and bake until the cheese is melted and the edges are beginning to char, 4 to 5 minutes. (This may take 8 to 10 minutes, depending on your oven.)

Using the peel, transfer the pizza to a cutting board (discard the parchment paper). Turn the burner under the skillet to high to get the scallions sizzling one last time, and as soon as they do, spoon the mixture over the kale. Season with one more pinch of flaky salt. Cut and serve.

Spring Wedge Salad
with Radishes, Egg, and Greek Yogurt Ranch

Serves 4

1 head iceberg lettuce (about 1½ pounds), cut into 8 wedges

Flaky sea salt or kosher salt

2 radishes, thinly sliced on a mandoline

2 ounces snow peas, thinly sliced on the bias

½ cup Greek Yogurt Ranch Dressing (page 40), plus more for serving

4 Hard-Boiled Eggs (recipe follows), peeled and finely chopped

4 scallions, finely sliced

Freshly ground black pepper

Having grown up with a mother who favored oil-and-vinegar-based dressings and who never stocked bottles of ranch or blue cheese dressing, I came to appreciate these sorts of dressings much later in life, often with pizza and wings by my side. Though today I still love a rich, creamy dressing, I can't ignore my mother's influence, and I do appreciate lightened-up versions, this Greek yogurt ranch being a prime example. It's bright with herbs and fresh lemon juice, and it's a perfect match for all the fixin's here: radishes, snow peas, and eggs. With a little less water, it makes a great dip for veggies, too.

Set the iceberg wedges on a large platter and season them on both sides with some sea salt. Arrange them wedge-edge up. Scatter the radish slices and snow peas over the wedges. Drizzle the dressing evenly over the top, being sure to dress each wedge generously—use more dressing as needed. Scatter the chopped eggs all around, along with the scallions. Season with pepper to taste. Pass more dressing on the side for serving.

Hard-Boiled Eggs

Makes 4 eggs

4 large eggs

Set up a bowl (large enough to submerge the eggs) with ice and water. Place a steamer basket in a pot. Fill the pot with 1 inch of water, cover, and bring to a simmer over high heat.

Uncover, carefully place the eggs in the steamer basket, cover, and steam for 10 minutes. Carefully transfer the steamed eggs to the ice bath.

Spanakopita-Inspired Spinach and Feta Pizza

Makes one 13-inch pizza

1 ball Thin-Crust Pizza Dough
  (page 26)

All-purpose flour, for dusting

Toppings

1 tablespoon olive oil

5 ounces baby spinach
  (about 5 cups)

Kosher salt

Assembly

Semolina flour, rice flour, or
  all-purpose flour, for the peel

1 cup shredded low-moisture
  whole-milk mozzarella cheese
  (4 ounces)

4 large eggs

Flaky sea salt and freshly ground
  black pepper

⅓ cup crumbled feta cheese
  (1½ ounces)

NOTE
An alternative and simpler method is
to eliminate the parbake, and bake
the pizza topped with the sautéed
spinach, mozzarella, and feta until
it is fully cooked. Out of the oven,
top with four fried eggs.

Whenever I return home to my parents' house for a big holiday, I can expect to find an enormous pan of spanakopita in my mother's fridge. It reheats beautifully, and while its main purpose is to provide lunch for everyone for the duration of our visit, it often gets broken out at breakfast because no one can resist. It never occurred to me until very recently that this might be because it's loaded with eggs. As I tucked into the crisp, buttery pastry one morning I thought, *Is spanakopita, hailing from the country that invented everything, the original breakfast casserole?* Hard to say, but what we do know is that spinach, eggs, and feta work famously together, especially at breakfast and not surprisingly on pizza, too. This pizza is a bit tricky to get right because it relies on a parbake to give the dough a jump-start before the eggs are added. If you like the idea of eggs on pizza but don't love the idea of maneuvering a round of dough topped with four jiggly eggs into a hot oven, try the Breakfast Pizza with Sausage, Eggs, and Pickled Banana Peppers (page 223), which calls for two beaten eggs and a lot less finesse. (See Note for another idea as well.)

Prepare the dough: Transfer the dough from its storage container to a roomier, lightly floured, covered container (see Dough containers, page 16) and allow it to proof at room temperature for 1½ to 2 hours.

Prepare the toppings: In a large skillet, heat the oil over high heat until it shimmers. Add the spinach and a pinch of kosher salt. Use tongs to immediately stir the greens and rearrange them in the skillet, helping them wilt down. When nearly all of the greens have wilted, 30 to 60 seconds later, transfer the greens to a plate to cool. Taste and adjust with kosher salt.

Prepare the oven and pizza peel: About 1 hour before you want to bake the pizza, place a baking steel in the top third of the oven and preheat it to 550°F convection roast (or as high as it will go). Dust a pizza peel lightly with semolina flour or top with parchment paper.

Roll the dough: Lightly dust a work surface and the dough ball with flour. With lightly floured hands, pinch the outermost edge of the dough to flatten and depress the air from the edges. Flip the ball and repeat the pinching at the edges. Using a lightly dusted rolling pin, roll the dough into a 13-inch round, flipping the dough every few strokes and using flour as needed. Transfer the stretched dough to the prepared peel and give it a shake to ensure it's not sticking.

Assemble the pizza: Spread the grated mozzarella over the dough all the way to the edges. Top with the spinach, again spreading it all the way to the edges. Crack each egg into its own small bowl and set aside.

Parbake the pizza: Shimmy the pizza (still on the parchment if using) onto the steel and bake until the edges just begin to lightly brown, 2 to 3 minutes.

Recipe continues

Using the peel, remove the pizza from the oven and close the oven door. Use two spoons or forks to pull apart the spinach to create 4 small "nests," one in each quarter of the pizza. Carefully pour an egg into the center of each nest. Season each egg with sea salt and pepper to taste. Crumble the feta evenly over the top.

Finish the pizza: Using the peel, carefully shimmy the pizza back into the oven onto the steel and bake until the eggs are just cooked, 2½ to 3 minutes—watch closely at the end.

Transfer the pizza to a cutting board (discard the parchment paper). Cut the pizza into 4 large slices with an egg in the center of each slice. Serve.

Baby Kale Salad
with Ribbony Carrots, Dates, and Sunflower Seeds

Serves 4

½ cup sunflower seeds

1 large fat carrot

2 green or purple radishes or whatever variety of radish you can find

6 ounces tender baby kale

Flaky sea salt or kosher salt

3 or 4 Medjool dates, pitted and finely diced

Freshly ground black pepper

⅓ cup Apple Cider Vinaigrette (page 37), plus more to taste

4 ounces honey (or regular) goat cheese, crumbled

I am always astonished by the vibrant storage vegetables I can find at my local farmers' market throughout the winter and spring: candy-striped beets, ombré pink turnips, deep purple carrots, and green and magenta radishes. Raw and thinly sliced, these roots bring so much to salads by way of color, texture, and flavor. This baby kale salad is inspired completely by what I picked up one Sunday morning in April at the Schenectady Greenmarket: tender sweet kale, purple carrots, green radishes, and locally made R&G honey goat cheese, which I love slathered over dates, hence their inclusion here, too. Sunflower seeds always remind me of summer, which I yearn for this time of year, but any toasted nut or seed would work well in their place.

In a small skillet, toast the sunflower seeds, stirring occasionally, slowly over low heat until golden brown and fragrant, 5 to 10 minutes.

Using a peeler, shave the carrot into long, thin ribbons. Shave the radishes using a mandoline (or thinly slice with a knife). Place the kale in a large serving bowl. Add the shaved carrots and radishes. Season with a pinch of salt and toss to combine. Add the toasted sunflower seeds, dates, and pepper to taste. Toss with the dressing. Taste and adjust with more salt, pepper, and/or dressing. Add the goat cheese and toss one last time.

Pineapple Pizza with Bacon and Jalapeños

Makes one 13-inch pizza

1 ball Thin-Crust Pizza Dough
(page 26)

All-purpose flour, for dusting

Toppings

¼ pineapple (6 to 7 ounces;
see Note)

4 ounces bacon, cut into ½-inch
pieces

1 tablespoon extra-virgin olive oil

Flaky sea salt or kosher salt

Assembly

Semolina flour, rice flour, or
all-purpose flour, for the peel

Extra-virgin olive oil

2 tablespoons finely grated
Pecorino Romano or parmesan
cheese (see page 19)

¼ to ½ cup ¼-inch-thick jalapeño
slices, to taste

4 ounces low-moisture whole-milk
mozzarella cheese, pulled into
½-inch pieces (about 1 cup)

Flaky sea salt

NOTE
To peel and quarter the pineapple,
first slice off the ends, then run
a knife down the sides, hugging the
flesh to remove the tough outer skin.
Stand the pineapple up on one of its
flat ends, then cut the pineapple
in half straight down through the
core. Cut each half in half again
through the core. Working with one
quarter at a time, stand each piece
up vertically, then cut away the
remaining core. You'll be left with
4 large wedges of pineapple.

The idea of pineapple as a pizza topping can incite extreme negative responses, from outrage to disgust, but I'm Team Hawaiian all the way, and I love seeing it featured on the menus of celebrated pizzerias from Nancy Silverton's Pizzeria Mozza to Franco Pepe's Pepe in Grani. Like other fruity pizza toppings, it pairs well with salty, fatty meats like bacon, prosciutto, and, famously, ham. Here the pineapple is cooked in rendered bacon fat and paired with sliced jalapeños, which Nancy Silverton uses in her take on the controversial pie, a combination I find to be *outrageously* delicious. I hope you'll agree.

Prepare the dough: Transfer the dough from its storage container to a roomier, lightly floured, covered container (see Dough containers, page 16) and allow it to proof at room temperature for 1½ to 2 hours.

Prepare the toppings: Cut the pineapple quarter lengthwise into three sections, then, keeping the sections together, cut them crosswise into ¼-inch-thick pieces.

Place the bacon in a large skillet and set over high heat. As soon as the bacon begins sizzling, reduce the heat to medium and cook until the bacon has rendered some fat but is not yet crisp, about 5 minutes. Transfer the bacon to a plate, leaving the fat in the pan.

Add the olive oil to the skillet and set over medium heat. Add the pineapple and season with a pinch of sea salt. Cook until the pineapple is beginning to brown, 2 to 3 minutes. Flip and continue to cook until the pineapple is fork-tender and the underside is beginning to brown, another 2 to 3 minutes. Lift the pineapple out of

the pan juices and transfer to a plate to cool.

Prepare the oven and pizza peel: About 1 hour before you want to bake the pizza, place a baking steel in the top third of the oven and preheat it to 550°F convection roast (or as high as it will go). Dust a pizza peel lightly with semolina flour or top with parchment paper.

Roll the dough: Lightly dust a work surface and the dough ball with flour. With lightly floured hands, pinch the outermost edge of the dough to flatten and depress the air from the edges. Flip the ball and repeat the pinching at the edges. Using a lightly dusted rolling pin, roll the dough into a 13-inch round, flipping the dough every few strokes and using flour as needed. Transfer the stretched dough to the prepared peel and give it a shake to ensure it's not sticking.

Assemble the pizza: Brush the dough with 1 to 2 tablespoons olive oil all the way to the edges. Sprinkle with the Romano. Scatter the jalapeños evenly

Recipe continues

over the top. Sprinkle the mozzarella evenly over the top all the way to the edges. Scatter the pineapple evenly over the top, followed by the bacon. Drizzle lightly with olive oil. Sprinkle with sea salt.

Bake the pizza: Shimmy the pizza (still on the parchment if using) onto the steel and bake until the cheese is melted and the edges are beginning to char, 4 to 5 minutes. (This may take 8 to 10 minutes, depending on your oven.)

Using the peel, transfer the pizza to a cutting board (discard the parchment paper). Cut and serve.

Market Salad with Greens, Radicchio, Fennel, and Hazelnuts

Serves 4

½ cup hazelnuts

6 ounces mixed green lettuces

½ head radicchio (about 4 ounces), roughly chopped

½ bulb fennel (about 5 ounces)

Flaky sea salt or kosher salt

⅓ cup Mimosa Vinaigrette (page 40), plus more to taste

4 ounces feta cheese

Freshly ground black pepper

My husband travels for work frequently and though he rarely has time to explore the local dining scene, when he does, finding good pizza is always the priority. On one visit to Portland, Oregon, Ben found a window of time to visit Ken's Artisan Pizza, run by pizza and bread baking legend Ken Forkish. No surprise, Ben loved every bite from the pizza to the meatballs to the market salad, a mix of farmers' market greens, radicchio, and fennel tossed in a "mimosa" vinaigrette with toasted hazelnuts and feta. The combination sounded so good, I set out to re-create it, making a simple dressing with fresh orange juice and champagne vinegar, sweetened lightly with honey. The whole combination was as lovely as Ben had described, and more than anything, it made me wonder why I don't use hazelnuts—which provide crunchy, toasty, and earthy notes all at once—more often.

Preheat the oven to 350°F.

Spread the hazelnuts on a sheet pan and roast until fragrant and lightly browned, about 12 minutes. Transfer to a wire rack and let cool for 5 minutes. Rub the hazelnuts in a dry kitchen towel to remove the skins. Roughly chop the hazelnuts.

Place the mixed greens and radicchio in a large serving bowl. Shave the fennel thinly on a mandoline (or thinly slice with a knife). Add to the bowl with the greens. Season with a pinch of sea salt and toss to combine. Add the dressing and toss. Taste and adjust with more dressing by the tablespoon until it is dressed to your liking. Add the feta and hazelnuts, season with pepper, and toss.

Breakfast Pizza with Sausage, Eggs, and Pickled Banana Peppers

Makes one 12-inch pizza

1 ball Neapolitanish Pizza Dough
(page 22)

All-purpose flour, for dusting

Toppings

2 tablespoons heavy cream

Flaky sea salt or kosher salt

2 large eggs

Freshly ground black pepper

Assembly

Semolina flour, rice flour, or
all-purpose flour, for the peel

3 ounces Gruyère cheese, grated
(about ¾ cup)

4 ounces bulk hot or sweet Italian
sausage

¼ cup packed pickled banana
peppers (1½ ounces)

2 tablespoons finely chopped
fresh chives

A few dashes of hot sauce
(optional)

One Saturday morning in a hockey rink in Rochester, New York, I bumped into a dear high school friend and his father, Mr. Paolini. As if no time had passed, we hugged, laughed, snapped photos, and, because I'm a softy, I also cried. Just a little. The next day, Mr. Paolini, hockey fan that he is, came to my daughter's game and brought us treats for our long car ride home: a loaf of bread from a favorite local bakery, a few clementines, and individual breakfast pizzas, which I devoured immediately. What I loved about those breakfast pizzas was the egg topping. I had only ever seen eggs on pizza with yolks still intact (see the Spanakopita-Inspired Spinach and Feta Pizza, page 214), but these eggs were beaten and spread over the dough, making the pizza a little easier to shimmy into the oven. I love this particular combination of eggs, sausage, pickled peppers, and Gruyère cheese, but you can adapt the formula to your tastes and preferences: Use any cheese or pickled chiles you like and swap in bacon (parcooked) for the sausage or omit the meat all together.

Prepare the dough: Transfer the dough from its storage container to a roomier, lightly floured, covered container (see Dough containers, page 16) and allow it to proof at room temperature for 1½ to 2 hours.

Prepare the toppings: In a small bowl, beat the heavy cream with a fork or small flat-bottomed whisk until it thickens and forms soft peaks. Season with a pinch of sea salt. In a separate small bowl, beat the eggs. Season with a pinch of salt and freshly ground pepper to taste.

Prepare the oven and pizza peel: About 1 hour before you want to bake the pizza, place a baking steel in the top third of the oven and preheat it to 550°F convection roast (or as high as it will go). Dust a pizza peel lightly with semolina flour or top with parchment paper.

Stretch the dough: Lightly dust a work surface with flour. Using lightly floured hands, pat the dough gently to flatten it, then stretch it into a 10- to 11-inch round by laying it on the back of your hands and gently rotating it, taking care not to depress the beautiful air pockets in the dough. If the dough begins resisting, set it down on the work surface to rest for 5 to 10 minutes, then continue stretching. Transfer the stretched dough to the prepared peel and give it a shake to ensure it's not sticking.

Assemble the pizza: Spread the whipped cream over the dough, leaving a ½-inch border. Top with half of the Gruyère. Pinch the sausage into small pieces and scatter them evenly over the dough. Scatter the banana peppers evenly over the top.

Parbake the pizza: Shimmy the pizza (still on the parchment if using) onto

Recipe continues

the steel and bake until the crust is light brown, about 4 minutes.

Finish the pizza: Using the peel, remove the pizza from the oven and close the oven door. Pour the eggs evenly over the dough. Top with the remaining Gruyère. Using the peel, return the pizza to the oven until the eggs are just cooked, 1½ to 2 minutes—watch closely at the end.

Transfer the pizza to a cutting board (discard the parchment paper). Sprinkle the chives over the top. If desired, splash a few drops of hot sauce over the top. Cut and serve.

Raw Asparagus Salad with Anchovies, Garlic, and Parmesan

Serves 4

¾ cup walnuts

1½ pounds fat asparagus spears, tough ends trimmed

Flaky sea salt or kosher salt

2 garlic cloves, peeled

6 anchovy fillets

¼ cup white balsamic vinegar, plus more to taste

⅓ cup extra-virgin olive oil, plus more to taste

¼ cup finely chopped fresh chives

1½ ounces Parmigiano-Reggiano cheese, shaved (about ½ cup)

Freshly ground black pepper

Upon reading about puntarelle alla romana (see Chicories alla Romana, page 118), I learned that asparagus could be given the same treatment, meaning the raw spears could be thinly sliced, dressed with a garlic/anchovy vinaigrette, and served as a salad. With puntarelle nowhere to be found, this alternative excited me, and so I set to work slicing the fattest asparagus I could find thinly on the bias and making the same punchy vinaigrette I used on the chicories. For fun, I added toasted walnuts and Parmigiano-Reggiano, ingredients not traditionally included in the classic Roman preparation but ones that always pair nicely with asparagus. I find this combination addictive, a treatment that works well even with subpar asparagus, the bold dressing making up for any lack of flavor and the thin slices hiding any stringiness. Using fat asparagus here makes the cutting process a little easier, though any size spear, of course, will work.

In a medium skillet, toast the walnuts over medium heat, stirring occasionally, until they smell and look toasty, 5 to 10 minutes, watching closely. Transfer to a cutting board and chop coarsely.

Using a sharp knife, slice the asparagus thinly on the bias. Transfer the slices to a large bowl. Season with a pinch of sea salt and toss to coat.

In a food processor or blender, combine the garlic, anchovies, and vinegar and puree. Scrape down the sides. With the machine running, stream in the olive oil until emulsified. Taste and adjust with more vinegar and/or oil. Taste again and add a pinch of sea salt if needed. (Alternatively, mince the garlic and anchovies together until they form a paste. Transfer to a bowl and whisk in the vinegar. Whisking constantly, stream in the olive oil until the dressing is emulsified. Taste. Add a pinch of salt if necessary.)

Add the chives, Parmigiano, and chopped walnuts to the bowl. Season with pepper to taste. Pour ¼ cup of the dressing over the asparagus and toss. Taste and adjust with 1 to 2 more tablespoons of dressing, if necessary, and more salt and/or pepper if needed. Toss one last time, then serve.

Salami and Red Onion Pizza with Calabrian Chiles and Hot Honey

Makes one 13-inch pizza

1 ball Thin-Crust Pizza Dough (page 26)

All-purpose flour, for dusting

Semolina flour, rice flour, or all-purpose flour, for the peel

¼ cup No-Cook Tomato Sauce (page 34)

2 teaspoons Calabrian chile paste

4 ounces low-moisture whole-milk mozzarella cheese, pulled into ½-inch pieces (about 1 cup)

⅔ cup thinly sliced red onion

2 ounces sliced salami or soppressata (see Note)

Extra-virgin olive oil

Flaky sea salt

¼ cup Whipped Ricotta (page 41)

Hot honey or regular honey, for drizzling

NOTE
Many grocery stores now carry more varieties of salami and soppressata. I love the flavor of salami Calabrese, which is a little bit drier and spicier than traditional varieties of salami. Depending on how thick the meat is sliced, you may need more or less than 2 ounces; the goal is to have enough slices to nearly cover the pizza in a single layer.

I first read about Calabrian chile paste in Missy Robbins's newsletter, *QB*, which stands for *quanto basta*, meaning "just enough" in Italian, a saying that captures her less-is-more philosophy, her belief that the most important ingredient is the one left out. Having just dined at her Brooklyn restaurant Lilia, where I had the grilled clams with bread crumbs and Calabrian chiles, I bought a jar of the chile paste immediately and soon found myself adding a spoonful to everything I was eating, from pasta to fried eggs to roasted vegetables of all kinds. The paste is spicy, but in addition to imparting heat, it also lends smoky and fruity notes, subtle flavors that will keep your pizza night companions wondering, *What am I tasting?* I always love that. Inspired by the beloved bee sting pizza at Roberta's in Brooklyn, this chile-spiked red sauce pizza bakes with salami and red onion and is topped post bake with whipped ricotta and hot honey, which perhaps pushes it out of the less-is-more category, but doesn't unbalance it—I hope you'll find this union of ingredients to be more than just enough.

Prepare the dough: Transfer the dough from its storage container to a roomier, lightly floured, covered container (see Dough containers, page 16) and allow it to proof at room temperature for 1½ to 2 hours.

Prepare the oven and pizza peel: About 1 hour before you want to bake the pizza, place a baking steel in the top third of the oven and preheat it to 550°F convection roast (or as high as it will go). Dust a pizza peel lightly with semolina flour or top with parchment paper.

Roll the dough: Lightly dust a work surface and the dough ball with flour. With lightly floured hands, pinch the outermost edge of the dough to flatten and depress the air from the edges. Flip the ball and repeat the pinching at the edges. Using a lightly dusted rolling pin, roll the dough into a 13-inch round, flipping the dough every few strokes and using flour as needed. Transfer the stretched dough to the prepared peel and give it a shake to ensure it's not sticking.

Top the pizza: In a small bowl, stir together the tomato sauce and Calabrian chile paste. Spread the tomato/chile sauce over the dough all the way to edges. Spread the mozzarella evenly over the top all the way to the edges. Scatter the onion evenly over the top, followed by the salami. Drizzle lightly with olive oil and season with a pinch of sea salt.

Bake the pizza: Shimmy the pizza (still on the parchment if using) onto the steel and bake until the cheese is melted and the edges are beginning to char, 4 to 5 minutes. (This may take 8 to 10 minutes, depending on your oven.)

Using the peel, transfer the pizza to a cutting board (discard the parchment paper). Drop small spoonfuls of the ricotta evenly over the top. Drizzle with honey to taste. Cut and serve.

Little Gem Salad with Avocado, Scallions, Cucumber, and Green Goddess Dressing

Serves 4

1 pound Little Gem lettuces or other salad greens

Flaky sea salt

⅓ cup Green Goddess Dressing (page 41), plus more to taste

½ English cucumber

8 asparagus spears, fat if possible, tough ends trimmed

4 scallions, thinly sliced

1 large avocado, thinly sliced

Freshly ground black pepper

One day on the photo shoot for my last cookbook, *Bread Toast Crumbs*, the food stylist, Jeffrey Larsen, introduced me to Little Gem lettuce. He had packed a few wedges in his lunch along with a little tub of homemade Green Goddess dressing—*I know, how cute?*—and he told me it was one of his favorite appetizers to serve when entertaining, because everyone could enjoy it: the gluten-free, the vegetarians, the paleos. I can almost never find Little Gems in their whole form, but when I do, I leap and make a batch of herby Green Goddess dressing to dip them into. When I can't find the whole Little Gem heads, I'll simply make a salad with the sweet, crisp leaves. For kicks, I've kept the color palette of the salad the same as the vibrant green dressing, adding avocados, asparagus, cucumbers, and scallions—and I can think of a few others that would work well here, too, namely snap or snow peas, edamame, and shelled fresh peas.

If you are using whole heads of Little Gems, trim away the root ends, separate the heads into leaves, and place in a large serving bowl. If you are using Little Gem leaves (or other salad greens), place the lettuce in a large serving bowl. Season with a pinch of salt and drizzle with the dressing. Toss until the leaves are coated. Taste and adjust with more salt and/or dressing.

Slice the cucumber into long, thin ribbons using a mandoline or a peeler. Add to the bowl of greens. Use a peeler to thinly shave as much of each asparagus spear as possible. Thinly slice what remains of each spear. Add the asparagus to the bowl of greens, along with the scallions and avocado. Season with pepper to taste and toss the salad gently. Taste and adjust with more dressing, salt, and/or pepper. Serve the salad with a knife and fork.

Classic Margherita Pizza

Makes one 12-inch pizza

1 ball Neapolitanish Pizza Dough
(page 22)

All-purpose flour, for dusting

Semolina flour, rice flour, or
all-purpose flour, for the peel

3 tablespoons No-Cook Tomato
Sauce (page 34)

3 ounces low-moisture whole-milk
mozzarella cheese (see Note),
pulled apart into ½-inch pieces
(about ¾ cup)

Extra-virgin olive oil

Flaky sea salt

Fresh basil leaves, torn if large

NOTE
If you have a pizza oven, you can
make this with buffalo or fresh
cow's milk mozzarella. Pull it
into ½-inch pieces and let drain
on a paper towel or kitchen towel
for 10 to 15 minutes. For baking
instructions, see Cooking Your Pizza
in an Outdoor Oven (page 46).

I have had one million Margherita pizzas in my lifetime, and yet every time I find myself at a pizzeria that serves Neapolitan pizza, I can't *not* order the Margherita. Why? Partly because the quality of a pizzeria's Margherita is a good measure of what's to come, but also because the Margherita is hard to beat: It's a simple but perfect pie. To this day, it continues to be one of my favorite pizzas, and it is unquestionably the pizza I make most often at home, because it's my children's favorite, too. With so few ingredients, to get it right, it's important to use high-quality ingredients: good tomatoes, good mozzarella, good olive oil, and fresh basil. When I make Margherita pizza in my outdoor oven, I love using buffalo or fresh cow's milk mozzarella, which retain their freshness and creaminess during the brief cooking time. In my home oven, however, I find using these cheeses to be a waste: They lose their nice texture, become rubbery, and can make the pizza soggy. For these reasons, I almost always use low-moisture whole-milk mozzarella—I love the Calabro brand—on all of my home-oven pizzas.

Prepare the dough: Transfer the dough from its storage container to a roomier, lightly floured, covered container (see Dough containers, page 16) and allow it to proof at room temperature for 1½ to 2 hours.

Prepare the oven and pizza peel: About 1 hour before you want to bake the pizza, place a baking steel in the top third of the oven and preheat it to 550°F convection roast (or as high as it will go). Dust a pizza peel lightly with semolina flour or top with parchment paper.

Stretch the dough: Lightly dust a work surface with flour. Using lightly floured hands, pat the dough gently to flatten it, then stretch it into a 10- to 11-inch round by laying it on the back of your hands and gently rotating it, taking care not to depress the beautiful air pockets in the dough. If the dough begins resisting, set it down on the work surface to rest for 5 to 10 minutes, then continue stretching.

Transfer the stretched dough to the prepared peel and give it a shake to ensure it's not sticking.

Top the pizza: Spread the tomato sauce over the dough, leaving a ½-inch border. Scatter the mozzarella evenly over the top. Drizzle lightly with olive oil. Season with a pinch of sea salt. Stretch the dough one last time by pulling outward on the edges. Redistribute the toppings as needed, then give the peel one last shake to ensure the dough is not sticking.

Bake the pizza: Shimmy the pizza (still on the parchment if using) onto the steel and bake until the cheese is melted and the edges are beginning to char, 5 to 6 minutes. (This may take 8 to 10 minutes, depending on your oven.)

Using the peel, transfer the pizza to a cutting board (discard the parchment paper). Sprinkle with basil. Cut and serve.

Spring Chopped Salad
with Edamame, Snap Peas, Endive, and Asparagus

Serves 4

1 cup shelled fresh peas

1 cup (½-inch dice) asparagus

1 cup frozen shelled edamame

2 heads Belgian endive (8 to 10 ounces total), halved lengthwise and cut crosswise into ½-inch half-moons

4 ounces snap peas, sliced on the bias (1¼ cups)

2 ounces salami, sliced into thin strips

4 scallions, thinly sliced

4 or 5 radishes, thinly sliced

½ cup cubed Manchego cheese (2 ounces)

4 pepperoncini, thinly sliced, or ½ cup black oil-cured olives

Flaky sea salt or kosher salt

½ cup Italian Dressing (page 39), plus more to taste

Freshly ground black pepper

From the moment the Vischer Ferry General Store opened its doors, I became a regular not only for their brioche egg sandwich and sea salt milk chocolate chip cookies but also for the welcoming, communal vibe I felt every time I visited. I soon became friends with the owner, Louise McManus, and before long we began collaborating on various events, from casual baking and cooking classes to community dinners. For one such dinner, I had the brilliant idea to serve a spring salad featuring fresh peas and fava beans. Shelling peas is not terribly laborious, but if you've ever prepped fava beans you know of their demands: They require an initial shelling from their pod, then a blanching, then a second peeling from another protective sheath. All of these efforts will yield a toddler-sized portion of favas, leaving you to wonder, *What for?!* This is how Louise and I felt as we stood over a stainless steel bowl, releasing favas from their little cells, the clock ticking by, panic setting in as our to-do list remained undiminished. Never again. Edamame, while not quite as enchanting, play the role of favas quite nicely in this spring chopped salad. Similarly, there's no shame in buying shelled fresh peas, which are readily available in many grocery stores during the spring and summer.

In a medium pot of boiling water, blanch the peas, asparagus, and edamame for 30 seconds. Drain and let cool briefly, about 5 minutes.

In a large bowl, combine the endive, snap peas, salami, scallions, radishes, Manchego, pepperoncini, and the cooled peas, asparagus, and edamame. Season with a pinch of sea salt. Add the dressing, season with pepper to taste, and toss to combine. Taste and adjust with more dressing, sea salt, and/or pepper.

Grandma Pizza with Broccoli Rabe and Sausage

Makes 1 sheet pan pizza

2 tablespoons unsalted butter, at room temperature

1 tablespoon extra-virgin olive oil, plus more as needed

One 525-gram ball Pan Pizza Dough (page 30)

Broccoli rabe

1 bundle of broccoli rabe (about ½ pound), ends trimmed

1 tablespoon extra-virgin olive oil

1 garlic clove, minced

Pinch of crushed red pepper flakes

Kosher salt

½ lemon

Toppings

3 cups shredded low-moisture whole-milk mozzarella cheese (12 ounces)

4 to 6 jarred Calabrian chiles, finely minced, or 1 to 2 tablespoons Calabrian chile paste, to taste

¾ cup Simple Tomato Sauce (page 34) or your favorite jarred sauce

8 ounces bulk hot Italian sausage or links with casings removed

Before the fall of 2022, I rarely cooked broccoli rabe. It's not a vegetable my mother ever made when I was a child, and I never taught myself to make it later in life because the sight of it always filled me with doubt: *Do I blanch it before sautéing it? Do I use the leaves and stems? Could I simply roast it?* All of my questions were answered when I made Deb Perelman's broccoli rabe with broken burrata from her cookbook *Smitten Kitchen Keepers*. Deb's method calls for briefly sautéing the rabe, stems and all, with garlic and pepper flakes, then adding a few tablespoons of water, covering, and cooking for 2 minutes. This no-blanching stovetop method yields perfectly cooked broccoli rabe I'd be happy to eat straight from the skillet, but Deb takes it one step further by finishing it with fresh lemon and burrata, which, as you can imagine, is delicious. More exciting than the discovery of a great side dish, however, was a new confidence for cooking broccoli rabe for other things, namely pizza. Here it's paired with sausage, homemade tomato sauce, Calabrian chiles, and mozzarella, *no doubt* a killer combination.

Prepare the dough: Grease a 12 × 16-inch grandma-style pan or a 13 × 18-inch sheet pan with the softened butter. Pour the olive oil into the center of the pan. Place the dough ball in the oil and turn to coat. Let rest uncovered until the dough has doubled in volume, 3 to 4 hours.

Prepare the broccoli rabe: Cut the broccoli rabe into 1-inch segments. In a large skillet, heat the oil, garlic, and pepper flakes over medium-high heat just until the garlic begins to shimmer and take on the slightest amount of color, 1 to 2 minutes. Add the broccoli rabe, season with ½ teaspoon kosher salt, and cook, stirring and rearranging frequently with tongs until wilted, about 2 minutes. Add 2 tablespoons water, cover, and cook for 2 minutes more. Remove the cover and squeeze lightly with the lemon. Stir, taste, and adjust with more salt or lemon to taste.

Stretch the dough: Lightly oil your hands and use your fingertips to dimple and stretch the dough to fit the pan. When the dough resists, let it rest for 30 minutes, then stretch it again using the same technique. Repeat this stretching and resting until the dough fits the pan.

Prepare the oven: If you have a baking steel, place it on a rack in the middle or lower third of the oven and preheat the oven to 450°F.

Assemble the pizza: Using lightly oiled hands, stretch the dough one final time to fit the pan. Sprinkle the mozzarella evenly over the pizza, spreading it all the way to the edges. Spread the broccoli rabe evenly over the cheese. Scatter the chiles or the paste evenly over the top. Drop spoonfuls of the tomato sauce over the dough in the empty spaces around

Recipe continues

the broccoli rabe, then smooth with the back of a spoon to spread. Finally, pinch the sausage into small pieces and scatter them evenly over the top.

Bake the pizza: Bake until the edges look very caramelized, 22 to 25 minutes.

Remove the pan from the oven. Run a paring knife or spatula around the pan's edges. Use an offset spatula to carefully transfer the pizza from the pan to a cutting board. Cut into 12 to 16 squares.

Spring Caesar Salad à la Speedy Romeo

Serves 4

2 heads romaine lettuce (1¼ to 1½ pounds)

Flaky sea salt

½ cup Caesar Dressing (page 39), plus more to taste

1- to 2-ounce block Parmigiano-Reggiano cheese, for shaving

Freshly ground black pepper

During spring break of 2021, Ben and I took our kids to Brooklyn for a few nights. As you might recall, this was when the world was beginning to open up, and for these upstate kids who hadn't traveled much beyond their hometown in over a year, well, Brooklyn felt like a complete party, from the bustling streets to the blossoming Botanical Gardens to the many delicious meals, including the one enjoyed in a dining shed outside of Speedy Romeo. Sitting on bar stools at a high-top table, we drank Coke in glass bottles and savored Neapolitan-style pepperoni pizza, gigantic meatballs, and Caesar salad, which emerged blanketed in shaved parmesan, the romaine lettuce leaves barely visible, like tree branches weighed down by fresh snow. Incredibly it did not taste too cheesy, due to the lightness of the cheese shavings, likely created by a Microplane grater, which has the effect of multiplying a small block of parmesan into what feels like three times its volume. Here, as at Speedy Romeo, the romaine leaves are cut into large segments, 4 to 6 inches long, so it's best to serve this salad with a knife and fork.

Cut off the root end of each head of romaine along with any raggedy, dark green tips from the other end. Cut each head in half crosswise. This will leave you with pieces roughly 4 to 6 inches in length.

Place the romaine in a large bowl. Season with a pinch of salt. Add the dressing and toss to coat. I find this easiest to do with my hands. Taste and adjust with more dressing and/or salt.

If you don't care about the presentation, leave the greens in the bowl and proceed with the recipe. If you do, find a serving platter— something long and shallow is ideal— and with clean hands pile the leaves on top.

To finish, use a Microplane grater to shave the block of Parmigiano over the salad until the leaves are blanketed with the white shavings. Season with pepper to taste.

5 Desserts Perfect for Pizza Night

Dessert need not be complicated to be satisfying. In this chapter you'll find five of my favorite, simple sweet finales, including a three-ingredient berry dessert (my British father's favorite), an affogato (the classic two-ingredient Italian gelato dessert), and a one-bowl chocolate chip cookie recipe that may become your go-to—on pizza night or otherwise—for its ease and deliciousness. The remaining two desserts will put to good use two ingredients you might have on hand for topping your pizza-night pizzas—mascarpone and ricotta—and each has its virtues: Loaf Pan Tiramisu (page 243) is a no-bake dessert that can be made days in advance, and the One-Bowl Lemon-Ricotta Pound Cake (page 247) comes together in minutes and gets better by the day. Of all the desserts that follow, only the tiramisu requires a little bit of work, but after you've made it once, you'll find yourself stocking your freezer with ladyfingers to ensure that espresso-spiked, chocolate-dusted goodness lies just a few (vigorous) whisk strokes away.

Berries and Cream

Serves 4

2 cups fresh berries, such as
raspberries, strawberries,
blackberries, or blueberries
(see Note)

8 tablespoons heavy cream

4 teaspoons sugar, or to taste

This three-ingredient dessert is something my British father served after every summer dinner: fresh berries + sugar + cream. When his mother was in town, there always was a wedge or two of cheese—often Stilton and Wensleydale—on the table as well, all of which comprised what my granny referred to as the "pudding." When the local strawberries begin arriving, this is one of the first desserts I make, and upon tasting one of those berries, with flesh brilliant red from stem to tip, I can't help but think of Willy Wonka: "The strawberries taste like strawberries!" Adored by adults and children alike, this simple "pudding" has become a summer staple, proven to please and delight just as effectively as its flashier fruit-filled brethren without all the work.

If using strawberries, core them and halve or quarter if they are large.

Place 2 tablespoons cream in each of four small bowls. Add ½ cup berries to each bowl and sprinkle 1 teaspoon sugar over the top of each. Add more sugar to taste.

NOTE
You can use a single berry for this or a mix of berries. Ripe stone fruit such as peaches and nectarines work well here, too.

One-Bowl Chocolate Chip Cookies

Makes 21 or 22 cookies

2 sticks (8 ounces/226 grams) unsalted butter, melted and slightly cooled

1 cup (200 grams) packed light brown sugar

½ cup (100 grams) granulated sugar

1 large egg

1 tablespoon (12 grams) pure vanilla extract

1 teaspoon (3 grams) Diamond Crystal kosher salt

1 teaspoon (5 grams) baking soda

2½ cups (320 grams) unbleached all-purpose flour

1¼ cups (215 grams) chocolate chips (see Note)

Everyone needs a simple, excellent chocolate chip cookie recipe in their repertoire. This one, which calls for two sticks of melted butter and one bowl, is just that. It's so simple, in fact, that my children have nearly memorized the recipe and have taken over as the cookie makers in the family. My older two love making the batter; my younger two love scooping and rolling. (If only divvying up the laundry duties could be so seamless!) Child- and adult-approved, these cookies are the perfect treat to cap off pizza night. Any unused cookie dough can be rolled into balls and stashed in the fridge or freezer to be baked on demand.

In a large bowl, whisk together the butter and both sugars. Add the egg and vanilla and whisk again to combine. Add the kosher salt and baking soda and whisk to combine. Add the flour and stir with a rubber spatula to incorporate. Finally, add the chocolate chips and stir again to incorporate. Refrigerate the batter for at least 30 minutes.

Preheat the oven to 325°F. Line a sheet pan with parchment paper.

If you have a scale, portion the dough into 50-gram balls: You will get 21 or 22. This is a tedious task, but it makes for beautiful and uniform cookies that bake evenly. Alternatively, use a 2-tablespoon scoop to portion the dough into 21 or 22 balls. The cookies are baked in batches of 6 to 8, so store any cookies balls you won't be baking in the fridge for up to 1 week or in the freezer for up to 3 months. There is no need to thaw before baking, though you may need to add a minute or two to the baking time.

Arrange 6 to 8 cookie dough balls evenly spaced on the lined pan. Bake until the cookies are evenly light brown around the edges, 16 to 18 minutes. Keep a close watch. You want to remove the cookies from the oven when they are puffed and still look slightly undercooked—you might think you are removing them too early. The cookies will continue cooking as they sit on the pan out of the oven. Let the cookies cool completely on the pan before removing.

NOTE

I love Guittard chocolate chips. If you like dark chocolate, try their 63% extra-dark chocolate baking chips, and if you like a sweeter chip, try their 46% semisweet chocolate baking chips.

Loaf Pan Tiramisu

Makes one 9 × 5-inch loaf pan

¾ cup (186 grams) heavy cream

3 egg yolks

½ cup plus 2 tablespoons (125 grams) sugar

½ cup plus 2 tablespoons mascarpone (155 grams or about 6 ounces)

1 teaspoon (4 grams) pure vanilla extract or (5 grams) vanilla bean paste

1 teaspoon instant espresso powder (see Notes)

⅓ cup (75 grams) boiling water

2 teaspoons brandy or rum

10 soft ladyfingers (see Notes)

A bar of dark chocolate, for shaving

NOTES

An alternative to instant espresso and boiling water is to simply use ⅓ cup brewed espresso from a home machine or purchased from your favorite coffee shop.

This recipe calls for soft ladyfingers, which are often found in the bakery section of supermarkets. Soft ladyfingers can be frozen for up to 3 months. I do prefer the soft ladyfingers for this recipe, but if you only can get the hard savoiardi-style ladyfingers, you'll need 12 total—6 whole for each layer—and instead of brushing with the espresso mixture you should dip each whole one very briefly—in and out—of the espresso mixture.

My grandmother loved tiramisu and always made one when she was expecting a house full of guests for the holidays. This is her recipe but made in a half portion, a perfect amount for pizza night with a perfect amount left over (for me in the morning with my coffee). Of the five recipes in this chapter, this one requires the most effort—but overall it's not hard. It's a no-bake recipe that can be made days ahead of time, and the effort is so worth it: espresso-soaked ladyfingers layered with custardy mascarpone cream all topped with shaved chocolate. Heaven.

Fill a wide-mouthed pot with a couple inches of water. Bring to a boil.

In a medium bowl, use a whisk or an electric mixer to beat the heavy cream until firm peaks form. Transfer to the fridge.

In a large bowl that can sit over (not in) the pot of boiling water, whisk the egg yolks vigorously for 1 minute. Add the sugar and beat until it becomes slightly thicker and lighter in hue, about 1 minute. (You can use a hand-held mixer here if you prefer.)

Set the bowl over the pot of water. Reduce the heat to medium so that the water is gently simmering below the bottom of the bowl. Stir the egg yolk/sugar mixture with a whisk until the mixture is light, ribbony, and warm to the touch, about 5 minutes. Remove the bowl from the heat and let cool for 5 minutes.

With a whisk, stir the mascarpone and vanilla into the slightly cooled egg yolk/sugar mixture until blended. With a spatula, fold in the whipped cream. It's okay if the mixture seems slightly grainy at this point—any graininess will disappear after the assembled tiramisu rests in the fridge for 12 hours.

In a small bowl, stir together the espresso powder and boiling water to dissolve. Stir in the brandy.

Line the bottom of a 9 × 5-inch or 8½ × 4½-inch loaf pan with a single layer of ladyfinger halves, about 10, halved-side down, going crosswise in the pan. Brush each with the espresso/brandy mixture. Be generous with the saturation—you should use half the amount or roughly 3 tablespoons.

Pour half of the cream mixture (about 1¼ cups) over the first layer of ladyfingers, spreading with a spatula to cover them evenly. Top with another layer of 10 ladyfinger halves. Brush with the remaining espresso mixture. Top with the remaining cream, spreading it to cover the area evenly. (Note: You may be tempted to add more ladyfingers, but as the tiramisu sits, the ladyfingers absorb the creamy mixture and swell like a sponge.)

Using a vegetable peeler or Microplane grater, shave the chocolate over the top of the entire dish. Cover the dish with plastic wrap and refrigerate for at least 12 hours before serving. This can be prepared up to 3 days in advance. If necessary, shave more chocolate over top before serving.

Affogato with Homemade Gelato

Serves 4

4 scoops (roughly ½ cup each)
Vanilla Gelato (recipe follows)
or No-Churn Vanilla Gelato
(recipe follows)

4 shots (roughly 2 tablespoons
each) of brewed espresso
(see Note)

In the summer of 2014, Ben and I dropped our kids off at my dear aunt Marcy's house in Vermont, then kept making our way north to Montreal. We spent three days cruising the streets and markets, eating kouign-amann and Montreal-style bagels, and watching World Cup soccer games at Café Olimpico, an Italian café in the Mile End neighborhood. One evening at the café, we noticed table after table ordering the affogato, a dessert I'd long known about but had never tried. It was time. When it arrived, the server set the bowl of ice cream before us, then poured the espresso over the top. As the hot liquid cascaded over the scoop, it melted the sweet cream beneath, causing a mocha-hued swirl to pool at the base of the bowl, a hot/cool, bitter/sweet dynamic I had never experienced. If you are a coffee-ice cream lover, this one's for you, and if you have an espresso machine at home, you're in for a treat (see Note). You, of course, can use store-bought ice cream here, but if you're up for it, make it from scratch. Whether you have an ice cream machine or not, it's easy and so, so tasty. There are two recipes below, one calling for a machine and one utilizing a no-churn method.

Place one scoop of gelato into each of four small bowls. Pour one shot of brewed espresso over each scoop. Serve immediately.

NOTE
If you don't have an espresso machine, you can use a French press or an Aeropress, or, in a pinch, instant espresso.

Vanilla Gelato

Makes 1 quart

2 cups (505 grams) whole milk

3 tablespoons (28 grams) cornstarch

¾ cup (150 grams) sugar

¾ teaspoon (2 grams) Diamond Crystal kosher salt

2 cups (473 grams) heavy cream

1 teaspoon (5 grams) vanilla bean paste or 2 teaspoons (8 grams) pure vanilla extract

In a small bowl, whisk together ½ cup (128 grams) of the milk and the cornstarch until the cornstarch is dissolved.

In a medium pot, combine the remaining 1½ cups (377 grams) milk, sugar, and salt and whisk over medium heat until the sugar is dissolved, 2 to 3 minutes. Whisk in the cornstarch/milk mixture and cook until the base thickens enough to coat the back of a spoon, 3 to 5 minutes.

Whisk in the cold cream and vanilla. Strain the mixture into a storage container and let cool to room temperature. Cover and refrigerate until completely cold, at least 8 hours.

Pour the base into the bowl of an ice cream maker and churn according to the manufacturer's instructions. Transfer the churned gelato to an airtight container and freeze until ready to serve.

When ready to serve, be sure to let the gelato sit at room temperature for 10 to 15 minutes until it reaches the appropriate serving temperature, which is typically about 16°F. I like to microwave my storage container in 15- to 30-second increments to get it to a soft, scoopable consistency.

No-Churn Vanilla Gelato

Makes 1 quart

1 (14-ounce) can sweetened condensed milk

2 cups (473 grams) heavy cream

1 teaspoon (5 grams) vanilla bean paste or 2 teaspoons (8 grams) pure vanilla extract

½ teaspoon (1.5 grams) Diamond Crystal kosher salt

In a large bowl, whisk together the condensed milk, cream, vanilla, and salt until emulsified. Using a handheld mixer, whip the mixture at high speed for about 3 minutes, until soft, billowy peaks form, like a fluffy frosting—the peaks will not be stiff.

Pour the mixture into a 9 × 5-inch loaf pan, cover with plastic wrap or tuck the pan inside an extra-large zip-top bag, and freeze until thick and creamy, at least 5 hours or up to 2 weeks.

Let the gelato sit at room temperature for 15 to 20 minutes or until softened to a scoopable texture before serving.

One-Bowl Lemon-Ricotta Pound Cake

Makes one 9 × 5-inch loaf

Softened butter and 1 tablespoon sugar for the pan

3 large eggs

1½ cups (365 grams) whole-milk ricotta cheese

¾ cup (164 grams) extra-virgin olive oil

Grated zest of 1 lemon

2 tablespoons (26 grams) fresh lemon juice

1½ cups (300 grams) sugar

1 teaspoon (3 grams) Diamond Crystal kosher salt

2½ teaspoons (9 grams) baking powder

1½ cups (192 grams) all-purpose flour

Fresh berries (optional), for serving

This is an adaptation of an old favorite Giada De Laurentiis recipe, reworked to make it a one-bowl job, allowing it to come together very quickly. Made with ricotta and olive oil, it's an exceptionally moist cake that stays so for days, and it's a dessert I love serving any time of year, at the height of citrus season in the winter months and in the summer with fresh berries alongside. I almost always make it in a standard loaf pan, but you can divide the batter among three small loaf pans, too. The smaller loaves are great if you want to freeze the cake for a future pizza night, and they also make great gifts.

Preheat the oven to 350°F. Grease a 9 x 5-inch (or 10 x 5-inch) loaf pan with butter. Sprinkle 1 tablespoon sugar into the pan, and shake and turn the pan to coat the sides in the sugar.

In a large bowl, whisk together the eggs and ricotta until blended. Whisk in the oil, lemon zest, and lemon juice until blended. Whisk in the sugar and salt to combine. Whisk in the baking powder to incorporate. Add the flour and use a spatula to incorporate until it is no longer visible.

Pour the batter into the prepared pan and bake until a toothpick comes out clean and the cake pulls away from the sides of the pan, 60 to 75 minutes. If you have an instant-read probe thermometer (such as a Thermapen), it should register about 200°F or above.

Let the loaf cool completely in its pan. Run a knife along the edges of the pan to help release it. Store in an airtight zip-top bag at room temperature for 5 days or freeze for up to 3 months.

To serve, cut into slices. If desired, serve with fresh berries alongside.

How-Tos

How to Freeze Pizza Dough

For all of the yeast-leavened pizza dough recipes, you can freeze the dough after the first rise. Deflate the dough, divide it into portions, ball up the portions, then transfer each portion to its own airtight container. Freeze for up to 3 months.

I do not recommend freezing sourdough pizza dough. It does not perform well after freezing for long periods of time. Even after short periods it will not rise as well in the oven or taste as light and airy. To preserve sourdough dough balls, see How to Parbake Dough below.

To thaw pizza dough, remove a dough ball from the freezer and thaw in the fridge for at least 12 hours or at room temperature for at least 4 hours.

How to Parbake Dough

For the recipes that call for the Neapolitanish Pizza Dough (page 22) or the Thin-Crust Pizza Dough (page 26), working with one dough ball at a time, stretch or roll it into its appropriate size as indicated by the recipe and place on a prepared peel. Transfer to a 550°F oven (convection roast if possible, otherwise as high as it will go) on a preheated baking steel or stone and bake for 1 to 2 minutes—the dough will be very pale and slightly bubbly when you remove it with the faintest browning on the edges and spots across the surface of the dough. Remove the parbaked dough round and let cool for 5 minutes. Repeat with any remaining dough balls. At this point, you can tuck the parbaked rounds into airtight bags and store at room temperature for up to 3 days or in the freezer for up to 3 months. Thaw frozen parbaked rounds at room temperature for 1 hour, then top and bake as directed in the recipe.

For Sicilian, Detroit-style, and cast iron-skillet pizzas, parbake as indicated in each specific recipe. Let the parbaked dough cool completely on a rack before storing in an airtight bag at room temperature for up to 3 days or in the freezer for up to 3 months. Thaw frozen parbaked pan doughs at room temperature for 1 hour, then top and bake as directed in the recipe.

How to Store and Reheat Day-Old Pizza

To store: Once the pizza has cooled completely, store it in airtight bag at room temperature for 2 to 3 days.

To reheat: There are several ways to reheat day-old pizza, but my favorite is on the stovetop, a method popularized by pizza consultant Anthony Falco. To reheat on the stovetop, place 1 or 2 slices of pizza in a skillet over medium-low heat. Let cook until the bottom begins to crisp, 2 to 3 minutes. Add 1 teaspoon of water, cover the skillet, turn the heat to low, and cook until the cheese and sauce begin bubbling, 1 to 2 minutes.

The toaster oven also works great: Place pizza directly on the oven rack and toast for 3 to 4 minutes, or until the cheese and sauce begin bubbling.

Finally, you can use your oven: Place slices of pizza on a sheet pan (parchment-lined for easy cleanup). Transfer the pan to a 400°F oven and heat until the cheese is bubbling and the crust edges begin to brown and crisp, about 10 minutes.

Troubleshooting

My pizza dough is so wet, sticky, and difficult to manage.

It is possible that given your environment and the type of flour you are using, you are using too much water relative to the amount of flour. First, ideally, you are measuring with a scale, so you can ensure you are measuring accurately and making meaningful adjustments. If your dough, upon being mixed, is unable to form a sticky dough ball, you'll need to reduce the water next time around. Hold back 25 to 50 grams (2 to 4 tablespoons) of water, and if that still is not enough, next time hold back more. To fix the current dough you are working with, simply add more flour 16 to 32 grams (2 to 4 tablespoons) at a time, until the dough comes together and forms a dough ball.

Every time I stretch or roll out my dough, it springs back.

If you have trouble stretching out your dough, it's possible it hasn't proofed long enough and simply needs more time at room temperature to relax. Check the recommended time in each recipe and be sure you are giving your dough that suggested time to rest. A properly proofed dough should expand with ease, but if you are still finding your dough to be resistant when you stretch it, let it rest for 5 to 10 minutes, then return to it and stretch again. This gives the gluten time to relax, which should help. For the Neapolitanish Pizza Dough (page 22), once you have your dough on your prepared peel and sauced and topped, always stretch the dough one last time: Simply tug gently at the edges to stretch it out.

My pizza crust is too soft.

There are several reasons your crust might be too soft:

- Too much sauce, cheese, and/or toppings
- Toppings released too much liquid
- Oven not hot enough
- Too short a baking time

Solutions:

- Use a lighter hand when topping.
- Be sure to use cooked ingredients as opposed to raw. Ingredients with high water content, such as mushrooms, spinach, and many other vegetables, will release liquid onto the dough. Cooking these ingredients prior to using them as toppings will remove much of their moisture.
- Invest in a baking steel, set it on a rack in the top third of the oven, and be sure to preheat your oven for long enough, ideally 1 hour or more.
- Consider the "upside down" method, which calls for placing the cheese on the dough first with the sauce on last. The cheese will provide some insulation from the sauce, thereby preventing the dough from getting soggy.
- Consider parbaking the crust (see How to Parbake Dough, page 248) before topping and baking as directed in the recipe.
- Use semolina on the peel.
- Before stretching the dough ball into a round, slick it lightly with a bit of olive oil.
- Try the recipe for Thin-Crust Pizza Dough (page 26), which is lower hydration than the Neapolitanish Pizza Dough (page 22) and will create a firm, crisp crust.
- For the pan pizzas, invest in Lloyd steel pans (see Pizza Tools, page 13).

Acknowledgments

Thank you to:

The readers of Alexandra's Kitchen, for your support and encouragement over the years. This book would not be possible without you.

My husband, Ben, for enthusiastically eating every pizza I made these past few years and for discovering that *toppings* from leftover pizza could be repurposed for eggs, snacks, and beyond. Thank you for bringing me home whole pizzas from San Francisco, Portland, and Chicago, and for your tireless appetite in Italy when the unimaginable happened: I could not take one more bite of pizza.

My children—Ella, Graham, Wren, and Tig—for never complaining when the answer to "What's for dinner?" was once again "Pizza!" I am never prouder than when you ask for fresh basil if you don't see it already showered over the pizza. You make me feel so lucky every day.

My mother, for prioritizing pizza every Friday at Clear View Drive, for introducing me to the joys of making homemade pizza from *The Figs Table* years ago, and for your love and support always. Papa, for your enthusiasm for every pizza recipe Mom tested and for always texting me the report. Your future in food journalism is bright! Dad, for the many Stouffer's French Bread Pizza dinners, followed by epic games of ping pong, bridge, and Journey Through Europe.

Little Lindis and Mr. T, for making your home my favorite place to be, where the idea for *Pizza Night* was born, when a storm canceled our camping trip, and we found ourselves eating pizza and Greek salad in your kitchen instead.

Nick Cobbett and Brittany Powers, for welcoming me into your beautiful home for many weeks and for sharing it (and your magical friends) for the photoshoot. I wish we could end every night watching Bad Sisters and eating just-baked (but rested!) chocolate chip cookies.

Auntie Marcy and Unclie Wade, for all of your outdoor oven pizza experiments. I wish I could live in your garage permanently and eat pizza with you nightly.

Carole and Richard Stafford, for all of your help with the children always. I'm grateful every day you live two blocks away.

To my recipe testers, for your honesty and insights, which have made the recipes magnitudes better. Thank you to: Derek Peterson for your enthusiasm for the Detroit-style pizzas I set out one Halloween and for becoming the DSP master in the weeks/months that followed; Christy Alia, for so generously sharing your extensive knowledge, for your honest feedback and insights, for your kindness and spirit; Laura McCarthy, for testing all of the salad recipes (and many pizzas and desserts, too) and for making every email I opened from you feel like an adventure. I loved more than anything when Conor especially approved; Erinn Johnson, for your incredibly speedy and thoughtful work, for your proactiveness and honesty, and for your insights and suggestions; Deb Haltzman, my pan-pizza champion, for your obsessiveness, attention to detail, and friendship; and Frank Wilk, for your enthusiasm for the thin-crust dough, for testing it on baking stones and overturned sheet pans, and for making it all work without a pizza peel. Thank you, too, to Dana Abate, Noelle Welk, Tara Carter, Amy Kaufman, Kristina Matsch, Teri and Matt Chapkosky, Sally Theran, Lydia O'Brian, and Renee Glass. I am overwhelmed with gratitude for all of you.

To many friends and advocates: Margaret Roach, Serena Wolf, Gena Hamshaw, Phoebe Lapine, Colu Henry, Ellen Yin, Andris Lansdin, Jim Fazzone, Uncle Tony, Louise McManus, Haley Priebe, Harry Whalen, Matthew White, Michelle Pollard (for making yoga feel like therapy, meditation, and comedy all at once), the Niskayuna Co-op, Kelly Lephart, Sandra Buchanan, Linda Lucca, and Lisa Malitz (still the best host in NYC).

To the photography crew: Eva Kolenko, Genesis Vallejo, Nicole Twohy, and Huxley McCorkle. You are a dream team, and I cherish every moment of being on set with you.

My agent, Berta Treitl, for being such a steady guide on this journey. The incredible team at Clarkson Potter: Lydia O'Brian, thank you for believing in the idea from the start, and Susan Roxborough for seeing it through. Thank you for helping me simplify a massive and overwhelming dough chapter and for so much insightful editing along the way. Many thanks, too, to Ian Dingman for your beautiful design sense, creativity, and patience. Thank you finally to Stephanie Huntwork, Natalie Blachere, Kelli Tokos, Chris Tanigawa, Kate Slate, Lauren Chung, Erica Gelbard, Chloe Aryeh, Francis Lam, and Aaron Wehner.

Index

Note: Page references in *italics* indicate photographs.

Library of Congress Cataloging-in-
Publication Data
Names: Stafford, Alexandra, author. |
   Kolenko, Eva, photographer.
Title: Pizza night / Alexandra Stafford ;
   photographs by Eva Kolenko.
Identifiers: LCCN 2023024022 (print)
   | LCCN 2023024023 (ebook) | ISBN
   9780593579947 (hardcover) | ISBN
   9780593579954 (ebook)
Subjects: LCSH: Pizza. | Sauces. | LCGFT:
   Cookbooks.
Classification: LCC TX770.P58 .S73 2024
   (print) | LCC TX770.P58 (ebook) |
   DDC 641.82/48--dc23/eng/20230524
LC record available at https://lccn.loc.
   gov/2023024022
LC ebook record available at https://lccn.
   loc.gov/2023024023

ISBN: 978-0-593-57994-7

Ebook ISBN: 978-0-593-57995-4

Printed in Canada

Editor: Susan Roxborough
Editorial assistant: Bianca Cruz
Designer: Ian Dingman
Production editor: Natalie Blachere
Production manager: Kelli Tokos
Compositors: Merri Ann Morrell and
Hannah Hunt
Food stylist: Nicole Twohy
Food stylist assistant: Huxley McCorkle
Photo assistant: Genesis Vallejo
Copyeditor: Kate Slate
Proofreaders: Kathy Brock and Jacob Sammon
Indexer: Elizabeth Parson
Publicists: Lauren Chung and Erica Gelbard
Marketer: Chloe Aryeh

10 9 8 7 6 5 4 3

First Edition